Thank you for making Renaissance ROM one of the most successful cultural fundraising campaigns in Canadian history.

"Renaissance ROM was a bold campaign that transformed the Royal Ontario Museum and sparked an exciting revitalization of arts and culture in the city of Toronto. The generous support of our donors and volunteers has beautifully crystallized, providing a truly inspiring place of wonder for generations to come. Together, the public and private sectors contributed $416 million in support of the ROM's many fundraising priorities, including the capital campaign, related projects, new acquisitions and operating funds. On behalf of the ROM Governors and the Renaissance ROM Campaign Cabinet, we sincerely thank you for your passion, vision and commitment to the Museum. Renaissance ROM grew to become one of the most successful cultural fundraising campaigns in Canadian history—and we could not have done it without all of you."

—The Hon. Hilary M. Weston
Chair, Renaissance ROM Campaign

Campaign Chair

The Hon. Hilary M. Weston

Honorary Patron

Her Imperial Highness Princess Takamado

Campaign Executive

Dr. Marie Bountrogianni
Rudolph P. Bratty
Jack Cockwell
John F. Driscoll
Linda Hasenfratz
John S. Hunkin
Michael Lee-Chin
G. Wallace F. McCain
James W. McCutcheon
David Palmer
Joseph M. Tanenbaum
James C. Temerty
William Thorsell
Rita Tsang

Honorary Cabinet Advisors

British Consulate General
Consulate General of the
    People's Republic of China
Consulate General of the
    Republic of Cyprus
Consulate General of Greece
Hong Kong Economic &
    Trade Office, Toronto
Consulate General of India
Consulate General of Japan
Consulate General of the
    Republic of Korea
Consulate General of Pakistan
Royal Nepalese Consulate
    General
Consulate General of
    Sri Lanka
T. T. Tsui
    Wanchai, Hong Kong

Countdown to Completion Task Force

Robert E. Pierce, Chair
Dr. Marie Bountrogianni
Jack Cockwell
Rebecca MacDonald
Jack F. McOuat
James C. Temerty
William Thorsell
Alfred G. Wirth

Campaign Cabinet

Shreyas Ajmera
Bluma Appel
Joe F. Brennan
Kelvin Browne
Monica Carr
The Hon. David Crombie
The Hon. William G. Davis
Michael E. Detlefsen
Roman Dubczak
A. Mark Foote
Robert T. Gillespie
The Hon. Edwin A. Goodman
Natasha Gurevich
Kenneth W. Harrigan
Patricia Harris
William B. Harris
Gwen Harvey
Martha J. Hogarth
John C. Hurd
Donna Ihnatowycz
Jennifer Ivey Bannock
The Hon. Henry N. R.
    Jackman
Peter S. Janson
Peter C. Jones
Chris Jordan
Bipin Khimasia
Thomas E. Kierans
Hiroshi Kobayashi
Stanley Kwan
Michael A. Levine
Elsie Lo
Susanne Loewen
Stephens B. Lowden
Bahadur Madhani
Malika Mendez

Jack M. Mintz
David Mirvish
Elizabeth Mitchell
Elizabeth Muir
Masaaki Murakami
Tamotsu Nakamura
Manabu Nishimae
Kazuto Ogawa
Terukazu Okahashi
Peter Oliver
Deanne M. Orr
Robert E. Pierce
Frank Potter
Jean M. Read
John A. Rhind
Earl I. Rotman
Hirohito Sakai
Noriaki Sakamoto
Elizabeth J. Samuel
Alan M. Schwartz
Irene So
Belinda Stronach
Shigeru Takagi
Suresh Thakrar
Yoichi Tomihara
Kenji Tomikawa
Sally Tuck
Harriet Walker
Kiyotaka Watanabe
Prem Watsa
Richard S. Wernham
Doug Wilson
Lynton R. Wilson
Robert C. Wong
Richard Wookey
Sharon Zuckerman

Occasionally, a group of individuals gathers around a common cause in a particular circumstance to make something special happen. So it was at the beginning of the 21st century in Ontario, and at the Royal Ontario Museum.

The times demanded bold action that would create higher expectations and set the course for a more vibrant and rewarding place to live and visit. Renaissance ROM, as the project became known, sparked a broader cultural revival in Toronto, and asserted our faith in the power of art, science and community to enrich the human experience.

Distinctly, it was the individuals in this group, rather than the group as an entity, that made the critical decisions required to invigorate the status quo. They clearly shared a vision, but acted on their own accounts to provide unprecedented resources in the service of change.

In this, the contributors to Renaissance ROM acted in the tradition of the Museum's founders—remarkable individuals themselves in their passion and commitment to create the Royal Ontario Museum. Rarely in the history of a place is such aspiring and forceful alignment to be found.

This book—*Bold Visions*—starts at the beginning but does not end. Rather, it continues into the current, wonderful chapter of the ROM's evolution, knowing that more will be done and written. But my, what was done and written in our time, by these individuals, to whom we are profoundly grateful.

Salvatore M. Badali
Chair, ROM Board of Trustees (2006 to present)

Jack Cockwell
Chair, ROM Board of Trustees (2001 to 2006)

William Thorsell
Director & CEO, Royal Ontario Museum (2000 to 2010)

With the incredible involvement of the community, the extraordinary generosity of our donors, patrons and volunteers, and vital support from the provincial and federal governments, Renaissance ROM became a brilliant reality. How fitting and touching to see a passionate group of people come together and imagine an even bigger and better ROM—a magical place that inspires more than a million visitors each year to dream and discover.

Launched in 2002 under the direction of David Palmer, former President & Executive Director of the ROM Governors, and the leadership of The Hon. Hilary M. Weston, Michael Lee-Chin, Jack Cockwell and Elizabeth Samuel, Renaissance ROM became one of the most successful cultural fundraising campaigns in Canadian history.

Today, the Royal Ontario Museum stands as a completely revitalized place of wonder—both inside and out—and the bold building serves as a reminder of the amazing achievements that took place during an exhilarating time of monumental change in the ROM's history. Congratulations on a truly breathtaking renaissance.

W. Robert Farquharson
Chair, ROM Board of Governors (2009 to present)

James C. Temerty
Chair, ROM Board of Governors (2002 to 2009)

Dr. Marie Bountrogianni
President & Executive Director, ROM Governors (2007 to present)

The Hon. Hilary M. Weston, Chair, Renaissance ROM Campaign

W. Robert Farquharson and Dr. Marie Bountrogianni

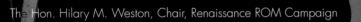

William Thorsell and Salvatore M. Badali

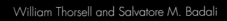

Jack Cockwell, Michael Lee-Chin, Elizabeth Samuel and James Temerty

Michael Lee-Chin Crystal

Inspired by the ROM's unique mandate—to build bridges of understanding, awareness and appreciation for the world's diverse cultures and precious natural environments—Michael Lee-Chin's extraordinary lead gift to Renaissance ROM is an act of both gratitude and hope: gratitude to this country for the opportunities it has given him and his family, and hope that his example might be an inspiration to Canadians from all backgrounds to act on their aspirations and become leaders in their own communities.

The Michael Lee-Chin Crystal is named in recognition of his exceptional generosity and the remarkable vision behind his gift to the Royal Ontario Museum.

Hyacinth Gloria Chen Crystal Court

The story of Michael Lee-Chin's extraordinary gift to the ROM is both personal and uniquely Canadian. From humble beginnings in Jamaica, eldest of nine children, Michael Lee-Chin received from his mother, Hyacinth Gloria Chen, a rich and enduring gift of belief—a belief, grounded in the values of respect, tolerance, empathy and charity, that there is no poverty that cannot be overcome except that of an impoverished spirit.

The atrium in the Michael Lee-Chin Crystal is named in honour of Hyacinth Gloria Chen. Her inspiring example as a devoted mother and successful businesswoman has never failed to lift the spirits and aspirations of all who have known her.

Michael Lee-Chin with his mother, Hyacinth Gloria Chen

RENAISSANCE ROM

The Royal Ontario Museum wishes to thank and acknowledge the many donors to Renaissance ROM who played a formative role in the Museum's transformation. Through their extraordinary generosity, they have helped unlock the full potential of the Museum's collections, galleries, programs and buildings, creating a lasting cultural, scientific and educational legacy for generations of Canadians and international visitors.

Cornerstone Gifts

Government of Canada
Government of Ontario
Michael Lee-Chin

Transforming Gifts

Jack Cockwell and Lynda Hamilton
Schad Family
Teck Resources Limited
James and Louise Temerty
Hilary and Galen Weston
The W. Garfield Weston Foundation

Principal Gifts

Shreyas and Mina Ajmera
Thor and Nicole Eaton
Elizabeth Samuel
Alex and Simona Shnaider
Joey and Toby Tanenbaum

Leadership Gifts

Bennett Family Foundation
Rudolph P. Bratty & Family
Brookfield Asset Management Inc.
CIBC
John and Merrilyn Driscoll
W. Robert Farquharson & Family
The Globe and Mail
William and Patricia Harris
Ian Ihnatowycz and Marta Witer /
    Ukrainian Canadian Community
Jennifer Ivey Bannock /
    Ivey Foundation
Richard M. Ivey and the late Beryl Ivey
Patrick and Barbara Keenan & Family
Loblaw Companies Limited
Manulife Financial
Judy and Wilmot Matthews
Mr. G. Wallace and
    The Hon. Margaret Norrie McCain
The R. Samuel McLaughlin
    Foundation
Peter and Melanie Munk
Sir Christopher Ondaatje, O.C., CBE
Power Corporation of Canada
RBC Foundation
Wendy and Leslie Rebanks
Ernest and Flavia Redelmeier
Nita and Donald Reed
ROM Department of
    Museum Volunteers

Sigmund Samuel Gallery Fund
Scotiabank Group
Shokokai
St. Joseph Communications
TD Bank Financial Group
Richard Wernham and Julia West
Red and Brenda Wilson
Alfred G. Wirth
Anonymous (4)

Founding Gifts

Bram and Bluma Appel
ArcelorMittal Dofasco Inc.
Shirley and Edward Barr
Roloff Beny Foundation
BMO Financial Group
Canon Canada Inc.
Cargill Meat Solutions
Jeanne Timmins Costello Trust
De Beers Canada Inc.
Department of Canadian Heritage –
    Virtual Museum of Canada
Fredrik S. Eaton
Murray Frum and Nancy Lockhart
GE Canada
Government of Ontario – Ministry of
    Culture Capital Rehabilitation Fund
Embassy of Greece
Adrian Hartog and
    Jasmine Vujasinovic Hartog
Alexandra and Julia Holgate
Philip N. Holtby
Honda Canada Inc.
HSBC Bank Canada
John Hunkin and Susan Crocker
Irving Tissue
Thomas Kierans and Mary Janigan
Kruger Products Limited
Estate of Campbell Alexander Leckie
A. G. Leventis Foundation
Linamar Corporation
Magna International Inc.
Maple Leaf Foods
Estate of Dorothy Muriel Matson
Brenda and James McCutcheon
Estate of John H. Milnes
Audrey and David Mirvish
Mitsui & Co., (Canada) Ltd.
Nienkämper Furniture
Robert E. Pierce & Family
Assuntino and Angelina Ricciuto
RioCan Real Estate
    Investment Trust

La Fondation Sackler
   (The Sackler Foundation)
Sony Canada
Estate of Henrietta E. Stevenson
The Dorothy Strelsin Foundation
Toyota Canada Inc.
Vale
W Studio Carpets & Alan Pourvakil
Estate of Isabel Carey Warne
John J. Wood
Estate of Jean Y. Wright

Major Gifts

Arius3D Canada
James C. Baillie
Marilyn and Charles Baillie
Bell Canada
Better Beef
Blake, Cassels & Graydon LLP
Fran and Lawrence Bloomberg
Jean-Raymond Boulle
Campbell Company of Canada
Cascades Tissue Group
Cathay Pacific Airways Limited
Colgate-Palmolive Canada Inc.
Commemorative Organization
   for the Japan World Exposition ('70)
Cultural Spaces Canada Program
David Chapman's Ice Cream Limited
Dimitra and Michael Davidson &
   Family
The DeGasperis Family
Glenna and George Fierheller
General Mills Canada Corporation
Bob and Irene Gillespie
Ira Gluskin and
   Maxine Granovsky-Gluskin
The Hon. Edwin A. Goodman and
   M. Joan Thompson
H.J. Heinz Company of Canada Ltd.
Hauser Industries Inc.
Higgins & Burke Tea & Coffee
Richard and Martha Hogarth
Margo and Ernest Howard
Inmet Mining Corporation
Rosamond Ivey
Suzanne Ivey Cook
Lassonde Industries Inc.
Donald R. Lindsay
Anne Y. Lindsey
Linda and Steve Lowden
John and Gail MacNaughton
Marsan Foods
The McLean Foundation

Marion Megill Trust
The Catherine & Maxwell Meighen
   Foundation
Metro Label Company Ltd. &
   The Lal Family
Ministry of Natural Resources
The Muzzo Family
Panasonic Canada Inc.
Hilda McLaughlin Pangman
Rosemary Rathgeb
Jean M. Read and
   the late Morris Appleby
John and Elizabeth Rhind
Alfredo and Moira Romano
Richard Rooney and
   Laura Dinner
The Salamander Foundation
Paula and Rudolph Schury
Sorrell Financial Inc.
Maureen and Wayne Squibb
Teradata Canada ULC
Mr. William Thorsell
John and Elizabeth Tory
Rita Tsang
Elizabeth M. Walter
Weston Foods Canada
Sharon Zuckerman
Anonymous (3)

Special Gifts

Aird & Berlis LLP
Mark and Gail Appel
Tony and Anne Arrell
Baker Real Estate Corporation &
   Invar Building Corporation
Bank of Tokyo-Mitsubishi UFJ
   (Canada)
Karen and Bill Barnett
Robert Barnett and
   Leslie Montgomery
J.P. Bickell Foundation
Blaney McMurtry LLP
John and Nancy Bligh
Borden Ladner Gervais LLP
Mary and Murray Bosley
Burgundy Asset Management Ltd.
Burnbrae Farms Limited
Centennial Foods
The Albert C. W. Chan Foundation
Dr. Martin Chepesiuk and
   Ms. Halyna Perun
CIBC Mellon
City of Toronto
Compass Canada

ConAgra Foods Canada
The Estelle Craig Family Trust
Estate of Lucille R. Davies
Michael and Honor de Pencier
Deloitte
DENSO Manufacturing Canada, Inc.
Michael Detlefsen and Louise Le Beau
Dorie Dohrenwend
The Dubczak Family
Dupont Corian / The Willis Group
E.D. Smith & Sons, Limited
El-En Packaging Company Limited
Andrew Faas
Anna-Liisa and Graham Farquharson
Farrow & Ball
Family and Friends of Cara Feldman
Dr. Madeline M. Field
First Gulf Corporation
Lloyd and Gladys Fogler
Robert and Julia Foster
Dr. Marian Fowler
Franklin Templeton Investments
Frito Lay Canada
Genuine Health
Gowling Lafleur Henderson LLP
John and Judith Grant
Scott and Krystyne Griffin
H. Donald Guthrie, Q.C.
Jean and Ken Harrigan
The Haynes-Connell Foundation
Hino Motors Canada
Hitachi Canada Ltd.
John E. Horton & Family
Mr. and Mrs. W. B. G. Humphries
Hussmann Canada Inc.
Ice River Springs Water Co.
Interforest Ltd.
The Ippolito Family
J & D Produce, Inc., Edinburg, Texas
Peter and Peggy Janson
The Jarislowsky Foundation
JNE Consulting Ltd.
JVC Canada Inc.
Kellogg Canada Inc.
Arthur P. Kennedy
Vera and Albert Kircheis
KPMG LLP
Kroll Computer Systems Inc.
Charles and Jane Kucey & Family
Ihor and Valentina Kuryliw
The S E Lam Family Foundation
Jack and Catherine Leitch
Dr. and Mrs. K. K. Leung
Michelle & Michael Levy
    Family Foundation

Myrna Lo
Wah Chee and Elsie Lo
Susanne and Charles Loewen
Mastronardi Produce Ltd.
Mazda Canada Inc.
McCarthy Tétrault
Robert R. McEwen
Paul and Martha McLean
Joann and Rodger McLennan
Jack and Vodrie McOuat
Merrill Lynch
Eleanor and Jack Mintz
Mizuho Corporate Bank (Canada)
The Honourable Robert S. and
    Dixie Anne Montgomery
Murphy's Food Sales & Marketing
Nestlé Canada Inc.
The Nielsen Company
Nissan Canada Inc.
Olymel, S.E.C./L.P.
Ontario Potato and O. P. D. I. Logistics
Mr. John G. B. and Mrs. Deanne Orr
David and Bernadette Palmer
Roger and Maureen Parkinson
Pepsi QTG Canada
Marilyn L. Pilkington and
    Wayne E. Shaw
Piller Sausage & Delicatessens Ltd.
Dr. Lloyd M. Piszel
Zenon and Sonia Potichnyj
Mary Jean and Frank Potter
PricewaterhouseCoopers LLP
Procter & Gamble Inc.
Bob Ramik
Joan R. Randall
In memory of Elizabeth Rhind
Estate of Norma Ruth Ridley
Mrs. Norman S. Robertson
Rosenbloom Groupe Inc.
Rotman Family
Arthur and Mary Sawchuk
Lionel and Carol Schipper
Shinkikai (Association of Japanese
    Canadian Businesses &
    Professionals)
Shiu Pong Group of Companies
Shoppers Home Health Care
SMBC Global Foundation Inc.
St. Helen's Meat Packers Limited &
    Lazar Yitzchok Kosher Meats
Barbara L. Steele
Estate of Donald and Frances Strudley
StuCor Construction Ltd.
Sumitomo Canada Ltd.
Symbol Technologies Canada, ULC

TD Friends of the Environment
Teknion Corporation
Thomas, Large & Singer Inc.
Richard Iorweth Thorman
Toronto Cathay Lions Club
Toronto Elegant Lions Club
Toshiba of Canada Limited
Towers Perrin
Toyota Financial Services/Lexus
    Financial Services
Trillion Financial Group
    - Kalano Y. L. Jang
Turner Fleischer Architects Inc.
UFJ Bank Canada
Ukrainian Canadian Foundation
    of Taras Shevchenko
Unisource Canada Inc.
Vanbots Construction
Phyllis and William Waters
Gary and Heidi Weddel
Dr. Fred Weinberg and
    Mrs. Joy Cherry Weinberg
Donald and Sally Wright
Roman (Moko) Wynnyckyj and
    Maria Lialka
Yamaha Motor Canada Ltd.
John Yaremko, Q.C. and
    Mary A. Yaremko
Simon and Jan Zucker & Family
Anonymous (3)

Department of Museum Volunteers Leadership Gifts

Lynn Ruth and
    Ronald Anson-Cartwright
Jacqueline and James Armstrong
Ann Walker Bell
Mary Bosley
Renee Bozowsky
Glad Bryce
Danuta Buczynski
Margaret Bush
Monica Carr
Jeanne Carter
Gloria In Chen & Family
Marilyn Cook
Estate of Lucille R. Davies
Dr. Nell Farquharson
David and Cara Feldman
The Honourable John J. and
    Joan Fitzpatrick
Everett and Frederica Fleming

Michael and Carla Foytenyi
Janet Genest
The Hon. Edwin A. Goodman
    and M. Joan Thompson
Elizabeth D. Hamilton
William and Patricia Harris
Patricia M. Haug
Richard and Martha Hogarth
Marjory Holmes
Margo and Ernest Howard
Diane Hughes & Family
Jane and Paul Jeffrey
Marion John-Postlethwaite
Les and Sandra Lawrence
Jasmine Lin and I-Cheng Chen
Anne Y. Lindsey
Myrna Lo
Susanne and Charles Loewen
Marguerite Low and Mark Winter
Jocelyn MacDonald
Diana and Ronald MacFeeters
Jack and Elizabeth McClelland
Brenda and James McCutcheon
John and Kay McKellar
Joann and Rodger McLennan
Malika Mendez
Elizabeth and Kent Mitchell
The Honourable Robert S. and
    Dixie Anne Montgomery
Ada and Hugh Morris
In honour of Mr. Hossein Mostafavi
Graham and Charlotte Mudge
Dr. Elizabeth (Liz) Muir
Joan Margaret Neilson
Corinne Nemy
Hilary Nicholls
Mr. John G.B. and Mrs. Deanne Orr
Eric Parker
Charlie and Sue Pielsticker
Joan R. Randall
Jean M. Read
Ernest and Flavia Redelmeier
Nita L. Reed
In memory of Elizabeth Rhind
ROM Department of
    Museum Volunteers
Tomo Sato & Family
Yoshiko and Takashi Sawa
The Dorothy Strelsin Foundation
Walter and Jane Tilden
Sally Tuck
Elizabeth M. Walter
Estate of Jean Y. Wright
Sharon Zuckerman
Anonymous

Public Campaign Gifts*

In loving memory of George Abady
Vanessa Abaya and Shawn Voloshin
The Abouchar Family
Dorothy and Sean Abraham
John Abraham and Linda Kurdydyk
Jerry Abramowicz
Accarrino-Marotta Family
The Achen Family
Gwen Brown Acker and Ian Ridge
Hy and Phyllis Ackerman & Family
Susan Ackerman and Donald Smith
John and Jo-Ann Ackery
Active Designers
William Acton and Susan Loube
Patricia S. Adachi
Alex Adams and Jesse Remington
Kathleen and Karen Adams
Ms. Laura Adams and
    Mr. Michael Serbinis
The Adamson Family
Alice Eiseman Adelkind
Tom and Mary Ann Adlhoch & Family
Margaret Agar
Blair, Kate, Calum and Ailsa Agnew
Emily and Adam Agouri
Maria and Ulpiano Aguilera
Radha and Dr. Jan Ahuja
James, Tuyet, Tiffany and
    George Aiken
Mr. Keith and Mrs. Sheila Ainsworth
Aird & Berlis LLP
Barbara A. Aitken
Shreyas and Mina Ajmera
Mohammad and Najla Al Zaibak
al-Ayedi/Williams Family
Donna, Lorne, Jamie and
    Ryan Albaum
Mark Powell Alchuk
Hilary Alderson and Burton Moon
Jonathan Alderson
Susan, Helen and Kerry Alexander
David Allan and Cynthia Young
Don, Elyse and Stuart Allan
Helen Katherine Allan
Clive and Barbara Allen
Drew and Susan Allen
Morgan Richard Allen
Peter and Claire Allen
Keith and Jan Allin Family
The Alqadhi Family
Drs. Howard and Bettina Alter & sons
    Jonathan and Daniel

Altus Helyar Cost Consulting
Francisco Alvarez
Lucien and Irene Amram
Colin and Trevor Anderson
Dale, Michele, Craig
    and David Anderson
In memory of Fred Anderson
Marcelene Anderson
Matt Andrews and Liz Wilson
Stephen Andrews & Family
Robert and Margaret Anglin
Adam and Jane Annandale
Lynn Ruth and
    Ronald Anson-Cartwright
Arlene and John Anthony
Yezdi and Perin Antia
Bram and Bluma Appel
Mark and Gail Appel
Tom, Will and Reed Trimble
    & Lisa Applegath
Cordelia Appleyard
Sebastian Appleyard
Titus Appleyard
Susan M. Arbuckle
ArcelorMittal Dofasco Inc.
James Archer
In memory of Alfredo A. Arenas
Steve Arenburg
Hinna, Neda, Haseeb, Hazeefa, Iqra,
    and Amet Arif
Arius3D Canada
A. R. Armstrong
Erin Armstrong
Isis Armstrong
Jacqueline and James Armstrong
Ken and Mary-Anne Armstrong
Mary K. Armstrong
Mr. & Mrs. R. G. Armstrong
Christiane and Gordon Arnold
Heather and Rick Arnone
Tony and Anne Arrell
Jonathan A. P. Arthur
Katherine V. N. Arthur
Matthew C. T. Arthur
Harvey, Ellen, Andrew and
    Rebecca Ash
Sue and Stewart Ash
Associated Brands
The Assunçao Family
Lloyd R. Atkinson
Robert and Wendy Atkinson
Sandra and Gordon Atlin
Glenda Au and Raymond Cheung
Mr. Hang Au and
    Mrs. Leung Pui Yin Au

Jonah Augustine
Peter and Rae Aust
John Ross and Ivy Florence Austen
Dr. Stephen Austin
Autism Treatment IMTI.ca
Automed Technologies (Canada) Inc.
Lora and John Avgeris
Peter and Joan Avirovic
Robert Ayling and Dr. Philip John
Sharon Aylsworth and John and
    Eric Barr
Betsy and Andrew Aziz

B

Jane Babiak
Bacon/Forrest Family
Salvatore M. Badali and Kim McInnes
George and Anne Bagosy
James C. Baillie
Marilyn and Charles Baillie
Alex Bain and Janet Rossant
Archie and Reta Bain
Peter and Nancy Baines
Baker Real Estate Corporation &
    Invar Building Corporation
Allan and Susan Baker
Anne C. Baker
Clarke and Pamela Baker
Dr. Gerald and Mrs. Nancy Baker
The J. L. Scott Baker
The K. F. Baker Family
Nancy Baker and Richard Shallhorn
Samuel, Naomi and William Baker
Barry Baldasaro, Mary McCullum
    Baldasaro & Family
Mr. & Mrs. Hugh Balders
Pam, Norm and William Baldoni
Vicki and Richard Bales
Helen G. Balfour
Ball Construction Inc.
The Ballantyne Family
Maryl Ballantyne
William and Renée Ballard
Barbara Ballentine
In memory of Michael Baltz
Husayn and Anne Banani
Jane, Mary and John Bancroft
Jane Banfield
Bank of Tokyo-Mitsubishi UFJ
    (Canada)
Jeanne Banka and Nickolas Kamula
Schuyler F. E. Bankes & Family
Jennifer Ivey Bannock
Michael William Bannock
Olivia Ivey Bannock

Stephanie Quinn Bannock
Frank and Sue Banwell
Joe A. Baptista, In memory of
    Victor Baptista
Mrs. Hiroko Barall
John and Maureen Barber & Family
Randy and Solveig Barber
I. W. Bardyn
Marilyn and Paul Barker
Alison Barlow, John, Evan and
    Logan Toews
V. B. Barnecutt
Stephanie A. Barnes
Karen and Bill Barnett
Michael, Jennifer, Madison and
    Jack Barnett
Robert Barnett and
    Leslie Montgomery
Nah-Amakuma Barnor Lamptey &
    Family
Jennifer Barr
Shirley and Edward Barr
Barrday, Inc.
The Barreto Ramos Family
Paul and Maggs Barrett
Kenneth and Gillian Bartlett
Patricia Bartlett-Richards
Ann Bartok-Venetis
Mara Bartolucci and Frances Share
Sherry Barton & Paul and
    Daniel Schmidt
Moira Bartram and Joseph Fantl
Florence Sharpe Barwell
Vincent and Bruna Barzotti & Family
Bill Baskin and Susan Blackburn
In memory of Verna Bast
Marilynn Bastedo and
    George Cooper
Drs. Ralph and Brenda Bastian
Eugene and Christine Batiuk
Mr. David Batten and
    Ms. Heather Banks
Michael, Lena, Vincent and
    Jacob Bauman
Will and Denise Bawden
Wayne Beach
Mitzi Beale
James T. Beamish and Gail D. Lilley
James R. Beattie
Karen and Fred Beattie
Kevin and Sarah Beauchamp
Paula Butler and Jocelyn Beaudoin
The Beaulieu Family
Jacqueline Beaurivage and
    Keith Wilhelm

* Alphabetical list of all donors who generously supported the Renaissance ROM Campaign with gifts of $500 or more.

Robert Boisvert
Debra Yeo Boland
Andre and Benjamin Bolton
Harriett and Gary Bomza
Andrea F. Bond
John and Cherise Bonin
Hugh H. Bonney
Borden Ladner Gervais LLP
Andrew Boright and
 Evelyne Bourrouilh
Mary and Murray Bosley
Sarah and Justin Boudreau
Jean-Raymond Boulle
Dr. Marie Bountrogianni &
 the Tsanis Family
Michael J. Bourassa
H. Blane Bowen
Dr. Arnold Bowers
Donald and Marjorie Bowman
Gary, Linda, Amanda and Naomi Box
Dana Boyko
Jane and Sergio Bozikovic
Bradey Family
Dianne Bradley
Ian W. and Sally B. Braff
Connor, Rhiannon and
 Ferguson Braid
Anna Maria and William Braithwaite
Keith and Anita Braithwaite
Hortense Bramhall
In memory of Brandy, Cricket
 and Lexi
Ann-Louise and Adam Branscombe
Rudolph P. Bratty & Family
Betsy and Carne Bray
Liam and Joseph Bray
Anne Brayley and Nanette Sanson
Jasenka Brcic and Steve Okun
Angelo and Elizabeth Breda & Family
Stephen Breen, Gillian Wan,
 Katherine and Adrian Breen
Sidney and Gladye Bregman
Jack and Margaret Breithaupt &
 Family
Margaret Dorothy Bremner
Allan and Freda Brender
Connor and Colin Brennan
Beryl and Bern Brenner
Edie and Shlomo Brenner
Cára, Aoífe and Caroline Brereton
Robert Brewer and Fionna Hanna
Charles and Samuel Breyfogle
David and Constance Briant
Shirley Bridges
Brendan, John Ross and Liam Briggs

Robert, Ben, Julia and Micah Britton
Kirby M., Sylvia B., Kirby J. and
 Andrew K. Brock
Robin and Margaret Brock
Peter Brodey, Quinn and
 Jaime Reetham-Clayton
Ava and Michael Brodsky
Bill Brokenshire
Brookfield Asset Management Inc.
Mr. J. Frank Brookfield
Laurel Brooks, Brad Cameron and
 Franklin, Lane, Malcolm and Blaire
Rick and Priscilla Brooks-Hill
Dwayne Brookson
Donald R. Brown, Q.C.
Joanne Brown and Kayla Brown
K. B. Brown in memory of
 Francis Bede Brown
Peter and Mary Brown
Robert and Wendy Brown
Sam, Jake and Libby Brown
Sandy Brown and Lara Henry
Bruce Edmeades Co.
Christian, Mitchell and Sian Bruce
Laura and Mitchell Bruce
Michael, Faith and Matthew Bruce
Harold and Ruth Brudner
Thomas W., Marilla G. and
 David J. Bruggenkoch
In memory of Joe Brummer
Frank, Rosa, Jessica and Phillip Bruno
Dr. John C. Bryan and
 Tamara Weir Bryan
R.A. Bryan
Kirk Bryant and Michael Trent
Glad Bryce
John Buchan
Louis, Christine, Clare and
 James Buchanan
Maureen Buchanan
Mr. Walter Buchwalder and
 Mr. Wayne Kerr
Kieran Alexander Mielke
 Buckingham
Lindsay Christianna Mielke
 Buckingham
Robert Buckman, Patricia Shaw,
 James and Matthew Buckman
Brian Bucknall and Mary J. Mossman
David and Lois Buckstein
Danuta Buczynski
Nina Budman
Klaus, Irene and
 Hazel Rose Buechner
Pym and Kathryn Buitenhuis

Chris and Debbie Buklin
Stephen Bulger and Catherine Lash
In memory of Ben G. Bull
Mary Bunnett
M. J. Petersen Burfield and
 The Burfield Family
Burgundy Asset Management Ltd.
Marie Luise Burkhard
Dennys Burkovsky
Leah Burkovsky
Burnbrae Farms Limited
Brenda J. Burnett
Hayden Burnett
Scott Burnett
Vanessa Burnett
Christopher and Audrie Burns
Clare Burns, Mark Hemingway and
 Fiona Burns-Hemingway
June F. Burnside
Deborah Burrett and Mario Possamai
William Reid Burridge
The Burton Charitable Foundation
Margaret Bush
Barb and David Butler
Fallon Butler
Deborah Butterfield
Gregory Buzbuzian

C

Franz, Rod, Edwin, Vita, Ian,
 Colin Caberoy and Miling Flores
Paul V. Caetano
Linda and Gord Caldwell
William J. Callahan
Archie, Sonia, Céline and
 Colin Callender
Lynn and Isaline Calliste,
 Nicholas Woollard & Family
R. Denys Calvin
Alicia, Horacio, Monica, George and
 Albert Calzaretto
Sidney and Liviana Calzavara
Craig Cameron
Jane Cameron
Margaret Harriett Cameron
Campbell Company of Canada
Christina Campbell and
 Barry McSherry
In memory of Hugh James
 Raphael Campbell
Jacqueline Campbell and
 Steven Boldovitch
James Edward Alan Campbell
Lincoln J. Campbell
Michael and Marianne Campbell

Michael and Marisol Campbell
Canadian General-Tower Limited
Jack Candido
Anne-Marie and Robert Canning
Canon Canada Inc.
Donna Capel
Arthur Caplan
Carmela Capone
Jacob and Thomas Cappadocia
Mrs. Coleman Cappe & Family
C.A.R.A.K.A.
Cargill Meat Solutions
Ken and Denise Cargill
Oscar and Angus Carlson-Whan
Leila Carnegie
J. Patrick Caron and
 Madeleine Comission Caron
Barbara and John Carpenter
Ellen and Brian Carr
Gerald and Betty Carr
Monica Carr
In memory of Katie Carrigg
Peter and Jagg Carr-Locke
C. E. Carsley
Auleen Carson and Paul Lupinacci
Barbara M. Carson
Charlotte and Brian Carter
Jeanne Carter
Graham and Barb Carver
Jessie Caryll & Family
Cascades Tissue Group
Mrs. Deborah and Mr. Dan Casey
Patrick and Annie Casey
Jerry, Marian, Alanna and
 Clint Cassells
Mrs. Betty Pat Cassels
Farren Catalano & Family
Cathay Pacific Airways Limited
The Catherwood Family
Dr. John Catherwood
Dorothy Catterson
Robert Cavanaugh
Centennial Foods
Margaret Chambers and
 Dr. Catherine Steele
The Albert C.W. Chan Foundation
Carl C.K. Chan
Chancery Mendez Holdings C. Ltd.
Chandaria Foundation
Amanda and Francis Chang
W. K. Chang Family
Pearl Pochu Chan-Hsing
Rose Marie E. Chapeskie
Dr. Paul and Joyce Chapnick &
 Family

Dr. Jerry and Justice Sandra Chapnik & Family
Farley Charad & Family
Robert and Lorraine Charbonneau
Richard and Jeanette Charron
Barbara, Pat and Duncan Charters
John and Vera Chau
Karen Cheah
Gloria In Chen & Family
Maureen J. Chen
John Chenery, Mary MacDonald and George Chenery
Cynthia Cheng
Randy Cheng
Dee Chenier
Dr. Martin Chepesiuk and Ms. Halyna Perun
Joanna Chesterman and Richard Betel
Kei Chicoy-Daban & Family
Amelia Chik
Kamal, Pia, Zain and Maira Chinoy
Barbara Chisholm
In memory of Donald Chisholm
Dr. Donald A. and Mrs. Marilyn Chisholm
But-Yau, Lucinda, Jonathan, Christopher and Christina Chiu
Dr. John H. C. and Yvonne Chiu, C. M.
Donald, Kelly and Kristen Choffe
Lucienne and Gregory Choryhanna
Ramesh Chotai & Family
Anne Choy, B'elanna and William Anderson
Barbara Anne Christie
Valerie and David Christie
Morgan and Quinn Christopher
Brian and Francine Chu
Gordon and Sandra Chu & Family
Linda Chu and John Donald
David and Sheila Chuang
Chubb Insurance Company of Canada
The Church Family
Frank and Alison Cianciolo
CIBC
CIBC Mellon
Mrs. Phyllis and Mr. Michael Cincinatus
Paolo Cini
Ioana Ciric
The CIT Group
City of Toronto
CKF Inc.
Faye Clack and Ewing Rae

Dr. Anne Claessens
Timothy Clague and Sharon O'Grady & Family
Fr. Donald Clark and Fr. David Mulholland
Linda J. Clark and Linda G. Stone
Lyn Clark
Damon and Karen Clarke
Michael and Linda Clarke
Giovanna, Ross, Daniel and Dominique Claybo
Matthew Cleland
Joanne E. Clement and D. J. F. Maltby
Pat and Geri Clever
Ditas and Geoff Cliffe-Phillips
Clifford Restoration Limited
In memory of Cameron Clifford
Dr. Cameron, Winnie, Duncan, Kayla and Colin Clokie
In loving memory of Betty Coatsworth
Anne Cobban and Edward Sitarski
John and Debi Coburn
Bernard Cocchiola and Richard Guisso
Caroline Di Cocco
Matt Cockburn, Sue Valencia, Adam, Megan & Jenna
Margaret E. Cockshutt
Jack Cockwell and Lynda Hamilton
Vincenzo Cocuzzoli
Muriel A. Code
Ronald A. Coffin
Eric, Michelle, Debra, Lisa Cohen
Dr. Zane and Joan Cohen and Jennifer and Allison
Claudia Colas
James and Janice, Jade, Jason Colbert
Marion Colbourne
Priscilla Cole
Ryan Cole, Hilary Cole, Maxwell Gaudet, Harrison Gaudet, Kasha Luis Gaudet, Andrea Luis Gaudet and Ethan Mark Luis Gaudet
Liam Coleman and Paul McGrath
Andre and Katharine Colenbrander
Jillian and Richard Coles
Colgate-Palmolive Canada Inc.
Shelly, sons David-Craig and Jonathan-Ashley Collard
Colley Insurance
Margaret Collier
Louisa Hurd Collins
Gloria Collinson and Frank Davies
Comisso Family

Commemorative Organization for the Japan World Exposition ('70)
Compass Canada
Dea Compton
Dr. Robin Compton
ConAgra Foods Canada
Kathy Condie and Jay Crockford
Nancy Conn and Douglas Grant
George and Sheila Connell
Joy and Paul Connelly
Dean Connor and Maris Uffelmann
Hugh and Janet Conover
Mr. Gerry Conway and Dr. K.V. Srinivasan
Lisa, Brendan, Rory and Aidan Conway
Jacqueline Cook and Eriks Rugelis
Gary and Benjamin Landrus and Lloy Cook
Marilyn Cook
Priscilla Cook
Barry and Susanne Cooper
Daniel Cooper
Dr. Deborah Chesnie Cooper
Elsie Cooper & Family
Kenneth, Kevin and Jackson Cooper
William and Susan Copland
Robert and Hazel Copp
Amalia Coppo
Paul W. Cornell
In memory of Jean Cornelson
The Honourable Peter Cory
Dr. Jane Coryell
Jeanne Timmins Costello Trust
Terence and Mary Cottrell
Barry and Linda Coutts
Maureen Couture
In memory of William Cowan
Ronald Cowell
Phil, Sue and Christian Cowling
Maurice and Elizabeth Cowper-Smith
Dr. Brian and Mrs. Irene Cox
Peter M. Cox
Patricia Coyne
Gloria Crabb
The Estelle Craig Family Trust
Sheilagh Crandall
Elizabeth L. Crane
In memory of Frank H. Crane
Sarah, Courtney and David Cranmer & Owen Taylor
Elizabeth Crawford
Jean Crawford
Edie and Eddie Creed
Robert and Jill Creighton

The Crerar Family
Amy and Barnie Crespi & Children
Peter and Margaret Crichton
Sheila M. Croft
Crombie Kennedy Nasmark Inc.
Shane and Brad Crompton
Diana M.T. Crosbie
Cross Hueller, LLC
Mr. Walter Cross
In memory of Ed Crossman
Anne Crowley
Mike, Judy, Micaela and Peter Crowley
Dr. James E. Cruise
Antonio and Purita Cruz
Rob Cudney
David M. Cullen
In memory of Grace and Bert Cullimore
Joanna, Maureen and Lynda Cully
Cultural Spaces Canada Program
Isabel Hadlen Cumandra
Barbara and Gordon Cummings
Ann I. Cunningham
Phil and Eva Cunningham
Ann Curran & sisters Nora and Mary-Pat
Dr. Daniel Curran and Mrs. Mary Curran
Chris Currelly
Marion E. Current
A. Blaine Currie and Terrance E. Smith
Dr. Douglas C. Currie & Family
Gabriel Declan Currie
T. Curry and L. Monteith & Family
John, Christine, Michael and Katelyn Cursio
Mr. Simon and Mrs. Michelle Curtis
Matthew, Leo, Michael Custode, Helen Bagshaw
Dr. Charles Cutrara and Karin Page-Cutrara
Michael and Patricia Cutting
Charles and Barbara Cutts
The Czegledy/Sorbie Family

D

The D. & T. Davis Charitable Foundation
Tim and Joanne Daciuk
Susan M. Dahlgren
Anita Levine Dahlin and Corrina Dahlin & In memory of Tula and Sam Levine

Natalie, Monica and Patrick Dale
Dr. Michael Dales and Angela Herwin
Camilla Dalglish
Christopher and Debra Dalton
Norma and George Dalton
Sandra Dalziel and Kevin Leonard
Evangeline M. Damian
The Danahys
C. P. and C. Scrafield Danby
Kimberly Danielson, Allen Zee,
    Annika and Kristopher Zee
Isobel and Barney Danson
Brian E. Darmos
Chandrika and Pradipta Datta
James and Marion Davey & Family
David Chapman's Ice Cream Limited
Bruce Davidson
Dimitra and Michael Davidson &
    Family
John Davidson and Irena Orlowski
Mary Davidson
Jane Davidson-Neville
Donald and Neli Davies & Family
Frances Davies
Dr. Joan Anne Moreland Davies
Estate of Lucille R. Davies
Bob Davis and
    Meredith MacFarquhar
Brian Davis
In memory of Carol Davis
George and Ulrike Davis
Joan Davis
Mary-Alice Davis
Richard Davis and
    Karen Rylander-Davis
The Hon. William G. and Kathleen Davis
Heather Davis-Buss
John and Shirley Dawe
Brian Dawson and John Therrien
Peter, Lucy, Katie Dawson
Sriram Dayanand and
    Gayathri Seetharam
De Beers Canada Inc.
Sue and Barry De Grandis
Robert and Evelyn de Langley
Michael and Honor de Pencier
Susan De Rosa
Donna and Bruce Deans
Yvette and Mike Debiasi
Andrew and Tracey Debnam
Raymond and Louise Decarie
    & Family
David, Kelly, Michael and
    Celeste DeFaveri
The DeGasperis Family

Vesna M. and Aloysia C. G. DeJulio
Delaney Family Foundation
Siobhan Delaney and
    Mariangeles Najlis
Ramon and Kimberley Delgado
Mr. David and Ms. Carolyn Dell
Aldo V. and Olga Dellidonne
Deloitte
Carol DelZotto
Leo and Sandra DelZotto
Vincent, Maude and Zoe DeMarco
Robert and Joanna DeMone
George and Leslie Denier, In memory
    of their grandson Benj Foster
Pearl and Harold Dennis & Family
Dennison Fowl Family
DENSO Manufacturing Canada, Inc.
Dentsu Canada
Department of Canadian Heritage –
    Virtual Museum of Canada
Tessa Derksen and John Brennan
In memory of Williamina, Francis and
    Vincent Dermody
Margaret and Douglas Derry
Sylvie Desfossés and Stephane Massé
David and Beverley Deslauriers
The Desrochers Family
Michael Detlefsen and
    Louise Le Beau
Michael, Patricia, Shannon and
    Matthew Deverell
Gerry Devette and James Jezioro
The Deviveiros Family
Dr. Tim and Carol Devlin
Jacqueline and Connor Dew
Eric and Martha Dewar & Jakob,
    Madelaine and Meghan Dewar
Jassodra and Ramdeo Dhanasar
Di Buono-Papamandjaris Family
The Di Giacomo Family
Morris and Daria Diakowsky
Dial Canada
Arthur and Denny Diamond & Family
Kelly Dickinson
Richard, Karen and Cole Didier &
    Casey and Jesse Massari
J. B. DiGiovanni
Nancy Dignam
Dorothy and George Dilworth
Martin Dimnik
Jane Dingle
Jessica Dinsmore
John and Fay Dirks
Sylvia and Bill Dixon
Glenn and Candy Dobbin

Rosemary Dobbin
In memory of Katherine Dobias
Geoffrey, Luisa, Sarah, Marc and
    Matthew Dobilas
Mary I. Dobson
Nancy Dobson
Susan L. Dobson (Art Students of
    Ridley & Appleby College)
Judge and Mrs. D.B Dodds
James Doherty
Jane K. Doherty
Ms. Lesley Doherty
Dorie Dohrenwend
Dole Packaged Foods Canada
Constance A. Donely
Steven D. Donohoe
Keshave H. Dookie
Marlies and Alfred Dookwah
Kathryn Doresco
In memory of Elizabeth and
    John Dorner
Mark, Rima and Hannah Dornfeld
Sylvie Doucet
Cheryl Douglas and Gerald Visc
C. Arthur Downes J.P. Litt.D
Laney Doyle
John and Merrilyn Driscoll
Mr. & Mrs. R.J. Drummond
Christopher Du Vernet
Ernest Du Vernet
Kaleigh and John David Du Vernet
Peter-Paul Du Vernet
Sylvia Du Vernet
Timothy Du Vernet
The Dubczak Family
The Duboc Family
Scott and Nancy Dudgeon
Barbara E. Duffus
Andrew Duffy and Ruth Richardson;
    Joshua, Rebekah, Samuel
Gillian Duffy
Lauren Duffy
Leslie Duffy & Family
Michael Duffy
Grainne Duggan, Brian and Ian Lasby
Kevin Duke and Meredith Meads
Loa Beth Dulmage
Mrs. Patricia Dumas
George and Linda Duncan
Mr. Wilfrid and Mrs. Barbara Duncan
Robert and Caroline Duncanson
F. Norman Dundas
Dorothy J. Dunlop
Mary, Zec, Eph, Man Dunn, and
    Norma Dunn

William M. Dunne & Associates Ltd.
K Dunnell and K Bateman
William, Susan, Andrew, Marlene and
    Zoë Dunsmoor
Dupont Corian / The Willis Group
Della Dwane
Dr. Daniel Dwyer and
    Mr. Michael Dwyer
Susan, Geoffrey, Emily and
    Elizabeth Dyer
Carolyn Dyke

E

E. D. Smith & Sons, Limited
E.R.A. Architects Inc.
Ken and Shura Eadie
Ms. Lynn Eakin and Mr. David Young
Barton J. Earle and Timothy D. Earle
Pamela and Richard Earle
Cléophée Eaton
Fredrik S. Eaton
Thor and Nicole Eaton
Thor Edmond Eaton
Frank and Anna Ebenhardt
William and Gwenda Echard
Letitia Edinborough
Dr. Brodie Edmonds
David Edwards
Nancy Susan Edwards PhD
Patricia and Peter Edwards
Irina Efimov
Linda Egan, Tara Egan Wu and
    Daniel McGinley
Dr. Judith Eger
Prof. C. S. Ehrlich and
    Rabbi M. Shekel
Heidi, Eric, Ingrid Eilbracht,
    Doug Burn
Joan and Hy Eiley
Brian and Laila Eiriksson
Dr. Ari and Mrs. Elisa Eisen
Irving Eisenberg, Elbert Lee Hoffman,
    Thomas Sullivan and Ron Wilson
John and Vera Elder
El-En Packaging Company Limited
The Eley Family
Elgammal Family, Tarek,
    Yasmine and Omar
Maria and Jack Elias & Family
Doug, Shirley and Philip Elliott
Elizabeth Elliott
Heather J. Elliott
Lynne and Jordan Elliott
Dr. Mary Elliott and
    Dr. Mark Minden

Mr. & Mrs. Daniel Ellis
Rodney, Neil, Bruce, Clare, Ian Ellis
Evelin Ellison
Jean and Adrian Emberley
Emergis Inc.
Raffi and Natalie Emirzian
Margaret E. Emmerson
Mary Eng
The Engstrom Family (Mark, Fiona,
    Holly and Ian)
Sharon and Larry Enkin
Susan and Bill Ennis
John, Nancy Enright and
    Abbygael Angle-Enright
Erie Meat Products Limited
Peter, Elda and Lee Eustace
Evans Industrial Installations Ltd.
Christine and David Evans
Donald G. Evans
George Evans
Sharon Evans
Verona May Evans
Gordon, Patricia, Sarah and
    Hilary Ewen
Ms. Marjorie Ewing
Exploration Production Inc.
Joan Eydt

F

Andrew Faas
Carol and Paul Fahey
Beverley Fainer
Heather Faire
Ms. Patricia Falck
Fallico Family, Giorgio and Frank
Anna-Liisa and Graham Farquharson
Dr. Nell Farquharson
W. Robert Farquharson & Family
Beryl Farr
Maral, Shant, Alec and Hrag Farra
Bernadette and Angela Farrell
Elizabeth Roias Farrell
Barbara Farrell-Drum
Berle Farrier
Farrow & Ball
The Feddoes Family
David and Cara Feldman
Michael, Lee Anne, Kirsten and
    Lauren Femson
Prof. William and Mrs. Jean Fennell
Dr. Ian and Mrs. Nadine Ferguson
Howard and Elaine Fergusson
Kathleen Fernandez, Douglas Gray,
    Hannah, Emily and Joshua
Anthony Ferrari and Karen Millon

Ferro Technique Ltd.
In memory of Michael Fershaloff
Roberta and Jon Fidler
Dr. Madeline M. Field
Robert and Mary Fielden
Glenna and George Fierheller
Frances Filegan
The Filippovitch Family
Keith, Sharon, Meagan, Scott and
    Laura Fillmore
Jack M. Fine
Cameron and Mary Ellen Finlay
Mary Finlay, William Riddell, Stephen
    Finlay, Catherine Riddell and
    Martha Riddell
Rod and Susan Finlayson
Ms. Elizabeth Finnie-Hunt
Dr. Gail Firestone
First Gulf Corporation
Beatrice Fischer
Judith E. Fisher and Helen J. Fisher
Ruth and Richard H. Fisher
Dr. Margaret I. Fitch
The Honourable John J. and
    Joan Fitzpatrick & Grandchildren:
    Rodger Seccombe, Jennifer
    Seccombe, Elizabeth Hanly, William
    Seccombe, Michael MacDonald,
    Drew Morrison, Brendon
    Morrison, Kaeli MacDonald,
    Patrick Stevens, Carl Romcolthoff,
    Teija Romcolthoff and
    Kathleen Stevens
Trent Flack Sr., Tiana Flack,
    Trent Flack Jr. and Sabrina Flack
Ana Flander
Dr. John and Mrs. Maria Flannery
Mr. Barry Flatman
Thomas Flatt and Paul Barkley
Paulette Fleary, Rowan and
    Rhece Holung
Charlotte and Nathaniel Fleming
Everett and Frederica Fleming
Lois Fleming
Alan and June Fletcher
Marna Fletcher
Paul Fletcher
Kimberly Flood and Andreas Kyriakos
Michael, Marnie, Ryan and Caitlyn Flux
Joshua Fogel and Joan Judge-Fogel
Lloyd and Gladys Fogler &
    Grandchildren: Laura Fogler,
    Katherine Fogler, Sarah Nadal,
    Samantha Nadal, Alison Levitt,
    Bradley Levitt and Carolyn Levitt

In memory of Herta and
    Konstantin Fokins
CM and L Foley
Dr. Peter G. Forbath
Johanne Forbes
Peg Forbes
James Ford and Brenda Coomber
Matthew John Ford, Joan Van
    Kralingen and Julia Van Kralingen
Philip and Margaret Ford
D. Scott Forfar
Marc Formosa
Gordon and Lorraine Forrest
Roberta Forrest
Jane and Larry Forster
Joyce and George Forster
The Fort Family
Ann Foster
Robert and Julia Foster
Jonathan, Rina and Eric Fowler
Dr. Marian Fowler
Mrs. Shirley Fowley
Margaret and Elizabeth Anne Fox
Fox-Burjaw Family
Michael and Carla Foytenyi
Mary Frances and Keith Hendrick
Antonio and Mariolina Franceschetti
Joan Francis
Lorna Francis and Jonathon Brooks
Julie and Patrick Franco
Franklin Templeton Investments
Gordon and Claudette Franklin
Janice Franklin and Dean Moratz
James D. Fraser and Suzan Khan
Madison Elizabeth Fraser, Brieanna
    Nicole Preston and Christopher &
    Marilynda Cunliffe
Mrs. Mary Fraser-Earl
Romano and Emilia Frasson
Dawn and Sidney Freedman
Stella and Gerald Freedman
J.V and E. Frei
Eva M. Fried
E.D. Friedlander
Dr. Brian and Mrs. Anna Friedman
Muriel and Colin Friesen & Family
Frito Lay Canada
Mary Louise Elizabeth Fritz
Jim, Judi, Emily and Sydney Frohlick
Lynn, Kathryn, Eric and Jeremy From
R. Derek Frost Family
Mrs. Myrna Frost
Murray Frum and Nancy Lockhart
Susan J. Frye
Fuchs Lubricants Canada Ltd.

Joanna and William Fuchs & Family
Carol Lynn Fujino and Ronald G. Mah
Michael and Wendy Fullan
Barbara, Andrew and Charles Fuller
Katherine K.Y. and
    Stephanie X.Y. Fung
Prof. John and Mrs. Alda Futhey
Ruth E. Fuyarchuk

G

Samuel and Melda Gabbidon
Leslie Galbraith & Rob and
    Boris Baker
Gamble Sperling Family
Robert L. Gambles
Anna and Sydney Gangbar
Eric Gangbar and Lisa Markson
Dr. Andres Gantous and
    Dr. Jennifer Anderson
Garber Kahn Family
The Gard Family - Brian, Lorraine,
    Natasha, Autumn, Edward, Zoe and
    Bradley
Helen E. Gardiner
Marian Gardiner
Roger F. Gardiner and
    Margaret Martin Gardiner
Thomas Gardiner and Adelaide Taylor
Douglas G. Gardner
Ellis and Pat Gareth & Family
Steve Garmaise, Sue Rebick Matan
    and Gabe
Peter and Shirley Garneau
The Garvey Family
Joseph and Mary Garwood
Bruce, Nida, Vanessa and Kelly Gates
Evelyn Gaye and Julie Crooks
Fiona Gazenbeek and Joe Przednicki
GE Canada
Linda Geddes
David Geen and Rita Krysak
General Mills Canada Corporation
Janet Genest
Genuine Health
Bernadette and Alexander Gerol
Mr. & Mrs. G.W. Getson
In memory of Judith Eve Gewurtz,
    Margo, Shalon and
    Michelle Gewurtz
Constance and Garnet Gibbon
Shirley Giblon
Lynda Giddings
Carolee Gilbert
Dr. David and Mrs. Diane Gilday
    & Family

Lucille Giles
Robert and Glennys Gill
The Gillam Family
Norman and Florence Gillanders
The Honourable Alastair and
    Diana Gillespie
Bob and Irene Gillespie
Karen L. Gillies
Peter and Dianne Gillin
Paul, Jennifer, Jessie and
    Emily Gillingham
Barry and Emilia Gilmour
Louise C. Gilroy
The Gindl Family of Ottawa
Eric and Susan Girard
Bria and Connor Gitt
The Gleasure Family
Joseph and Velma Glesta
The Globe and Mail
Sylvie and Peter Glossop
Robert and Hannah Glover and
    Martha McOuat
Wayne and Mary Glover
Alexander Gluskin and
    Shauna Sexsmith
Ira Gluskin and
    Maxine Granovsky-Gluskin
Mr. & Mrs. J. Lawrence Goad
Leo, Lisa and Justin Godfrey-Nodwell
Dorothea Godt and Ulrich Tepass
Vincent Gogan
Elaine and Peter Gold & Family
Martin and Joan Goldfarb
Louise and Mark Golding
Goldman Sachs Canada Inc.
Murray and Sheila Goldman
Sheba and Herb Goldstein
Apolonia Golen
Della Golland
Peter Gooderham/Michele McCarthy
The Hon. Edwin A. Goodman and
    M. Joan Thompson
The Wolfe and Millie Goodman
    Foundation
In memory of James Duncan
    Goodwin
Mary Gooley
Kamala-Jean Gopie O. Ont.
Charlotte Gorbet & Family
Debbi Gordon
Joan and Gregg Gordon
In honour of Landers and
    Le Dain Gordon
Lynn and Maryon Gordon
Ron and Estelle Gordon

Sarah and Claire Gordon
Ross Gorrie
Tayte, Flynne, Reed and
    Tilly Gossling
Marion, Leo, Rachel and
    Jacob Gotlieb
In memory of John M. Gottschalk
Marcia W. Gould
Alan and Judith Goulding
Ms. Ina Govan
Government of Canada
Government of Ontario
Government of Ontario - Ministry of
    Culture Capital Rehabilitation
    Fund
Gowling Lafleur Henderson LLP
David Grader, Q.C.
Bill Graesser
Senator Jerry and
    Carole Grafstein, Q.C.
For Andrew and Emma Graham
Brent Graham and Helen Macrae
Helen E. Graham
Janet and David Graham
Kitty Graham
Melba Graham, Penny and Shannon
Messrs Graham and Greaves
Michael and Nancy Graham
Robert, Denise, Michael and
    Peter Graham
Hamlin Grange and Cynthia Reyes
Grant & Bernhardt
Barry, Gayle, Britt, Tucker and
    Morgan Grant
John and Catherine Grant
John and Judith Grant
Kenneth and Candace Grant
Margaret R. Grant
In memory of Marjorie Helen Grant
Mark Grant and Karim Eid
P.A. Gravel
Brian and Rosemary Gray
Donald and Margaret Gray
Malcolm M., Betty W. and
    Karen Gray
J. Grayson, E. Miller, Grayson and Ryan
Greater Toronto Airports Authority
Dolores, Michael, Andrea, Vanessa and
    David Greco
Embassy of Greece
Carrie and Frank Green & Jackson
    and Clayton Howe
Katherine Green
The Patrick and Freda Hart Green
    Foundation

Ene Greenaway
Wendy Greene, John, Sam and
    Daniel Dupuis
Brian H. Greenspan and Marla Berger
William L. Greenwood
John and Geraldine Greey
Dr. Keith and Mrs. Sheila Gregoire
Greg's Ice Cream
Ralph and Jayne Gresham
Allan Griffin and
    Christine McClymont
Andrew Griffin
Scott and Krystyne Griffin
Frieda A. Griffiths
Trevor, Marilyn, Jo-Anne, Barbara,
    Christopher and Michael Grimwood
Rani, Jan-Willem, Nils and
    Liam Gritters
Profs. Michael Kirkham and
    Ruth Grogan
Susie Gromit
Nick Groocock and Liz Stupavsky
Carl and Wilma Groskorth Family
William and Frances Gruber
Julia Grunau and Greg Smith
Matthew Gryschuk
Nicholas and Stella Gu
In memory of Roma M. Gunning
The Gunter Family
Natasha and Mark Gurevich
H. Donald Guthrie, Q.C.
Elizabeth Gutteridge
Allan and Helen Guttman
George and Beverly Guy
Linda Arlene Guz
Jack and Judy Gwartz
Michael John Gwynne
Ms. Shirley Gwynne-Smith and
    Mr. Malcolm Smith

H

H. J. Heinz Company of Canada Ltd.
Priscilla Y. Sau Ha
Gudrun Hackert
Rainer K. Hackert
Ryan, James and Wendy Hadcock
Paul Haggis
Isabella and Nora Hahn
Haidasz-Cybulski Family
Leslie, Bill and Geoff Hajdu
Ralph and Roz Halbert
Michael and Marjorie Hale
Harry and Susan Hall
Lyle Hall
Jim Halliday

William and Daphne Halloran
Michael A. Halls
Halton Imaging Associates
Everard N. Hambro
Betty and Bob Hamilton
Elizabeth Hamilton
Lisa Hamilton and Mark Quail
The Hammond Family
Chase and Curran Hanchar
Scott and Ellen Hand
Jacqueline Hanley, Sinead and
    Gavin Wheleham and
    Richard Thomas
Dr. Brian and Mrs. Isabelle Hanna
The Hannon-Cobb Family
Helen and Bert Hanratty
Judith Zeisler Hans and
    Sherman Hans
Prof. Roger and Mrs. Mary Hansell
Ms. Cheryl Hanson and
    Dr. Ronald A. Kuipers
Kirsten Hanson and Sandy Houston
Sharon and Michael Hanson
Thomas W. Hanson
Di and Simon Hardacre
Frank and June Harding
Michelle, Christy, Joel and
    Shane Hardy
Donald L. Hargrove and
    Gloria Jane Hargrove
Anne and William Harker
In memory of Jean Winston Harlock
Gerry and Janis Harlos
Barbara Harold
Bruce T. Harpham
Jean and Ken Harrigan
Allen S. Harrington
Daniel, Bailey, Kyle, Sarah, Caitlyn &
    John and Diane Harris
Jennifer and Bill Harris
Penny and Bill Harris
Robert W. Harris
William and Patricia Harris
Mary Lee Harrison
The Hart Family
Bardy and Ronald Hart
Dr. Gerald and Mrs. Lilian Hart
R. Allan and Georgia Hart
Darlene and Kathryn E. Harte
Kendra Hart-Lee, Corinna Lee and
    Bradd Hart
Adrian Hartog and Jasmine
    Vujasinovic Hartog
Lindsey Hartshorn and
    Toby Hartshorn

Richard and Gwen Harvey,
   Scott Harvey, Jacqueline Harvey,
   Patrick Harvey
Sarah Harvey, Alyssa Harvey,
   Idamae Joyce
Tom Haslett and Sunny Mills
Ruth E. Hastie
Daniel and Noah Hastings
Sylvie and Cliff Hatch & Family
Ms. Sheila Hathorn
Patricia M. Haug
Hauser Industries Inc.
Gordon and Lorna Hawkett
The Hayes Family – Dennis and
   Dianne Hayes
Lydia Hayne-Jenkins
Gordon, Linda and Susan Haynes
Laurie and Richard Haynes
Ronald M. and Sherry L. Haynes
The Haynes-Connell Foundation
Barry Kenneth Haywood and
   Doreen Rapport
Judith Hazen and Greg Lappan
Frank and Heather Heaps
William and Linda Hechter
Harold and Emmeline Hedley
Judith and Edward Heffernan
The Heggie Family
Annemarie and Kurt Heinze, Simone,
   Paul, Reece and Bryce Robson
Barcley Ann Heisey
Fern Hellard
In memory of Ellen J. Hellyer
Pamela, Jennifer, Cassandra, Derek
   and Kevin Helt
Ann and Lyman Henderson
Barbara Henderson
Dianne W. Henderson
Ewan Leslie Henderson
Pamela and Gordon Henderson
George M. Hendry
Lorna and Robert Hendry
Ross A. Hennigar
Susan, Harcus and Colin Hennigar
Paul, Jennifer, Elenor, Madeleine,
   Duncan, Julia and Naomi Henry
Doreen Henwood and
   Michael Wilmot
Adela Hepburn
Calum Hepburn
Magnus Hepburn
Herbert-Robertson Family
Alix Hersak and Rubsun, Sophie and
   Noah Ho
Fred and Mara Herscovitch

Paul Hess and Katherine Childs
Estate of Helen S. Heward
Ms. Margaret Hicks
Higgins & Burke Tea & Coffee
Brenda, Stephen, Sarah and
   Graeme Higgins
Fiona Highet, Andrew, Stirling and
   Alistair Scott
Dan Hill and Lisle Christie
Miss Dorothy Hill
Kate, Jennifer and Laura Hill
Nancy Hill, Timothy Boyd,
   Isabel Hill Boyd
Paul and Rhoda Hill & Family
Eldon and Norma Hillyard
Kate Hilton, Rob Centa and
   Jack Hilton-Centa
Althea and Adelaide Himel
Donald Himes
Barbara Hinds
James and Susan Hinnecke & Family
Hino Motors Canada
The Hipp Family – Hedwig, Bernard,
   Lore, Sonia, Valerie, Paul
Mr. Leslie Hipson
Hitachi Canada Ltd.
Belinda and Kenneth Ho
Mr. Kim Yim Ho and
   Walter Frederic Thommen
Matthew Ho, Sadamu and
   Shigemi Imaoka
Harry J. Hodge, P. Eng.
Marjorie I. Hodges
Terri, Ronald and Geoffrey Hodges
John and Joan Hodgson
Norbert, April, Geoffrey and
   Kristen Hoeller
Gloria Hoflezer
Lena Hogan
Siobhan and Kathleen Hogan
Richard and Martha Hogarth
Erin M. Hogg
Frances and Peter Hogg
The Honourable Stanton and
   Mrs. Elspeth Hogg
Kathleen H. Hohner
Richard and Donna Holbrook
John and Genevieve Holden
John and Kathryn Holden
Rudolf and Myrna Holder
The Holdway Family
Alexandra and Julia Holgate
Emma, Matthew, Andrew and
   James, Rebecca and Aidan Holland
Nancy Holland

Marjory Holmes
Tyla Holmes
Philip N. Holtby
Adam and Adrienne Holzapfel
Bruce and Candy Homer
Honda Canada Inc.
Florence Honderich
Sarah and John Honey
Anne Hope-Brown
David and Lynn Hopkins
Oksana Horbach and
   Irfon-Kim Ahmad
Lee and Barbara Horigan & Family
Ralph R. Hornell
Sjouke, Petra and Derek Horopw
Roland and Rae Horst
John E. Horton & Family
Jim, Margaret, Jack, Peter and
   Charlotte Hoskins
Mrs. Barbara Houlding
Chris Hourmouzis
Alan C. and Phyllis A. Houston
Margo and Ernest Howard
Dale and Barbara Howey
Barbara Howlett
Christina, Michael Howlett & Family
Audrey Hozack
HSBC Bank Canada
William Wei Jan Hsing
Margaret Huckle & Family
Diane Hudson
Ally Hughes
Diane Hughes & Family
Evan Hughes
Kaela Hughes
Teagan Hughes
Ann Hughson
Ms. Paz Humana
Karl and Beverley Hummitzsch
Mr. and Mrs. W. B. G. Humphries
John Hunkin and Susan Crocker
Marguerite Emma Moogk Hunt
Martin and Judith Hunter
Robert and Helvi Hunter
John and Helen Hurd
Tim Hurson, Franca Leeson & Family
Fazal, Maryam, Yasmeen, Sarah,
   Mahmoud and Khadijah Husain
Hussmann Canada Inc.
Michael and Linda Hutcheon
Mr. T. D. Hutchen
The Hutchison and Kearns Family
Kay G. Hutton
Margaret Huybers
Roy N. Hyer

J. Alison Hymas
Barbara Ann Hynes

I

IBM Canada Ltd.
Ice River Springs Water Co.
Ian Ihnatowycz and Marta Witer
Ilona, Erica, Heidi, Ashley, Kylee
   and Dylan
Patricia Rawlings Ing & Family
Sam and Jill Ingram
Inmet Mining Corporation
Interforest Ltd.
Jay Ionson
William W. K. Ip and
   Kathleen A. Latimer
The Ippolito Family
IPSCO Charitable Foundation
James and Patricia Ireland
Takao and Kazuko Irizawa
R. J. Irvine
Irving Tissue
James Irwin
John and Eleanor Irwin
Joy, Bryon and Orin Isaacs
Dr. Melvyn Iscove
Sheila and Seymour Iseman
Rokuzo, Mieko and Masaaki Ito
Ivey Foundation
Barbara C. Ivey
Richard M. Ivey and
   the late Beryl Ivey
Rosamond Ivey
Suzanne Ivey Cook
Mary Etsuko Izawa
Stephen Izzard, Elizabeth Lorincz,
   Colin Izzard, Brendan Izzard,
Brandon Lorincz

J

J & D Produce, Inc., Edinburg, Texas
J. J. Barnicke Limited
Joe and Stephanie Jackman
Alan and Isabel Jackson
Barbara L. Jackson
In memory of David Lorne Jackson
Diana and Philip Jackson
Elizabeth Jackson
H. Kent Jackson
Janice Jackson & Family
Marjorie Jackson
Peter and Nancy-June Jackson
Ruth Zaryski Jackson and
   David Jackson
Neil Jacoby and Karen Brown

Lenniel S. Jacques
Dr. Alejandro Jadad, Martha Garcia,
    Alia and Tamen Jadad Garcia and
    Jessie Venegas Garcia
Florence N. Jagdeo & Family
Hans and Leslie Jager
Hans and Panya Jain
Vip and Jill Jain & Family
Neera, Munir, Ela and Rohan Jamal
Thomas A. Jambro
Heather James and Richard Livesley
Judith Morrow James
Brittany and Daniel Jamieson
Mrs. Dawn Jamieson
Mohammad and Farida Jamjoum
Jan, Mike, Sophie and Max
Peter and Peggy Janson
Sandra Janzen and David M. James
Japanese Canadian Cultural Centre
The Jarislowsky Foundation
Joseph B. and Elizabeth R. Jarvis
Jaworski and Pitre
The Jeans Family
Jane and Paul Jeffrey
Naomi and Terry Jeffs
Janine, Assen, Josh, Jake, Erik and
    Jefi Jelezarov
Calvin Jen and Bill Wyatt
Chris and Jeanne Jennings & Family
Mr. & Mrs. W. Laird Jennings
Audrey and Kurt Jeppesen & Family
Kenneth and Edith Jewett
JNE Consulting Ltd.
Ulrica Jobe and Daniel Antonios
Ursula Jochimsen-Vogdt
Elisabeth Jocz
Marion John-Postlethwaite
Anna and Francesca Johnson
Mrs. Elspeth Johnson
Frances E. Johnson
June Johnson
Mary and Art Johnson
In memory of Mary D. and
    Douglas A. Johnson
Peter James Johnson
Debbie and Bob Johnston
E. A. Owen Innes Johnston
Sue, David and Elizabeth Johnston
William Johnston
David, Selena, Spencer and
    Kaitlyn Jolly
Andrew Jones and Jo Tomsett Jones
Bob and Paula Jones
Carleen Jones and Bob Kanarek
Christopher R. Jones

Doreen S. Jones
Elizabeth and Martin Jones
Jim Jones and Colin Gruchy
Joyce Jones
Leslie Jones and Ross Henderson
Madeline and Cate Jones
Peter C. Jones
Mrs. Velma Jones
Dr. Brian C. and
    Mrs. Bonita L. Jordan
John Jordan and Dennis Keefe
Llewellyn and Margaret Joseph
Michelle and Cheryl Joseph
Merryl Josephson-Conway
Andrea and Peter Journeaux
Geoffrey and Lorraine Joyner
Caroline and Janet Julian
Joan Jung, John Lee, Bryan and
    Austin Lee
Diane J. Jurkowski and
    David L. Jurkowski
Dr. Wilfrid Jury
JVC Canada Inc.

K

Dr. Walter Kahr, Dr. Carolina Landolt,
    Olivia and Matias Kahr-Landolt
Anna Marie Kalcevich
Terri, Kumud, Jake, Josh and
    Seth Kalia
Toomas and Leone Kalm
Karl and Kathleen Kamper
Kirsten Kamper and Gabe Juszel
Karl and Karin Kampnich & Family
The Kanargelidis Family: Greg,
    Toula, Constantine, Demetre and
    Audromache
Sagar, Uma and Mihail Kancharla
Dr. Brenda Kane and Jozef Cipin
Seymour Kanowitch and
    Heather Brade
Mima Kapches
Mrs. Andree Kaplan
William Kaplan and Susan Krever
Berta Kaplow
Leonard Kaplow
Tammy Karaim, Brydon and
    Alex Parsons
Christine Karcza
Susan Karol
Emerich and Draha Kaspar
Marvin and Estelle Kates
Barbara Anne Kato
Dr. Christine Kato and
    Katrina Kato-Kelly

Ann Katrusiak and John Waldie
Jotinder Kaur and
    Harlean Kaur Tiwana
Mark Kawaja
Miriam and Henry Kedward &
    Family
In memory of Douglas R. Keedwell
Robert and Penny Keel
Josephine Keenan
Patrick and Barbara Keenan & Family
George and Donalda Kelk
Ethel Kellen & Family
In memory of our special Uncle,
    Doug Kellestine. Darren and
    Matthew Calas
Thomas and Milou Kelley
Kellogg Canada Inc.
Hubert and Dianne Kelly
Inez Kelly
Kelvin Family
Alexandra and Madeleine Kennedy
Arthur P. Kennedy
Christopher J. A. Kennedy
Louise Kennedy
Kelsea Kenny
Kristin Kenny
M. Kenny and J. McDonald
Evelyn Kent
Mary and David Kent &
    Grandchildren: Caroline Kent,
    Charles, Oliver and Hilary Kent
Dr. Rosemary Keogh
Ruth Kerbel
Mr. Norbert Kerber
In memory of Sandra Kerr
In memory of Paul and Hilda Kertes
Morris and Miriam Kerzner
Jan and Saskia Kessler
Dr. Raymond Kevork & Family
Imtiaz and Shaheen Khan
Samina Khan and Basharat Mirza
Shehla Adil Khan and Ali Adil Khan
Kidder and Krysmanski Family
Grace Kidney and Geoff Morris
Thomas Kierans and Mary Janigan
Brent and Barbara Kilbourn
Philippa Kilbourn
Bistra Kileva and Thomas Skimming
Harold and Nancy Kimberley
Warren and Debbie Kimel
    Family Foundation
Ms. Carol King
Diane and Jim King
Elizabeth J. G. King
Malcolm and Lorraine King

Sarah King and Nicholas Bolden
Glenn Harold Kingston
June Kingston and David Rosen
Vera and Albert Kircheis
Neville and Lorraine Kirchmann
Gary, Illona, Marissa and Joanna Kirsh
Lea Kirsten and Jason Mogg
Sally Kirszbaum and
    Renata MacMillian
Karen Kitchen & Family
The Kiwanis Club of
    Kingsway Humber
Riina Klaas
Herman and Audrey Klausen
Dr. Harvey and Mrs. Gloria Kline &
    Adam and Kimberley Kline
Sophia Knapik and Alexander Levert
Wayne and Irene Knapp
M. June Knudsen
Marilyn Kobayashi
Norma Kobe
Dr. Liz Koblyk and Dr. Scott Bunyan
Pamela Koch, Holly and
    Jude Koch-Nobbs
Olga, Aron and Tiiu Koel
Chris and Maribeth Koester
Mr. Sam and Mary Kohn
The Koleff-Bristow Family
Ania and Walter Kordiuk
Henrietta Kostman
Richard J. Kostoff
George, Amy and
    Christopher Kousinioris
Rosemary Kovac & Family
Adrienne and Amanda Kovacs
Marina Kovrig
Elizabeth K. Kowalczyk
Koyo Canada Inc.
Patricia, Robert and Alyssa Koziol
Valarie E. Koziol
Andrew and Elizabeth Kozlowski
KPMG LLP
Trudy Kraker
Emil and Jean Kramar
Dr. Roselynn Krantz
Rolf, Georgette, Matt and
    Sarah Kreher
The Kriss Family
Deb Kritzer
Edward, Leona, Chris and
    Hillary Krofchak
Bronwyn Krog and Paul Taylor
Kroll Computer Systems Inc.
Joe and Doreen Kronick
Kruger Products Limited

Nien-Pin Ku, Ryan, Andrella, Cecilia
    Manuel and Jonathan Chung
Leonard, Kathleen and
    Christopher Kubas
Robert, Becky, Jackson and
    Mason Kubbernus
Charles and Jane Kucey & Family
Walter and Dale Kucharczyk
    & Family
Ernst and Moni Kuechmeister
Joanne and Martin Kuhn
Christine Kujus-Fuhrmann
Roman and Marion Kulyk
Dr. Donald and Mrs. Mary Kulyski
Dr. Naresh and Mrs. Poonam Kumar
Amy Kung and Franklin Kung Oliver
The Kuplowsky-Biskup Family
Newman and Ruth Kurtz
Ihor and Valentina Kuryliw
Kwan-Hick Family
Andrew, Christine, Monika and
    Katya Kwiatkowski
Kyocera Mita Canada Ltd.

L

Louise Labrosse
Joan Laidlaw
Ben, Matthew, and Megan Laing
In memory of
    Mrs. John A. Laing (Betty)
Charlie B. Laister
James Lake and Wendy Ratcliff
Robert and Eileen Laker
Shashank, Navin and Renu Lal
The S E Lam Family Foundation
Dr. Peter and Mary Lamantia
In memory of Nicholas Lambden
Marion Lambert
Claire and Archie Lamont
Jacqueline, Robert Lamont & Family
Barbara, Sy, Daryl and Nicole Landau
    & Paul Lampert
Joan Lampkin
Brian Lampole and Vicky Marchant
Famille Lamy-Douville
Richard, Pearl, Laura, Jeffrey, Jordan
    and Anthony Lande
Michele Landsberg and
    Stephen Lewis
Catherine E. Lane and Clive Ellis
Margaret Whalley Lang and
    Kirstie, Tamaryn and Angus Lang
Trisha A Langley and
    Kathryn E Langley Hope
Elena and Ryan Langlois

Lynda Languay
Richard, Deborah, Caitlin and
    Dylan Lanktree
In loving memory of
    Dr. B. W. Lapp, D.V.M.
Jonathan, Nora, Leann, Lisa,
    Anthony Lapp
Robin Larocque-Ethier
Sylvester and Anne Lasby
Ruairi and Deirdre Laski
Lassonde Industries Inc.
Laterna Group
Amy Lathrop and Brad Hubley
Gregory Latiak
Nick Latinovich
Susana and Pak Lau
Lisa and Dick Lauckner
John and Linda Laurie
Nancy Lavalle
Patrick and Linda Lavelle
Carol Lawlor and Basil Rodomar
Allan, Debra and Crystal Lawrence
Antony and Jennifer Lawrence
Sandra D. Lawrence
Mary Ann, Robert and
    Gregory Lawrie
Donald and Lorraine Lawson
Ms. Jane Lawson
Joannah, Brian, Tristan, Alexander and
    Gillian Lawson
Stefanos, Pamela and George Lazakis
Gerald Lazare
Colin and Jocelyn Lazier
Lyle, Lorence, Chantal, Adam and
    Alysha Le Drew
Roger Le Roy and Jane Campbell
Patricia Leary and Jerry Teitel
Peter and Sara Lebensold
Janine LeBlanc-Gagné
Madison Lecakes and
    Naomi Burgess
Timur Leckebusch Family
Estate of Campbell Alexander Leckie
James Ledford
Josée Ledoux
Daniel and Soren Lee
Fei Yin Lee and Sau Wah Chan
Frank, Angela, Brendon and
    Melissa Lee
Jeffrey Lee, Anik Gaumond and
    Abbey Lee
Mark Lee and Nathan Lee
Dr. Ming J. Lee and Dr. Wen Su Lee
Nicole and Kaitlyn Lee
S. H. K. Lee

Marguerite Low and Mark Winter
Mary and Christie Low
Charlie Lowden
Hayley Lowden
Linda and Steve Lowden
MacKenzie Lowden
Gladys M. Lowe
Mrs. B.H. Lowry
Vidor, Eva, Kaitlin, Lorissa and
    Calista Lowy
The Loyalty Group
Robert and Gail Luckhart
Donald R.L. Ludlow
The Lueth Family
Walfun and Judy Luey
Bruce Lum
Patrick and Alexandra Lum
Margaret Luxton
Marian M. Lye
Drs. Beverly and Charles Lynde
Toni and John Lyng
Edward W. and Maisie Lyon

M

Constance MacDonald
Duncan and Marie MacDonald
    & Family
Ian and Janette MacDonald
Mr. J. Bruce and
    Dr. Mary Lu MacDonald
Jocelyn Macdonald
In memory of John A. MacDonald
Kenneth MacDonald
Mary E. Macdonald
Molly Anne and Bill Macdonald
Shannon and Breydon MacDonald
James and Connie MacDougall
Sean Mace and Susan Done
John and Carol Macfarlane
In memory of
    Dr. Philip R. Macfarlane
The MacFarquhar Family
Diana and Ronald MacFeeters
Yvonne MacGowan
Betty H. MacGregor
Dr. Jeffery J. Machat & Family
Frank, Dale, Robin and
    Lauren Macina
Charles MacInnes
Dr. Cameron MacInnis and
    Mary MacInnis
Ms. G. Z. MacIntosh
In memory of Marjorie E. Mack
In memory of Audrey Mackenzie
Lindsay, Tasha and Sandy MacKenzie

Louise and Raymond Mackintosh
Nan Mackintosh, Colin and
    Daniela Smith
Peter MacLachlan and
    Enid MacLachlan
The MacLean Family
Estate of Florence L. MacLean
Vaughn MacLellan and Tiffany Jay
Virginia MacLennan
Julia (Boody) MacLeod
Dr. Stuart Macleod and
    Dr. Nancy McCullough
The MacMillan Family, In memory
    of Alec J. R. MacMillan
Malcolm and Lesley MacMillan
MacMull Family
John and Gail MacNaughton
Dr. Alexander Macpherson
Mary I. MacRae
Bahadur Madhani & Family
Mani and Vasanth Madhava
Marion E. Magee
Magna International Inc.
Audrey L. Mahaffey
Shobha Maharaj & Family
In memory of William R. Mahon
Luke and Liam Mahoney-Donato
Joan and Jim Main
In memory of Dibs Rhind, the Mains
Darius Majlessi, Manuela
    Marcheggiani-Majlessi, Kian
    Majlessi and Arman Majlessi
Mrs. Joan B. Singer Makuch and
    Mr. Henry Makuch
Alex, Dianne and Stefan Makuz
Monica J. Malkus
Michael Mallinos & Family
Dr. R. Malone and
    Dr. E Oliver Malone
Sharon Maloney, Alix Rutsey and
    William Rutsey
The Manarin Family
Jane W. Manchee and J. Joseph Paul
Gino and Eda Mancini
Edward Mandel
Diane, Peter, Gabrielle and
    Danielle Mandell
Frances Mandell-Arad
Barbara and Bill Mann
Marion Mann
Paige and Brooke Manning
Robert Manson
Manulife Financial
Maple Leaf Foods
Mary Louise March

Juleen Marchant
Ruth and Simon Margel
Joseph Mariani and Sandy Fusca
Boro, Cheryl, Nikolas and
    Alexander Marinkovich
Patricia Mark, Christine Oliver,
    McKenzie and Miranda Oliver
Marsan Foods
Patricia and Bruce Marshall
Betty J. Marson
Stephen and Sandra Marson
Denise Martin and Jim Chung
Florence Martin
Margaret Martin
Lillian Martingano
Terry Mash and Anne Sowden
Boris Masip and John Gerhardt
Erika and G Maskobi
The Mason Family
Robert and Janet Mason
George and Patricia Massarella
Muriel Masson
Monique Massue & Children
Mastronardi Produce Ltd.
The Mathers Family
Kathryn and Virginia Matheson
Estate of Dorothy Muriel Matson
Mickey and Laiko Matsubayashi
James Matsumoto and Chako Setoyama
Judy and Wilmot Matthews
Robert and Renwick Matthews
Peter W. Maxwell
Rod and Barbara Maxwell & Family
Claire, Aline, Aidan Maybank
The John Mayberry Family
Helmut and Anke Mayer
John and Susan Maynard
Andrew, Katie, and Jake Mayo
Ms. Nadia Mazaheri
Mazda Canada Inc.
Mr. Gregory Mazur
Timothy and Kathryn McAleece
Anne, Kate and Emma McArthur
In memory of A. May McBeth
Mr. G. Wallace and
    The Hon. Margaret Norrie McCain
Mary McCall
David and Heidi McCallen
The McCallum Family
For Matthew and Ethan McCallum
Ron and Maureen McCallum
Richard, Tarja, Daniel McCammon
Louise McCann
W. Kenneth McCarter and
    Dianna Symonds

McCarthy Tétrault
Francine McCarthy and
    Mike MacKinnon
Michele and John McCarthy,
    In memory of John and Kathleen
    McCarthy
Richard and Sharon McCarthy
Glenn McCauley and Dean Smith
Jack and Elizabeth McClelland
Marcia McClung
Dawn and Malcolm McConnell
Jean McCorkle
Lorna and Amanda McCormick
Mr. Max McCraw
Ronald K. McCuaig
In memory of Dr. Elgin McCutcheon
James W. and Brenda J. McCutcheon:
    Frederick W. and Dale S.
    McCutcheon, F. Angus McCutcheon,
    J. Brenda McCutcheon, Julian
    J. McCutcheon & Madison
    S. McCutcheon; J. Grant and
    Sharon Lavine McCutcheon &
    Henry D. McCutcheon; Douglas
    F. and Deborah J. McCutcheon,
    Bryn V. McCutcheon, James D.
    McCutcheon & Maxwell W.
    McCutcheon; Murray W. and
    Nicole J. McCutcheon, Mark
    R. McCutcheon & Luke G.
    McCutcheon
Patricia and William McDermott
Alison, Bruce, Jack and
    Zoe McDonald
Barbara McDonald
Enid M. McDonald
William J. McDonald and
    Linda Ruth McDonald
McDorman Family
Grant and Katherine McDorman
Margaret Jean McDuff
The McElcheran Huff Family
Margaret, Carolyn and
    Peggy McEwan and Sandra Cook
Robert R. McEwen
Nancy and John McFadyen
Ivan and Harriet McFarlane
Joan McGill
Jennifer and Mark McGinnis
Mary McGowan and Michael Levine
Mrs. Jean McGrady
Catherine McGregor
Mr. Ian McGregor & Family
Margith Aalto McIlveen

Patricia A. McInnis
Eleanor McIntyre
Morris McKay
Patricia J. McKay
Sean, Ian and Madeleine
    Pounsett McKee
Thomas and Leila McKee &
    Family, Jillian and Brittany
John and Kay McKellar
Wayne McKelvey and
    Deb McKelvey-Cleveland
Michael and Jeryn McKeown
Kenneth I. McKinlay
Marjorie McKinnon, Barry, Bruce,
    William and Connor McKinnon
Norman and Martha McKinnon
McKinsey & Company, Inc.
Nestor Rodriguez McKneally
Fianna McKnight
Linda E. McKnight
Mr. Michael and
    Mrs. Mary McLaughlin
The R. Samuel McLaughlin
    Foundation
S. McLaughlin & Children
The McLean Foundation
Paul and Martha McLean
Joann and Rodger McLennan
Jane and Ian McLeod
Keith A. McLeod
Margaret McLeod and Victoria Snook
Marilyn and Iain McLeod
The McMahon Family
Brian, Lynn and
    Courtney McManaman
In memory of
    Joseph and Margaret McMinn
Ria and Roy McMurtry
Andy and Olga McNeill
Jeannie McNicol
Jack and Vodrie McOuat
Larry and Patricia McPhail & Family
Pete McPhedran and Wendy Samulski
Marian McPherson
Mary Ann McPherson and
    Walter Ridley
In honour of
    Monica Joan McPherson
McPhun Family
Barry McQuade and Albert Koebel
Catherine McRae
James, Gloria, Sarah and
    John McSherry
Mr. & Mrs. R. C. Meech
Marion Megill Trust

The Catherine & Maxwell Meighen
    Foundation
Michael and Kelly Meighen
Dr. Don Melady and
    Mr. Rowley Mossop
Patricia and Jean-Louis Melanson
Stewart J. Melanson
Hiltrudis Haley Meligrana
Roman and Tania Melnyk
Usamah, Marian, Safiyyah and
    Aaminah Memon
Malika Mendez
Maj. Gen. F. J. and T. Mendies
Mrs. Joanne and Mr. Alex Menzies
Mr. Alim Meralli
Mercer Human Resource Consulting
Anwar (Andy) and Fatima Merchant
G. G. Lee Ann Mercury
Anne Meredith
Pamela Meredith and Jamie McDonald
Merrill Lynch
Maureen E. Merrill and Val P. Merrill
Drs. Richard and
    Nancy Smith Merritt
Suzanne Mess
Johanna Metcalf
Metro Label Company Ltd. &
    The Lal Family
Matthias, Patrick and James Meusel
The Mews Family
Christine Meyer
Winston Meyer and
    Marie-Claude Larose
Meyers-Henderson Family
George J. Mezgirts
The Micheaux Family
Tristan Michela
In memory of Charles Michener
V. Mickevicius and F. Slayton
Mrs. Pamela Mignon
Tania, Larissa, Terry and W. Mihowich
In memory of Bill Mikkila
Greg and Linda Miklas & Family
Emily and Claudia Milana
Dino Milanese, Brigitte Roberge,
    Alexandre Roberge-Milanese,
    Olivier Roberge-Milanese
    and Vanessa Roberge-Milanese
Dan and Nancy Miller
Helen Davies Miller, David, Haley
    and Whitney Miller
Jim and Lynda Miller
Mrs. Marjorie S. Miller
Susan, Mike, Natalie and
    Nicole Miller

Frank Milligan & Family
Chris, Noella, Shane, Craig and
    Natasha Milne
Estate of John H. Milnes
Peter, Susan and Nikki Milovanovic
Barbara Milstein
Minaco Equipment Limited
Beatrice and Arthur Minden
Anne Minguet
Ministry of Natural Resources
Bruce G., Victoria and Hilary Minnes
James and Cindy Minns
Eleanor and Jack Mintz
Abby, Perry and Jordan Minuk
In memory of Julius Minuk
Audrey and David Mirvish
Andrew and Lexie Misterski
Christopher Mitanidis
In memory of Grozde and
    Tina Mitchell
Liz and Kent Mitchell
Lorelie Mitchell and Piet van Dijken
Randall S. Mitchell
Mrs. Anica Miter
Luigi, Christian and Monica Mitrache
Mitsui & Co., (Canada) Ltd.
Mitsui Sumitomo Insurance Co., Ltd
Mizuho Corporate Bank (Canada)
Garry and Fanny Moddel & Family
Donley and Bette Mogan
Mr. & Mrs. Moher
Emily-Jean and William Molls
Christopher and Jonathan Monaghan
William S. Monk
Michael and Mathew Monteith
Shirlee McEdwards Monteith
The Montgomery Family
The Honourable Robert S. and
    Dixie Anne Montgomery
Delia M. Moog
Andrew and Lauren Mooney
Joan and David Moore
John and Dorothea Moore
Sandra C. Moore
John F. and Gillian Brooks Moorecroft
Ashley Moraca
Katie Moraca
Irene Morales
Ellie Morch and Jason Baker
Mary Jane Moreau and Bill Bruce
Valerie Morelli
The Moreno-Valverde Family
In loving memory of Brian Morgan
Darren and Marissa Morgenstern
    & Family

Anne and Charles Morison
Ms. Arlene Morlidge
Jack and Estelle Morris
Donald E. Morrison
Mallory Morris-Sartz and John Sartz
Dr. F. W. Orde Morton
Larisa and Brad Morton
Mrs. Lucy Olesa Morwick
Allison F. Mosher and
    Moira W. Mosher
Patrick and Nora Mossman
Gail and Alex Motzok
Linda and Michael & Matthew and
    Nicholas Mountford
Dr. Charlotte (Zuppinger) Mudge
Stephen Karl Mueller
Antony Muhitch
John Muhitch
Elizabeth Muir
Susan Muir
Jennifer and John Mulholland
Catherine Mulkins
Mulvey & Banani International Inc.
Stanton and Kathleen Mulvihill
Marijan Munjic
Peter and Melanie Munk
Julia Munro
Erika Murata and François Passet
Patricia J. Mure
Dr. Patricia Murphy
Murphy's Food Sales & Marketing
Blake Murray and Nancy Riley
Gary and Shirley Murray
Jessima Murray & Family,
    In memory of Eric Murray
Ken Murray and Emma Robinson
Michael Murray
The Murrell Family
Pardo Mustillo & Family
The Muzzo Family
Ethel and Earl Myers
Maureen Myers
Joel Myerson & Family

N

Frank and Lidija Nadj
Eleanor Nadler
John and Sarah Nagel
Aliya Nandy-Frendo
The Napier Family
Samantha Napier
Dr. Martin and Georgine Nash
    & Family
In loving memory of Yetta Nashman
Ursula K. Nau

Douglas R. Neal
Mackenzie, Ryerson and
    Geneva Neal
In loving memory of Don Neheli
    from your children, Emmet and
    Maeve and wife, Nicole
Joan M. Neilson
Gary and Judy Neinstein & Family
Gerald Nemanishen
Catherine Nemes
Corinne Nemy
Nestlé Canada Inc.
Nestlé Waters Canada
Olympia Neuperger and
    Michael Simko
Christine E. Newhouse
Amanda Newhouses
Janet R. Newman and
    Ronald E. Rutt
Paul Newman
Ronald and Barri Newman
Stephen Newman
The Newstead Family
Emily Newton
Katie Newton
Luka and Katija Newton
Olivia Newton
Tommy Newton
In memory of Mr. & Mrs. Kwan-Foo Ng
Siu Lai Ng & Family
Yvonne T.Y. Ng and Sonja S. Ng
NGK Spark Plugs Canada Limited
Hilary V. Nicholls
Margaret, Ian, Brian, David and
    Emma Nicholls
Ms. Shannon Nichols
Aideen Nicholson
Robert Nicholson
Blair and Lisa Nicol
Mrs. Ingrid Nicolai
The Nielsen Company
Donna Fraser Niemy and
    Taylor R. Stark
Nienkämper Furniture
Gloria Nightingale,
    In memory of Percy Nightingale
Nikon Canada Inc.
Nippon Express Canada
Nissan Canada Inc.
Nissin Transport (Canada) Inc.
Gordon and Janet Nixon
E. U. (Lalo) Nixon-Pastén
Robert, Frances and Elizabeth Nobes
Elizabeth Noble
George, Betty and Kenneth Noguchi

Mary Nokes
Mr. Michael Norgrove
Noritake Canada Limited
Rodney V. Northey
Mr. Scott Northey and
    Mrs. Christina Northey
Betty-Lou Northway
Wendy Nott
Robert and Alexandra Nourse
Nova Machinery & Eng. Inc.
Iris Nowell
NSK Canada
NTN Bearing Corporation of
    Canada Ltd.
Nu-Life Nutrition Ltd.
Keith and Liam Nunn & Beth and
    Morgan Baskin
Marcia Nutley
NYK Line (Canada) Inc.
Judy Nyman and Harley Mintz

O

Clive Oakes
Carline, Paul and Graham Oakley
Dr. Christopher O'Brien
Roberta M. O'Brien and
    Jane Sacchetti
Ocean Spray International
George and Jean Ochrym
Mary O'Donoghue and
    Paul Reinhardt
Penny and Martin Offman & Family
In memory of Eileen and Ross Ogilvie
Dawn and Geoff Ogram
Susan and Stephanie Ogurian
Susan O'Hara
Mary and Tom O'Hearn
OK Gift Shop Ltd.
Ian and Yvonne Oldaker
In memory of Donna Oldfield
Elke and Melville Olsberg J.P.
Olymel, S.E.C./L.P.
Michael and Anne O'Mahoney
Sir Christopher Ondaatje, O.C., CBE
Keiko and Seiya Ono
Ontario Potato & O.P.D.I. Logistics
Optimal Group Inc.
The Orbanic and Ciccarelli Families
Kevin, Sheila, Cian and
    Brianna O'Reilly
Sharon O'Rourke and Fred Newey
Frances Orr
Mr. John G. B. and Mrs. Deanne Orr
Maureen and John Orton
Josephine M. Osadec

Abby and Liam Osborne
Orville and Susan Osborne
Brian and Nancy O'Shaughnessy
Hugh and Ann Osler
Lisa, Gary, Adam and
     Emma Ostermeier
Sam and Tom Outerbridge
Marie José Overweel
Ed and Etta Ovsenny & Family
John Oxenbury & Family

P

PACART Art Transportation Services
Al Pace and Kristin Morch
Margie Ryrie Pacini
Joy and Randy Packham
The Page Family – Jonathan,
     Stephanie and Jonathan
In memory of John E. Page
Shirley Page and Herbert E. Parker
Dagmar Pagel and Richard Trupke
Heather, Katerina, Marco and
     Stefan Pagura
Brian, Elaine and Tom Palmer
David and Bernadette Palmer,
     Alexander, Michael and
     Maeve Palmer
Godfrey and Patricia Palmer
Panasonic Canada Inc.
Anita and Hari Panday
Anshul Panday
Arjun Panday
Larissa and Joshua Panetta
Hilda McLaughlin Pangman
Panigas
The Pansieri Family
Deno and Linda Papageorge
Ken and Bette Ann Paradine
Clive, Vicky, Nathalie, Simon and
     Jonathan Parham
Eric Parker
Garrah, Helaena and Jonathan Parkes
Roger and Maureen Parkinson
Parmalat Canada
Michael and Patricia Parrett
Richard Partington and
     Chloë Bisaillon
Sabrina, Carlo and Ciro Pasini
Carol, Dylan and Caitlin Pask
Rev. Kathryn and Prof. Calvin Pater
     & Family
Ms. Roslyn Patrick and
     Mr. Keith Goobie
Yvonne Patrick-Ross and
     Yolande Grant

Rose M. Patten
Dee Patterson, Tony, Colin, Owen
     and Ciara Gaffney
Ray Patterson & Family
Viola H. Patton
Victoria Paul
Mr. John W. Pavey
Dr. Leo Pavone and
     Dr. Rosemarie Lall
Elizabeth Payea-Butler
Barbara and David Payne
PCL Packaging Corporation
David Peachey and
     Georgia Henderson
Margaret Peacock
Susan Peacock and Roger Hughes
Liz Pead and Don Eady
Peak Financial Services Inc.
Malcom and Frances Peake
Michael and Elizabeth Pearce
Ruth Peckham and Beyer Family
Stephanie Pellow
Ms. Katherine Pemberton
John and Eudora Pendergrast
Dr. G. Allan Pengelly and
     Dr. Bette Stephenson
Gordon and Marilyn Penley
Dr. Edwin M. Pennington
Pepper/Tattersall Family
Pepsi QTG Canada
Paul R. Perchaluk Family
Mrs. Paula and Mr. Gary Percy
Dena and Rachel Perlmutar
Andre, Terry and Beatrice Perusse
Petch Family
Jack Petch & Family
The Peters Family
Mr. & Mrs. Joel and Jayne Peters
Dennis and Maria Peterson
Neil and Leanne Petroff & Family
Joanne Pettigrew
Melvyn John Peverley
John, Natalie, Anna, Aidan and
     Cole Pezacki
Dr. James, Joann, Joanna and
     Tony Pfaff
Ruth Pfaff
Dorothy and Peter Pfahl
Inez E. Phair
John and Laurena Phelan
Ms. Batia Phillips
Cassandra Phillips
Judi Phillips
Jack and Victoria Phipps
Don Piafsky

Charlie and Sue Pielsticker
Lindsay Pierce
Martha Pierce
Matthew Pierce
Robert E. Pierce & Family
Andreas and Catherine Pierratos &
     Family
Piersanti Family – Chris, Terry, Justin,
     Morgan and Tara
Jacqueline Piggot
Joseph, Nigar, Aleeza, Sheniz and
     Mel Pilarski
Marilyn L. Pilkington and
     Wayne E. Shaw
The Pilkington-Henniger
     Charitable Trust
Piller Sausage & Delicatessens Ltd.
William and Monika Piller
Ron and Elsie Pines & Family
Gordon and Charmion Pinsent
Dr. Lloyd M. Piszel
Robin B. Pitcher
Gladys Pitman
Paul and Ruth Pitt
The Pittman Family
Jillian Pivnick
The Plant-Weir Family
Philip Playfair
The Plunkett Family
Irene and Wilf Podolak
Sandy, Mike, Christian, Danielle and
     Ryan Poitras
Paul Policaro & Family
Barbara Elaine Pollard
Barbara and John Pollock
John and Barbara Pollock
The Mimi and Sam Pollock
     Foundation
Rita Pool
Joseph and Claudine Pope
Mary-Ann Poplar
Mr. Justin M. Porter
Gary and Ann Posen
Wietse and Kathryn Posthumus
Zenon and Sonia Potichnyj
Mary Jean and Frank Potter
Gary Pottruff and Marie Verschuuren
J. C. Potvin & Family
Power Corporation of Canada
Powis Family Foundation
Santosh N. Prasad
John F. Prato
Alan and Louise Preddie
Sally Preiner
David W. Pretty

Charles Price
Erica, Holly, Gregory, Amy, Scott and
     Ethan Price
In memory of Dr. Ralph Price,
     Patricia, Kimberley, Taylor and
     Matthew Price & Families
PricewaterhouseCoopers LLP
Mark, Esme, Alex and Liam Prieditis
Andrew and Valerie Pringle
Douglas L. Pringle
Mark Prior and Luc Bernard
Mossie Prior
Rrain Prior
Dr. Sandy James Pritchard
Procter & Gamble Inc.
Dianne Proctor
Pro-Motion Transportation
James and Irene Proudfoot
Victor and Sheila Prousky & Family
Diana, Louis and Nicholas Provenzano
Professor Olga Zorzi Pugliese
Dr. John, Sarita, Sarah and
     Serena Purdy
Jaak, Cindy and Valek Purres
Elvira Putrus

Q

Barbara J., Nancy A. and
     Wendy J. Quaintance
Quality Home Products
Mayor Kate Quarrie
Tony Quarrington and
     Colette French
Stuart M. Quick

R

The Rabideau/Bode Family
Merle and Theodore Rachlin
John and Phyllis Rae
Don and Elaine Rafelman
Dan Rahimi and Julie Comay
Olivia and Claire Rakic
Ralph, Lu, Flaminia, Dante, Luciano
     and Ryan
Bob Ramik
Gloria Ramsay-Hall
J. Cal Ramsden
Joan R. Randall & Grandchildren:
     Barney Guillermo Williams,
     Rainbo' Clifford Williams,
     Oliver Alan Williams,
     Liberty Joan Angelique Williams,
     Tavin Alexander Hammersmith
     Williams, William Carr Walwyn
     Randall, Jesse Rae Randall, Kieran

James Randall, Jay MacLean Gould,
  William Merritt Randall Gould
Audrey and Colin Randall-Smith
Loretto Ann Rankin
Mrs. Elinor Ratcliffe
Rosemary Rathgeb
Dr. Ely and Mrs. Rose Ravinsky
D.G. Ray
The Raynham Family -
  Philip, Anna, Julia
Razin
RBC Foundation
Leith Rea
Jean M. Read and
  the late Morris Appleby
Oliver Rebanks
Wendy and Leslie Rebanks
Zuleika Rebanks
Almerinda, Luis and Miguel Rebelo
Shelagh J. Reddy
Ernest and Flavia Redelmeier
Mrs. Theresa Redelmeier
Mrs. D.B. Redfern
Robert and Sharon Redhead
Dr. Marshall and Mrs. Linda Redhill
Donna Reece and Drew and
  Madeline Phillips
Gordon A.D. and Joyce A. Reed
Nita and Donald Reed
Connie Reeve and Bonnie Tough
Marion Jean Reeves
Diane Reid
George Fraser Reid and Jane Reid
Graham and Anne Reid
Mrs. Helenmarie Reid
Holly Reid, Bruce, Simon and
  Sean Rayment
Janette Reid
Joan L. Reid
Kenneth and Teresa Reid
Nancy and Jim Reid
Mr. Max Von Reimann and
  Mrs. Jean Reimann
Ernest and Mary Reinhart
Piroska Remenyi, Niina Saarendi and
  Giselda Rossi
Salman Remtulla and
  Sabrina Ahmed and Raheem
The Rennie Family
Grant L. Reuber
Ann Reynolds
Eric and Patricia Reynolds
Roger and Elaine Reynolds
Dr. Tom Reynolds and
  Thomas W. Sparling

In memory of Elizabeth Rhind
John and Elizabeth Rhind
Assuntino and Angelina Ricciuto
Rob and Penny Richards
Don and Eleanor Richardson
Hannah Mackenzie Richardson
Jane Richardson, Kevin, Jack and
  Chloe Fine
Dr. Peter Richardson
Rachel Anna Richman and
  Taylor Jill Richman
Lorne Richmond and Karen Krupa
Norman Rickaby
John and Marvi Ricker
Jacqueline and Jack Riddell
Maegan and Luke Ballantyne
  Ridgway
Estate of Norma Ruth Ridley
The Ridsdale Family
Douglas Rienzo and
  Timothy Johnson
Daniel and Andrew Riley
Ernie and Tara Rinomato
RioCan Real Estate Investment Trust
Rippey, Takacs and White
Gary and Karen Ritchie
Mark, Ana, Sofia, Carla and
  Isabela Rittinger
Harry J. Riva and Ghislaine Page
Pierre and Catherine Rivard
Nancy and Bruce Rivoire & Family
Jackie, Max and Griffin Roach
In loving memory of Robbie
Robert, Martha, Katie, Robert
  and Annie
Cynthia Roberts
Liam Wood Roberts and
  Aleda Wood Roberts
William and Jean Roberts
Bruce and Karen Robertson
In loving memory of Don and
  Hazel Robertson
David S. Robertson
Janice Huff and Alex Robertson
Mrs. Norman S. Robertson
The Honourable Sydney Robins and
  Mrs. Gloria Robins
Bernadette Robinson
Donna Robinson and
  Robert Bauer Family
Richard and Pauline Robinson
  & Family
Eric and Terri Robitaille
The Robson Family
Dr. Charlotte Robson

J.T. Robson
Gerry Rocchi
Geoffrey and Marie Claire Roche
Gerry and Eileen Rochon
Ruxandra Rodgers and
  William S. P. Rodgers
The Rodrigues Family-Cathy, Levi,
  Lisa, Jessica and Michelle
Mary-O and Richard Rohmer
Polina, Irina and Alex Roitman
Margaux Rolston
ROM Department of
  Museum Volunteers
Katie and Becky Romanchuk
Alfredo and Moira Romano
Fay and Aldon Rooke
Richard Rooney and Laura Dinner
Dr. Betty I. Roots
George, Victoria, Glorianne, Susan
  and Vivian Ropchan
Lee, Cheri, Benjamin and
  Sophie Rorabeck
Anne and Dan Roscoe
Rose Family Fund at the Toronto
  Community Foundation
Denzil and Nathaniel Rose
Eric P. Rosen
Harry and Evelyn Rosen
Jennifer T. and David M. Rosen
John M. Rosen and Hannah Rosen
Karen Rosen and Andrew Bernstein
  & Children
Mrs. Annellen Rosenberg
Mrs. Beverly Rosenberger
Rosenbloom Groupe Inc.
Jack Rosenfeld and Jennifer Morritt
Shirley and John Rosenfeld
Edward Rosengren
Iqbal, Tanzila, Yusuf and Nabila Roshd
In memory of Mary Rosko
Paul Rosner and Janet Rosner
Eileen and David Ross
Hedy Ross and Family
Helen Josephine Ross
Dr. Miriam and Mr. Renato Rossi
Kenneth Rotenberg
Carol Rothbart
Paul and Gella Rothstein
Rotman Family
Carl and Donna Rotman
Brad and Dianne Rotteau
In memory of Anna Rotzinger
Amy, Andrew, Sarah and
  Catie Rowbotham
Cynthia Rowden

Timothy and Helen Rowswell
E. Roy and Mary Harvey
Marc Roy and Vicky Zeldin
Rae and John Rozenberg
Andris Rubenis and Erika Yost
Arnold Rubinoff & Family
Robert Rubinoff and Espie Chan
Joel L. Rubinovich and
  Heather M. Caple
Stephen and Susan Rudin & Family
Caitlin and Morgan Rueter
Robert and Kathleen Rueter
Francine and Bob Ruggles
Mr. Rolando Ruiz-Cepeda
Arnold and Gloria Rumm
Mary Anne Runnalls
Stephen Rupp and Alison Keith
Rev. Alan Rush and
  Rev. Mary-Jane E. Rush
Diana, John, Christine and
  Emily Russell
David and Ella Ruston, Justin
  Graham, and Aaron Graham
Arlene and Bob Rutherford
Ms. Tracey Rutledge

S

Jeanne Sabourin
La Fondation Sackler
  (The Sackler Foundation)
Dr. Mitsuko Sada
John, Michelle, Julie and
  Gillian Sadler
Ben and Jordan Sadowski & Joshua,
  Jeremy and Jordan Stein
Rochelle and Calvin Sager & Family
In memory of Ben Sakamoto
Dr. & Mrs. K. K. Sakamoto
The Sakauye Family
The Salamander Foundation
Dr. Kevin and Mrs. Lisette Saldanha
Ian, Anne, Andrew and
  Katherine Salgo
Dr. J. Douglas Salmon and
  Beverley Salmon
Dr. Barry Salsberg
James and Suzanne Salter
Marguerite, Claude and
  Pascale Sam-Foh
Elizabeth Samuel
Sigmund Samuel Gallery Fund
Robert and Jeanie Sanderson
William and Diana Santo
Carl and Aggie Santoni & Family
John, Lisa and Shaké Sarkhanian

Mary and Norman Satterfield
Paul and Mardi Saunders
The Savoy-Pitfield Family
Yoshiko and Takashi Sawa
Arthur and Mary Sawchuk
Ramasar and Ruth Sawh
Richard G. Sayers
Ralph and Joyce Scane
Dr. Philip Scappatura
Liborio Scelfo and Franco, Maria,
    Vanessa, Jason and Alexander Sivilla
Anya, Reva, Jonathan and
    Danny Schachter
Schad Family
Theresa Schaden and Eric S.T. Herauf
Fred Schaeffer
Adrian Schauer and Theresa Schauer
Hyla Scherer
Del Schinkopf
Lionel and Carol Schipper
Hermann, Elke and Wenke
    Schliemann
Sylvia Schmid
Robert Schmidt, Irene Wintersinger
    and Monika Schmidt
The Schmied-Pape Family
Mr. Timothy and Mrs. Kimberly-Ann
    Schneider
Mr. & Mrs. Ernest Scholten
Evelyn McIntyre Schulenburg
Deborah Schulte and David Schenck
Sophie and Chloe Schultz
Paula and Rudolph Schury
Dr. Andrea Schutz
The Schwab Family
Ronit, Miriam and Yara Schwabe
Scotiabank Group
Erik N. Scotney and Annette Shaw
Amy Scott
Bev and Milly Scott & Family
David Scott and
    Gwen Zezulka Family
Derek Scott
John E. Scott and Joyce Sullivan-Scott
Nelson Scott and Melanie Mader
Paul, Judith and Daniel Scott
Susannah Scott, Kyle Stuart and
    Samantha Stuart
David Sealy & Family
Diana and Paul Sealy
Craig Sebastiano
Amanda, Noah, Liv and Beck Segal
Dr. Marianne Seger
Eva Seidner and Michael Kedar
Ralph and Mary Selby & Family

Steve and Janice Semelman
Sentry Select Capital Corp.
Colleen Sexsmith
The Harry T. Seymour Family
SGH Design Partners
SGNC Charitable Trust
Eric B. Shackleton, Ruth and
    James Geddes
Wajid, Farida, Faisal and
    Jameel Shaikh
Al Shaikoli
Roselind and Fred Shapero
Fred and Rosslyn Sharf
Mr. Gan Sharma and
    Mrs. Madhu Sharma
Rosalie and Isadore Sharp
Lynda Sharpe
Marjorie J. Sharpe
Dr. David L. Shaul & Family
Katherine, Gary and Mark Shaw
Mr. Michael Shaw
Sir Neil and Lady Shaw
Roberta Lawrie Shaw
William and Elizabeth Shaw
Mr. Gerard Sheerin and
    Mr. David Sheerin
Jerry and Barbara Shefsky
Dr. Peter Sheldrick
Robert and Jessica Shelley
Elizabeth and Andrew Shepherd
Allison and Rick Sheppard
Judy B. Sheppard and James Sheppard III
J. P. Sheridan and Christa Sheridan
Jessica and Morgan Sherk
Carole and Marvin Sherkin
Miriam Shiell
Gwendolyn and Aiden Shin
Shinkikai (Association of Japanese
    Canadian Businesses &
    Professionals)
Shiu Pong Group of Companies
Alex and Simona Shnaider
Shokokai
Shoppers Home Health Care
Jerome and Marjorie Shore
Gloria Shulman
John and Barbara Sibbald
Gary Siepser and Laurie Siegel
June M. Sifton
Julian Siggers and Marianne Lovink
Rocco, Marion and Gregory Silvaggio
Dr. Julie Silver, Dr. Arthur Helman
    & Family
Dr. Malcolm D. and
    Dr. Meredith Silver

Alana Silverman and Dani Frodis
Dr. Ezra and Mildred Silverstein
    & Family
Dr. Cristoforo Silvestri, PhD
The Silzer Family
Judy Simmonds
Audra Simmons, Mark, Marcello,
Massimo and Angelo Ferraro and
    Davida Walker
Cori Simms and Alex Last
Emil Simon and Lesley Simon
Dr. Jerome and Mrs. Pamela Simon
Renate S. Simon
Walter and Cheryl Simone
Dr. Alan and Mrs. Elizabeth Simpson
Dale and Margaret Simpson
Ms. Irene Simpson
Janet E. Simpson
Maureen Simpson, Almos and
    Rory Tassonyi
Thomas and Beverley Simpson
Tracy and Bruce Simpson
Sueann and Henry Singer & Family
In memory of Dr. Pratima Singh
The Sirna and Hunt Families
Susan Sivrić
Robert and Berneice Skelly
Eric and Judith Skeoch
Denyse Slack
Abigail Slater, Morry Guttman, Maya
    and Emma Guttman Slater
Elaine Slater and James Slater
Mark Slone, Karen Tisch Slone and
    Isabella Slone
Mr. Sean Slowey and Carolyn Wood
The Smart Family
SMBC Global Foundation Inc.
Arthur M. Smith
Beverly Smith & Allyson and Michael
Brian Smith, Judy Wingham, Alison,
    Lindsay and Lauren
Connie, Ciara and Connor Smith
Mrs. Dorothy J. Smith
Emily Smith
Gerry and Sylvia Smith & Family
Ibolya Smith
Jay Smith and Laura Rapp
Jeff Smith Family
Jennifer Smith
Judy and Hume Smith
Leo and Elizabeth Smith
Mrs. Pauline and Mr. David Smith
Russell and Pam Smith
Shelia Smith
David and Patricia Smukler

Tatiana Smunchilla
Helene and Derek Snider and
    Emmett Johnston
Sam Sniderman and Janet Mays
Stanford Snyder
Dr. Ion and Mrs. Nelia & Clea and
    Kasy Soare
Joan Soble & Family
Joan Sohn
Janet Solberg and Henry King
Manuel and Gilma Soler
Mr. Jules and Mrs. Harriett Solomon
Joan Soloninka
Joan and Geoffrey Somers & Family
Sally Somers
Rev. Maryann Somerville Family
William W. Somerville
Martin Sommerfeld and
    Tracy Paulenko
Bob and Linda Sommerville
Sony Canada
Dr. Marja Soots
The Sorger Brock Family
Sorrell Financial Inc.
Sigmund and Linda Soudack
Sound Insurance Services Inc.
Wendy and Jim Southey
Pina Spatari Angela and Noah Ruiz
The Spaull Family
Leigh and Carole Speakman
Mrs. Margaret Spence
Edward and Carol Spencer
Nina Spencer, Kathryn Stephens
    and In memory of Beryl Miseldine
    Spencer and Desmond Spencer
Sheila Ruth Spergel
Erik Spicer, CM, CD and
    Helen Spicer
Bernard and Adrienne Spiegel
Serena, Brahm, Toni and
    Sidney Spilfogel
Paul and Andrew Spill
Nigel, Rebecca, Rob and Chris Spink
Danny Spinosa
Edward T.C. Spooner
Joe Springer
Nancy Sprott
Bruce and Fay Sproule
Maureen and Wayne Squibb
St. Helen's Meat Packers Limited &
    Lazar Yitzchok Kosher Meats
St. Joseph Communications
Gillian, Jennifer, Gavin and
    Kieran Stacey
Ronald Stagg

Bernard and Shirley Staiman
Ashley Stanley
Doreen L. Stanton
In memory of Amy Doreen Stanway
Caitlin Starr
Connor Starr
Steve and Sally Stavro Family
  Foundation
Barbara L. Steele
Greg and Anne Steers
Margaret Steger
Cecile Kaufman Stein
Jeremy, Jonathan and Karina Stellato
Regina Stemberger
Diane and Gary Stemerdink
Josephine Stemerowicz
Sonya, Dennis, Maksim Stepanov
In memory of R.T. Stephens
Dylan James Stephenson
Robert, Nancy, Lindsay, Jennifer,
  Peter Stephenson
Walter and Alexandra L. Stepura
Steve Steranka
Karen J. Sterling
Floyd and Barbara Stern
David Sterns
Ann and Robert Stevens
John A. Stevens
Margaret Stevens
Allan and Judi Stevenson
Bruce and Eleanor Stevenson
  & Family
Emma and Chelsea Stevenson
Estate of Henrietta E. Stevenson
Jack and Sam Stevenson
Alycia M. Stewart
Amy and Clair Stewart
Gloria Dow Stewart
Dr. Jim and Mrs. Maryln Stewart
Mrs. M.D. Stewart
Nalini and Tim Stewart
Shirley and Ronald Stewart
Allen Stewart-Coates
Dr. Niclas and Audra Stiernholm
Anne Stinson
Ross and Cindy Stirling
Michelle Stockwell, Paul, Braedon,
  Duncan and Madison Links
Jack and Beverley Stodgell
John D. Stokes & Family
Roselyn Stone
Marilyn Stonehouse
Janet Stovel
In honour of Fred Stow
Harold and Angela Straker

Mary and Bill Strangways
Jane and John Strathy
Wayne Stratton
Louis A. Strauss
The Dorothy Strelsin Foundation
Frances M. Stretton
Harold Strom and Susan Biggar
Roger and Susan Stronell
Estate of Donald and Frances Strudley
Trudy Struebing
James M.K. Stuart, Mala Thapar and
  Diya Thapar
Terry and Lilla Stuart
StuCor Construction Ltd.
Barbara Stymiest, James Kidd and
  Siobhan Kidd
Styrsky-Elwood Family
Mr. Sam Su
Subaru Canada, Inc.
Susan and Peter Sudbury
Alan and Mary Suddon
Margaret Y.K. Suen
Malcah and Mel Sufrin
George and Stephanie Sugar
The Suissa Family
Kathleen Sullivan and Meaghan
  Sullivan Klie
Mike, Kelly and Matt Sullivan
Sumitomo Canada Ltd.
Gregory and Lucy Sun
Ho K. Sung, Kim Shannon and
  Cailin Sung
Rayne, Daeja and Ciele Sutherland
Sutherland-Schultz Inc.
Michael, Julie, Garion and
  Spencer Sutton
Malcolm Sutton and
  Ms. Sandra Weissman
Suzuki Canada Inc.
Fred M. Swaine
Susanne and Scott Sweatman
Dr. David M. and
  Mrs. Ethelmae Sweeney
James Michael Sweeney
Symbol Technologies Canada, ULC
John and Margaret Symons
Ella and Eva Szabo
Ms. Christina Szweda
Marek and Elizabeth, Aaron, Jonas,
  Nicolas Szymanski

T

Sheila Tait
Peter, Rena, Grace MacLean Tallis
Madis J. Tambre

Aino Roos Tammerk
Chai Hong and Raymond Tan
Howard and Carole Tanenbaum
  Family
Joey and Toby Tanenbaum
Wai-Cheung, Mylene, Jennifer and
  Julie Tang
Arthur and Bea Tannenbaum
Tanner Goad Family
Mrs. Anne Tawadros
Alec and Eulaline Taylor
Lee T. Taylor
Philip, Eli, Ben, Kate, Harrison and
  Paulina Taylor
TD Bank Financial Group
TD Friends of the Environment
Teck Resources Limited
Teknion Corporation
James C. Temerty, Louise Temerty,
  Melissa Temerty, Leah Temerty
  Lord, Ludmilla Temerty, Nicola
  Temerty Canta, Kalyna Temerty
  Canta, Eliah Canta Monnoyer, Illia
  Temerty, Raissa Temerty, Alyna
  Temerty
Alan and Susie Tenenhouse
Ken Teng, Brenda Kapasky, Emma
  and Matthew Teng
Emil and Molly Tennenbaum
Roderick C. Tennyson and
  Daphne Lavers
Vera Teophil-Naber, In memory of
  Natalie Percuklijevic (Perklin)
Y.F. and K.S. Teow
Teradata Canada ULC
Dr. & Mrs. Karel Terbrugge
Mrs. Therese Thackray
Suresh and Urmila Thakrar
In memory of Mr. & Mrs. V.
  Tharmasangary
The Tokio Marine and
  Fire Insurance Co., Ltd.
John R. Theriault & Family
Suzanne Theroux
Colleen Thomas
Elijah, Joshua, Noah and
  Jacob Thomas
Thomas, Large & Singer Inc.
Brian J Thompson
Mrs. Des Thompson
Elizabeth R.S. Thompson
James A.S. Thompson
Judith, Gerard, Kathlyn, Matthew,
  Andrew and Jonathan Thompson
Ms. Madeline Thompson

Roberta and Heather Thompson
In memory of Dr. Joan Thomson
Kiera M. R. Thomson
Richard Iorweth Thorman
Kathryn J. Thornton
Mr. William Thorsell
John R. Thurner
Sean, Ellen and Amy Tidy
Anita and Bob Tiessen
Alfred and Roberta Tilbe
Lillian Tilbrook & Family
Jane B. Tilden
Mrs. Pixie Tilden
Walter and Jane Tilden
Wanda Timmins
Ann C. Timpson
Jaan and Tiina Timusk & Family
David and Janet and Paul, Jonathon,
  Theresa, Patrick, Andrea, Emily,
  Daniel Tingey
John B. Tinker
In memory of Lilly Tisch
Atul and Roisin Tiwari
In memory of Masaji and
  Hiro Tokiwa
Eric and Margot Toller
Mark and Vanessa Tomas
Ron Tomblin, Janice James, Paul,
  Christine, and Jonathan Tomblin
Peter G. Tomlinson
Tomo Sato & Family
Mrs. Kelly and Mr. Peter Tompkins
The Tong Family
In memory of Lawrence Toothman
Victor and Renee Topper
Ernesto Torchia
Morley and Anna Pearl Torgov
Toronto Cathay Lions Club
Toronto Elegant Lions Club
Toronto Hong Kong Lions Club
John and Elizabeth Tory
Toshiba of Canada Limited
Mary Tournour
Mr. Michael Toussaint
Towers Perrin
Jody Townshend
Toyota Canada Inc.
Toyota Financial Services/Lexus
  Financial Services
Clare Tremain and Graeme Tremain
Lahring Tribe
Trillion Financial Group
  – Kalano Y. L. Jang
Dr. Oleh A. and Mrs. Anna Trojan
In memory of Frances Trojek

Terry and Anitta Trotter
Cristina Trozzo and Elena Trozzo
Shawn and Alexis Truax
Dr. Maureen Trudeau and Jon and
  Jason Mergler
Dr. Ka Bo Tsang
Rita Tsang
Yuen Tse and Shui Chu Fong
Mr. & Mrs. Christopher Ttooulias
Sally Tuck
Robert G. Tucker
Lynne and Bob Tuer
Olive Tull
Maria-Lynn, Tibor, Tobias and
  Sophia Turi
The George and Mary Turnbull
  Foundation Fund at the Toronto
  Community Foundation
Turner Fleischer Architects Inc.
Barbara Turner
Carol Turner & Family
Kristina Turner
Mary Turner and Ron Bob and
  David, Madison and Benjamin
Jacob and Joshua Turriff
Julie Turylo
Dr. A. Douglas and
  Mrs. Margaret M. Tushingham
John and Mary Twomey
Darren, Marie, Harry and
  Charlotte Twyford
Tim and Irene Tyhurst
Elizabeth and Renée Tysiaczny
Bela and Anna Tyukodi

U

UFJ Bank Canada
Ukrainian Canadian Community
Ukrainian Canadian Foundation of
  Taras Shevchenko
Ukrainian Credit Union Limited
John, Karin and Mark Ungar
Unisource Canada Inc.
Skaidrite Upans
Guy and Sandra Upjohn

V

Ila and Paul Vaculik
Ashok Vadekar
Vale
Lesley Valentine-Anand and
  Raj Anand
Betty Van de Pol-Kea
The Van Dorp Family
Mr. Robert Van Dusen

Elbert and Eleanor Van Evans
Cheryl Van Horn & Family
Nicholas and Matthew Van Sloten
Vanbots Construction
Lucinda Vandenieuwegiessen
Bill and Sarah VanderBurgh
Joan and Jill Vanderkooy
Patrick Vandesompele, Lara Atlas,
  Beverley Jones, Dale and
  Taryn Atlas-Jones
The vanGansewinkel Family
Sylvia and Ed Vanhaverbeke
Elizabeth Vanstone
Joan and Ron Varley
Vasyl Shumskyy
Elliott and Geoffrey Vavitsas
Yuri and Lea Velsher
Dr. Bruno Vendittelli and
  Jane Halverson-Vendittelli
Ms. Anita Verstraete
Samantha, Thomas and Jessica Vertolli
Sam Vesuna
Isabel, Gino and Christian Vettoretto
Mark Anthony Vicari
Vidal-Ribas Smith Family
Bruce Vidler and Betty Mason
Raymond and Penelope Vigneault
Dr. Johan Viljoen and
  Dr. Inge Schabort
Kathleen Viner
Jane Vining
Susanna Vipond & Family
Mr. William J. and Ms. Regina Virgo
Joan L. Vitalis and Daniel Mastri
In memory of Nicola Vittorio
  Palladino and Carmela Palladino
Gary and Catherine Vivian & Family
Mr. Michael Vormittag
Sandra and Leo Vos
Trevor Vosu

W

W Studio Carpets & Alan Pourvakil
Delaney and Sacheen Waddell
Robert and Marion Waddell
Janet and Dennis Waddington
Margaret C. Waddington
Sheila Waengler
Elisabeth F. Wagschal
Alice, Richard, Jason and Jaime Wah
Sam and Martin Wakim
Sylvia and Henry Waks
Michael, Gail, Erica and Lucas Walden
Donna and Philip Walker
Elizabeth Walker & Family

Harriet and Gordon Walker,
  Wynsome and Melanie Walker
Ian L. Walker
Jeffrey and Anne Walker
Rick and Virginia Walker
Ruth, Cameron, Alexis, Charles,
  Bronwyn and Piers Walker
Wes and Margaret Walker
John Wallace and Bob Hambleton
Kenneth and Karla Wallace
The Klaas Walma Family
Robert and Ruth Walmsley
Teresa Walsh and David Kines
Family of Dan Walshe and
  Linda McCain
Patricia and Patrick Walshe
Elizabeth M. Walter
Mr. John Walter
Dr. John A. and Mrs. Pamela Walter
Margaret Walter & Family
Peter and Louise Walter
Diane and Paul Walters & Family
Lenore Walters and Sarah Beales
Robert Walters
J. Brian Walton and Alison Walton
David, Anne-Marie, Kristian,
  Bonnie Warburton
Gilbert and Marion Warburton
Damon G. Ward
Michele Ward
Estate of Isabel Carey Warne
L. Alan Warren
David and Melissa, Daniel, Micah,
  Matthew, Hannah and Riley
  Warry-Smith
Marvin M. and Tanya F. Warsh
Al and Marika Warson
Colleen and Hubert Washington
Dr. Maria Ellen Waslen
Robert May and Anne Waterhouse
Dr. Fern Waterman
Phyllis and William Waters
Gordon and Faye Watson
Irena Watson
Mac and Rena Watson
Sylvia Watson
Claire Watts
Cindy A. Waugh
Margaret Wayne
Gladys Weatherill
Judith Weaver
In loving memory of
  James Charles Webb
Elizabeth Webber and
  David Illingworth

Peter Weber
Robert and Patricia Weber
Elsie P. Webster and Jennifer Wilson
Marjorie Katheleen Webster
Mr. Paul Webster
Terence Victor Webster
Gary and Heidi Weddel
The Wee Tom Family
Robert and Menna Weese
WEEVAC-W. Murphy Enterprises Inc.
Edward Weinberg and Barbara Berson
Dr. Fred Weinberg and
  Mrs. Joy Cherry Weinberg
Howard and Faith Weinberg
Larry and Debbie Weinberg & Family
Dr. Edwin and Mrs. Judith Weinstein
Dr. Ruth Weintrop and
  Mr. Eli Naiman
Gren, Barb, Alec and Dylan Weis
Dr. Gerald and Mrs. Sally Weisbrod
Laura Weiss and Elizabeth Priori
Mr. Michael Weissenborn and
  Ms. Cathy Kozma
Avril Wendt
Christopher, Michael and
  Meagan Wenkoff
Christopher and Monique Wernham
Richard Wernham and Julia West
Douglas and Victoria West
Katri, Gordon, Tom, Anneli and
  Ross West
Western Creamery
Arnold and Margaret Westlake
Hilary and Galen Weston
The W. Garfield Weston Foundation
Dr. William Weston
Weston Foods Canada
Gordon and Jane Wetmore
Earl and Terry Wexler
Tina and David Whalen
Deborah White
Denise White
Derek White & Family
Mr. Leslie E. White
Mervyn, Gisele, Liz and
  Andrew White
Mr. William White
Sandra Whiteley
George and Fran Whitney
Eva Whitwell
Doreen Whyte
Karin Wiens
R. H. Wiens
The Wiggan Family
Diane E. Wigginton

Daniel and Marilyn Wigglesworth
  & Children
Ms. Linda Wigington
Jennifer Wilcox, Linda Webb,
  Christine L. MacNeil and
  Kenneth G. MacNeil
Martha H. Wilder
Mr. & Mrs. William P. Wilder
Libby Wildman
Judith and Michael Wiley
Diane Wilford
In memory of Noreen Wilkey
Barbara and Douglas Wilkins
Donald A. E. Williams
Kathy and Doreen Williams
Ruth and Hugh Williams
Lorraine M. Williamson
Prof. Nancy Williamson
Stephen and Barbara Williamson
John and Cheryl Willms
Colin Willows
Mrs. Georgina Wilmot Woods
In memory of Basil T. Wilson
Freda and Dale Wilson
Mr. George Wilson
Kathy Wilson
Linda Wilson
Pamela Wilson, Mitchell Wilson,
  Mathieu and Zachary Sheridan
Paul and Sue Wilson
Red and Brenda Wilson
W. R. Wilson
Florence and Mickey Winberg
Windfields Farm
Marjorie Wingrove, Felix, Reilly and
  Kate Brown
Jack and Betty Winston & Family
Brock Winterton and Janet Heisey
Alfred G. Wirth
Richard and Margaret Wise
Robert Wiseman and Virginia Roy
Marcia Wiseman
Nan and Jack Wiseman
Mr. & Mrs. Stanley Witkin
Zishe Lawrence and
  Eleanor S. Wittlin
Barbara and Harvey Wolfe
F. J. Wolff and Family
Judith Wolfson and Stanley Zlotkin
The Honourable William Wolski
The Women's Association of the
  Mining Industry of Canada
Arthur Wong and
  Kevin de Courcy O'Grady
Cheuk and Anne Wong

Harry Wong, Ruby Kung,
  Christopher and Matthew Wong
Robert C. Wong
Steven K. Wong
Suzie Wong
Dickson and Penelope Wood
Mr. Gary Wood
John, Paden, Sarah and Joshua Wood
John J. Wood
Dr. Lawrence Woodley and
  Ms. Susan Litt-Woodley
Thomas, Georgia, Siobhan, Zoe and
  Owen Woods
William, Sarah, Zoe and Ella Woods
The Worden-Colledge Family
World Salon
Richard Worr and Donna Murdoch
Donald and David Worth
Marylou Wratten
Donald and Sally Wright
Estate of Jean Y. Wright
Peter and Samantha Wright
Robert and Joan Wright
Diana Wronski and David and
  Kira Dorward
WService and Design &
  Wieland Family
Eva, Edmund and Adrian Wu
In memory of Mr. & Mrs. John
  Chang-Fu Wu
Diana Wurtzburg
Greg, Stephanie, Declan and
  Sarah Wylie
Roman (Moko) Wynnyckyj and
  Maria Lialka
The Wysocki-Bienko Family

Y

Jo-Anne Yale
Yamaha Motor Canada Ltd.
Soichiro Yamamoto and
  Junko Yamamoto
Yamato Transport U.S.A. Inc.
Mrs. Maureen Yang
Brandon and Cameron Yap
Robin Yap and Edward Perry
John Yaremko, Q.C. and
  Mary A. Yaremko
David and Patricia Yerzy
Deanna Yeung
Paul and Cici Yeung
Burle and Louise Yolles
The Young Family Foundation
David Young
Eleanor Young

Yuet Fai Young and Hou Sung Young
Bernadette Yuen & Family
Yuki, Ernie and Esmé
Yum, M.L.
Jessie Yurman

Z

Kate Zankowicz
Maria W. Zaremba
Geoffrey and Ellen Zeiss
Beate Ziegert
Wilf and Helen Ziegler
J. D. Lampard and R. D. Zigrossi
Helen Zinkargue
Robert and Delores Zinn
David Zitzerman and
  Karen Friedman
Jacob and Trinity Zucchiatti
Carole and Dr. Bernard Zucker
Simon and Jan Zucker & Family
Mrs. Arthur David Zuckerman
Sharon Zuckerman
Marvin and Brenda Zuker
Sabrina, Juan Carlos, Nicolas and
  Alicia Zuniga
Barrie and Jean Zwicker
Bernard and Miriam Zylberberg

Photography by Brian Boyle, Tom Sandler, Jeff Speed and Russell Vance

Published by the Royal Ontario Museum with the generous support of the Louise Hawley Stone Charitable Trust

Cristal
Michael Lee-Chin
Crystal

BOLD VISIONS

I THE ARCHITECTURE OF THE ROYAL ONTARIO MUSEUM I

Page 6: Study model of the dinosaur galleries, second floor, Michael Lee-Chin Crystal. *Page 8:* Second floor, Michael Lee-Chin Crystal, as built, now named the James and Louise Temerty Galleries of the Age of Dinosaurs.

BOLD VISIONS

| THE ARCHITECTURE OF THE ROYAL ONTARIO MUSEUM |

KELVIN BROWNE

24

27
he Roy
ntario M
st wing
designed
nto arch
Darling

60

118

124

136

145

156

McLAUGHLIN PLANETARIUM

CONTENTS

13 | Foreword

24 | Museum Builders 1906/1907, 2006/2007

27 | The Idea of Museum

60 | 1914: The Original ROM

80 | 1933: Queen's Park Building and Centre Block

118 | 1968: McLaughlin Planetarium

124 | 1984: Curatorial Centre and
Queen Elizabeth II Terrace Galleries

136 | 2007: Renaissance ROM: Heritage Building
Retrieval and the Michael Lee-Chin Crystal

 | Building the Royal Ontario Museum (fold-out)

145 | Bold Vision: Interview with Daniel Libeskind

156 | 2001–2007: The Michael Lee-Chin Crystal Emerges

174 | Renaissance ROM: A Tour

FOREWORD

The creators of the Royal Ontario Museum have always been conscious of the role of architecture in fulfilling the ROM's mission. The investment in a master plan and the ambitious first wings of the ROM in 1914 and 1933 spoke forcefully to the importance of architecture in meeting the Museum's goals, both practical and symbolic. In its physical form, this was to be a classic museum in the great tradition of the Metropolitan Centre—London. It was to look and feel like an archetype, creating an appropriate sense of respect, mystery and even awe for what a museum embodied. By 2001, our concept of the museum had evolved, and thus our aspirations for its architecture. The museum will always be a place of scholarship, collection, conservation and education, and its physical facilities must serve these purposes. But the museum—especially the ROM—now plays additional roles in public life.

The ROM is a universal museum of cultures in a diversifying country—and so emerges as a new "agora"—a common ground for encounter and social integration, rooted in its mandate, but beyond its original terms of reference. The ROM is a significant museum of natural history—and is thus a centre for public understanding in the newly urgent debate about the environment and our place in shaping it. The ROM occupies a dominant corner in the centre of Canada's largest city—and so is a defining part of the city by its very presence.

In this context, we felt that the architecture of the ROM's new expansion should be deeply urban, as well as institutional in character. It should transcend colonial archetypes and traditional institutional needs. In our view, the new building needed to be a distinguishing act of originality serving more complex public purposes—more publicly.

Our "Vision for Architecture" of May 2001 sought first the retrieval of the heritage buildings, which had been compromised by renovations over many years. These earlier "bold visions" justified every effort at their revival. That done, we also foresaw "a much more accessible, dramatic, transparent and modern complex integrated into the urban fabric around and through it," as a foil to, and in dialogue with, our heritage wings. This was to be an act of city-building as well as an effective museum expansion. In a sense, this new wing and main public entrance on Toronto's "high street" would turn part of the Museum inside out and make an irresistible claim to broader social purposes.

Daniel Libeskind responded to these aspirations with deliberation and passion. The Michael Lee-Chin Crystal recalls no other place or time in its form, urban stance, and mythology: it is both universal and intensely local as a work of public art. It serves both the vision for architecture and the program for meeting the Museum's needs. Coincidentally—and wonderfully—it recalls the crystalline shapes of the ROM's authoritative mineral collections—and of Canada's natural environment. The Lee-Chin Crystal arises from Daniel Libeskind's singular imagination, but if you wish, you might see a Lawren Harris painting in three dimensions—an Arctic mountain glistening in an urban sea, quintessentially Canadian beyond the colonial context at last.

Architecture is the most public of the arts, and the ROM is the most public of museums. Museums should be creators of art as well as guardians of artifacts and specimens. The architecture of museums must serve classic purposes, but should also contribute iridescently to the identity of the cities and societies in which they exist—thus the requirement for bold visions in museum-making, whatever the place or time.

William Thorsell,
Director and CEO, Royal Ontario Museum

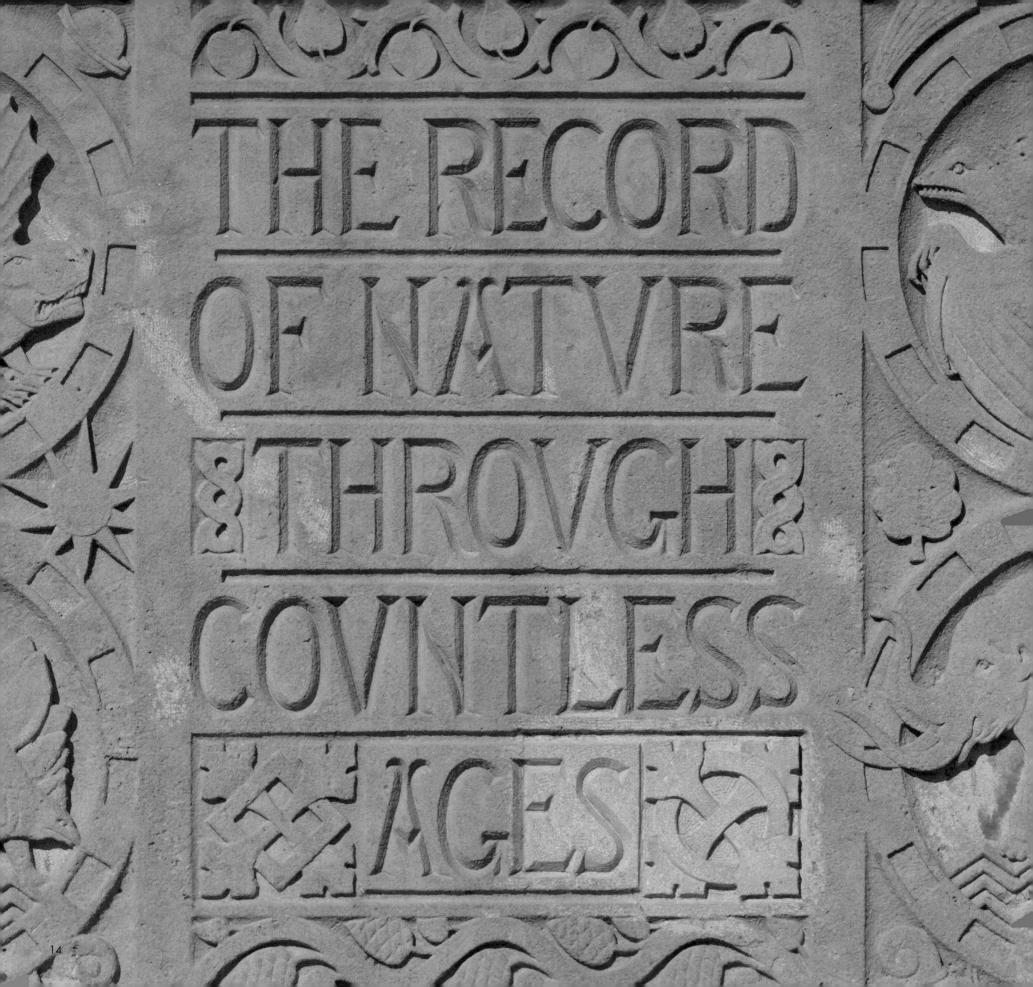

THE RECORD
OF NATVRE
THROVGH
COVNTLESS
AGES

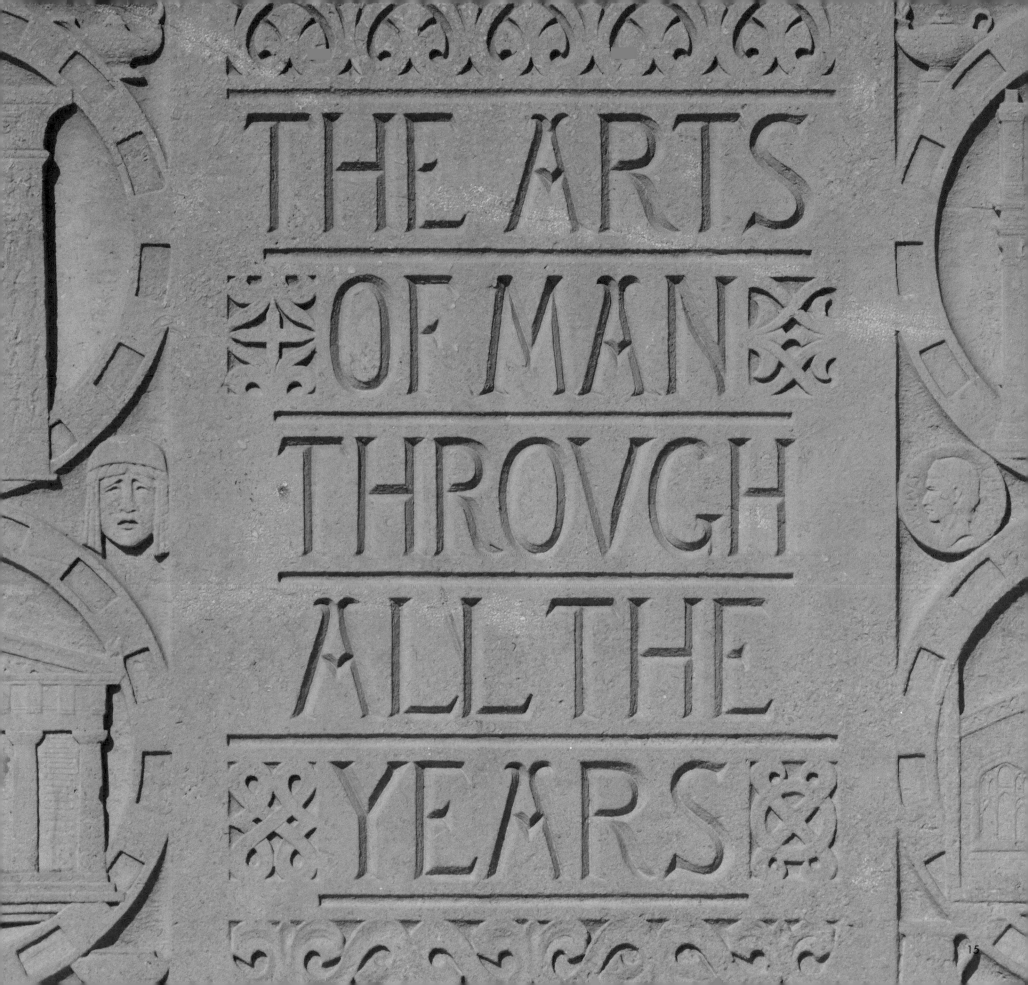

THE ARTS
OF MAN
THROVGH
ALL THE
YEARS

15

NATVRE

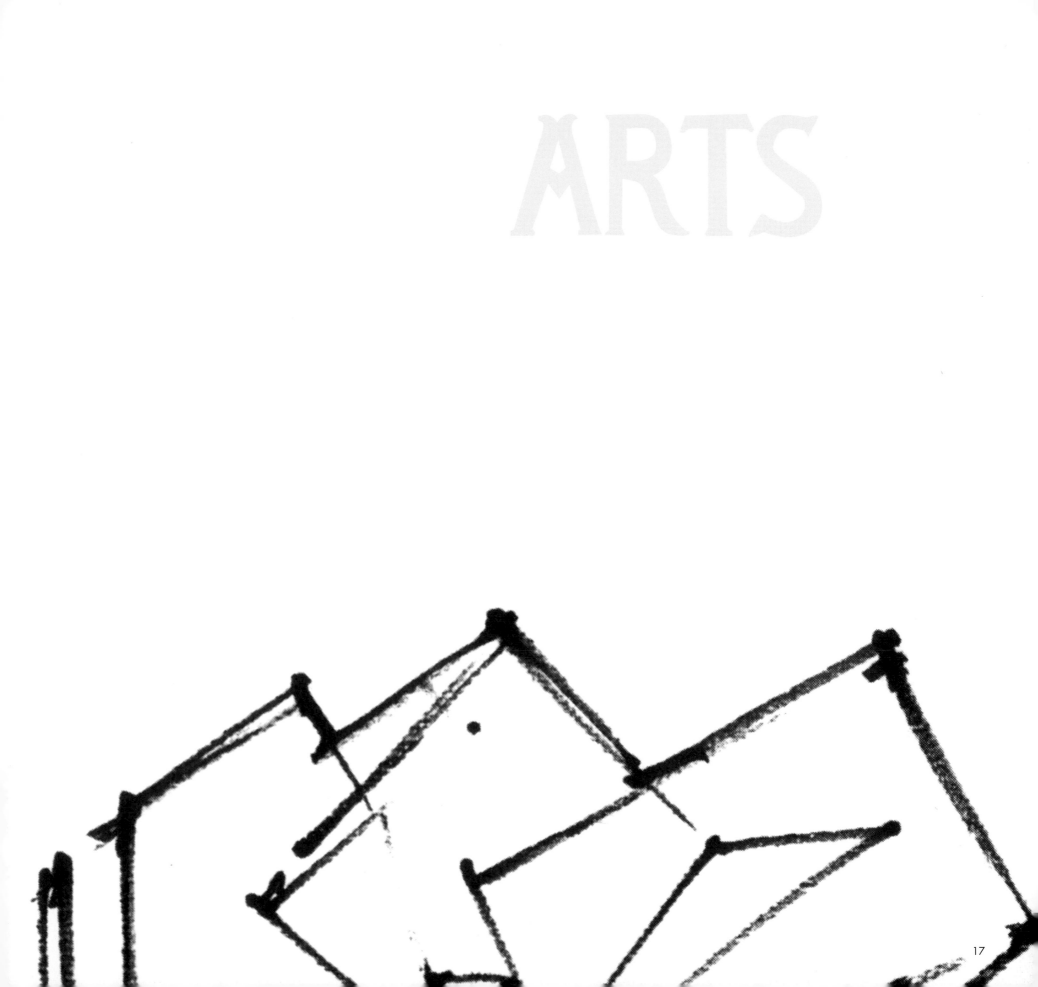

ARTS

ROM COLLECTS

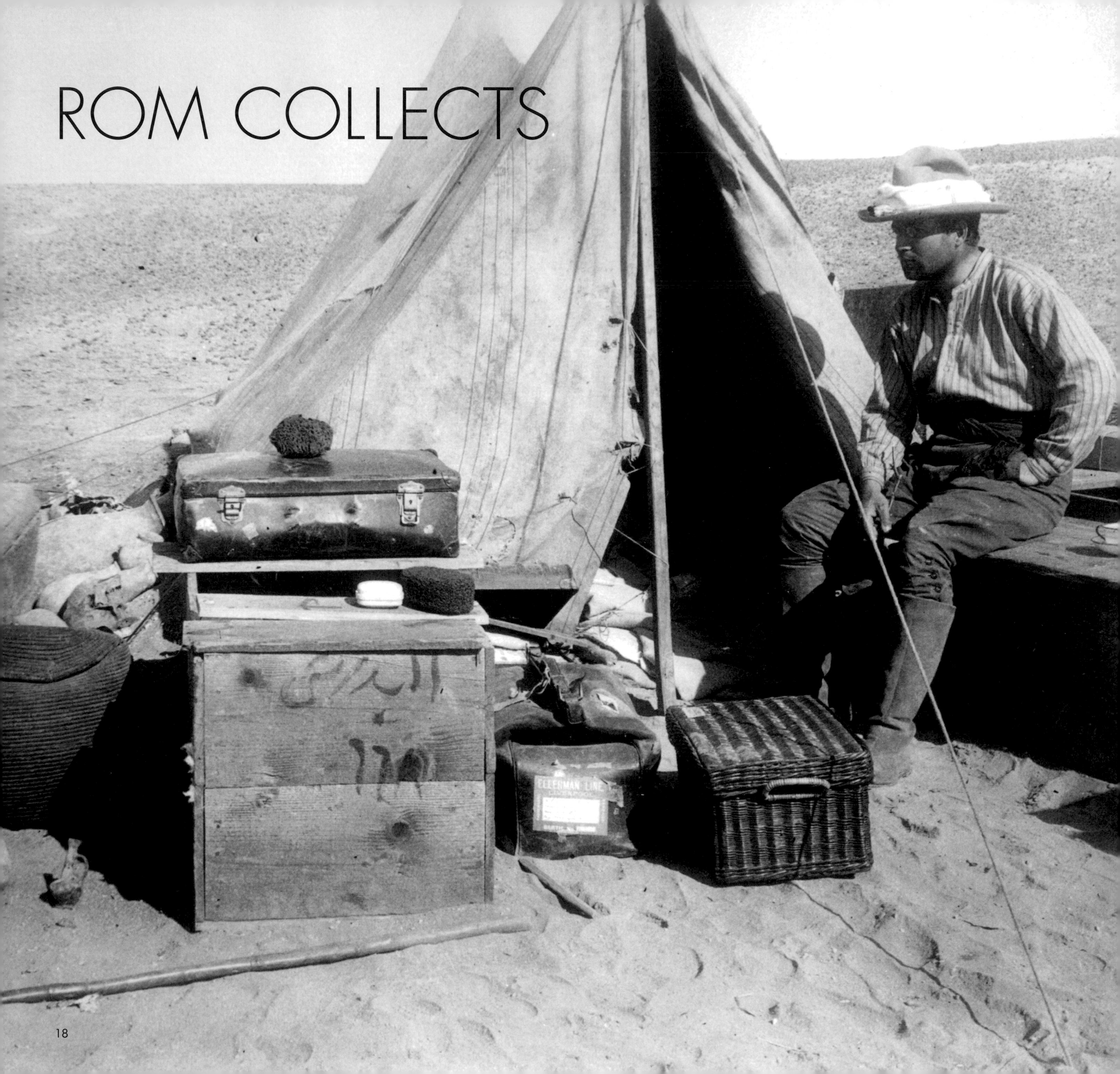

ROM RESEARCHES

Page 18: Charles Currelly on expedition in Egypt, 1903. *Page 19:* Katherine Dunnell, a technician, studies mineral specimens in the Louise Hawley Stone Curatorial Centre. *Page 20:* Daphne Cockwell Gallery of Canada: First Peoples, 2007. *Page 21 (left and right):* The ROM Digital Gallery, 2006.

19

ROM DISPLAYS

ROM EDUCATES

ROM CELEBRATES

Page 22: Dancing in the ROM's Rotunda, Hungarian Ball, c. 1965. *Page 23:* The *shishi*, the ROM's celebrated stone lions, from Beijing in 1922 to their 2007 location on either side of the Weston Entrance.

ROM EVOLVES

23

Page 24: Torontonians at the pyramids, winter 1906/7; some of them went on to visit Charles Currelly, first director of the Royal Ontario Museum of Archaeology, at his excavations at Deir el-Bahri. The party includes (left to right) Charles Cockshutt and significant ROM supporters Mrs. H. D. Warren, Gordon Osler, Mrs. G. Osler, and Sir Edmund Osler. *Page 25:* The architecture of the ROM has depended on the vision and support of each generation's leaders. Museum leaders of the 21st century, supporting the vision of Renaissance ROM, are honoured as "New Century Founders." A photomural installed in the Michael Lee-Chin Crystal's Spirit House shows ROM Director and CEO William Thorsell (upper left) with the New Century Founders (left to right): Mina and Shreyas Ajmera, James and Louise Temerty (seated), Robert and Elizabeth Schad, Elizabeth Samuel (seated), Nicole and Thor Eaton, Michael Lee-Chin, Galen and Hilary Weston (seated), The W. Garfield Weston Foundation (not pictured), Simona and Alex Shnaider, Joey and Toby Tanenbaum, Jack Cockwell and Lynda Hamilton (not pictured). In the foreground is the Spirit House Chair designed by Daniel Libeskind.

Architecture is the manifestation of many intangibles. An architect's vision, a client's ambition, and a community's resolve, for instance, can all play a role in shaping a structure. The Royal Ontario Museum illustrates many such intangible forces—as well as ones assumed to be more tangible but likely as elusive, such as budget, site, and program—coalescing over time to create a building. From the long list of factors contributing to the ROM's architecture, two are particularly influential, and they are among the most ephemeral.

The first is that the ROM reflects the vision of its leaders. Each generation has molded the Museum's physical form, from Sir Byron Edmund Walker (1848–1924) at the beginning of the 20th century to William Thorsell at the start of the 21st. The second is the evolving notion of what a museum should be. The ROM's various iterations beginning in 1914 have been shaped by museum trends, most as contentious now as they were when planning for the first wing began. The ROM's architecture illustrates much of the history of museum design. Perhaps this should not be surprising since the idea of *museum* itself is relatively new.

The Museum

Although the ceremonial display of accumulated treasure has prehistoric origins, the ROM's antecedents are more recent. Until the 16th and 17th centuries, objects were seldom displayed as orderly collections or viewed in buildings contrived expressly for this purpose. Palaces of this period reveal the origins of both museum architecture in general and the ROM's in particular.

Galleries in palaces initially had little to do with hanging pictures; they were primarily circulation spaces connecting one area to another, or they were used as reception rooms for official ceremonies. But as large, empty spaces, often forming routes, they were ready-made for the display of trophies and they came to be used for this. Eventually, enlightened noble families displayed their collections and bolstered their prestige as savvy collectors, powerful community leaders, and magnanimous citizens by allowing a wider audience to see their possessions. Better to give the appearance of sharing, of course, than actually having to do it.

In 1793 the Louvre became an early example of a private gallery—Louis XVI's—that made the transition to public amenity, albeit in a revolutionary manner. A less violent example, the Villa Borghese in Rome, became accessible to the public in the late 1700s also and was subsequently made a completely public gallery with the participation of its owners. This strategy was good for the Borghese family, allowing them to retain control of the property while minimizing their financial burden.

Between 1750 and 1800, palaces that housed important private collections became the de facto models for museums, whether these museums were conversions of existing buildings or new purpose-built structures. While modern museums may strive to be peoples' palaces, the connection to royal palaces and wealthy benefactors remains unshakeable. Because of this many visitors are simultaneously fascinated by and detached from both the objects and the institution itself: This is interesting but what does it have to do with me? And a few visitors, especially when the venue is a retrofitted palace, may feel anger or resentment toward much of what the museum represents—a way of life and a social system that may have oppressed them or their ancestors.

The plan derived from the palace format is easy to recognize: long corridors with rooms opening onto them, or an enfilade, a row of rooms connected via openings in line with each other. These are the kinds of spaces we have come to assume are most suitable for the orderly display of artifacts and specimens. One of the earliest museums in which a progression of spaces was used to illustrate the progression of time and styles—when this became the predominant organizing principle of display—was the Louvre.

Using the Louvre as his prototype, French architectural theoretician J. N. L. Durand (1760–1834) published his landmark museum plan in 1802. (He eventually provided ideal plans for most building types, not just museums.) His ideal museum was a square with long corridors running along the perimeter giving access to relatively small rooms. Inside this square was a Greek cross, with a similar arrangement of corridors and rooms, that created four courtyards. The centre of the cross, and of the museum, was a domed rotunda. Given the emphasis on symmetry of the prevailing Beaux Arts style of the 19th and early 20th centuries, Durand's ideal was embraced by architects and remained influential for nearly 150 years.

Durand's plan was predicated on a larger-scale museum building, but the concept was well suited to a modular approach. Architects could build from the plan in stages, or they could adapt the plan, using only a portion of it to design smaller buildings. The Altes Museum in Berlin designed in 1823 by Karl Schinkel (1782–1841), for example, represents only half of Durand's model—in plan it looks like a rectangle with a line bisecting its middle. Schinkel compensated for the building's reduced size by adding a monumental grand stair, and soon a grand staircase became an expected feature in any significant new museum.

The ROM's DNA

The ROM's original master plan was created by the Toronto architectural firm Darling and Pearson, with planning likely beginning in 1906. (University of Toronto professor and museologist Lynne Teather's 2005 book, *The Royal Ontario Museum: A Prehistory, 1830 to 1914*, offers a vivid account of the events and people connected with the ROM at this time.) A hand-lettered and illuminated document presented to the Duke of Connaught (then Governor General of Canada) to commemorate his visit when he opened the Museum in 1914 gloriously presents this plan. It is clearly derived from Durand's ideal and is another example of the use of half his prototype. If the ROM had been fully realized as the illuminated plan suggested, it would be a classic Beaux Arts building in plan but with a rather more eclectic façade treatment.

The Louvre, Paris.

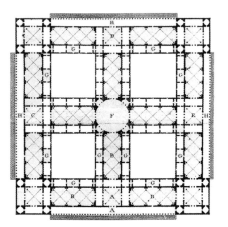

J. N. L. Durand, museum plan, 1802.

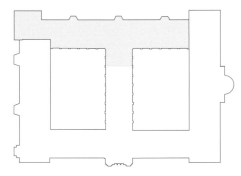

ROM master plan, Darling and Pearson, 1909, with the 1914 section shaded.

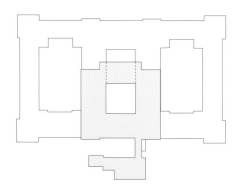

Art Museum of Toronto master plan, Darling and Pearson, 1918, with the initial building shaded.

Interestingly, the original 1918 plan for the Art Gallery of Ontario, then the Art Museum of Toronto, was based on a master plan with a configuration similar to the ROM's. It, too, was conceived by Darling and Pearson and in its original version the centre axis was a large sculpture court with galleries to either side. At the ROM, this central circulation area is a single, large east-west gallery, now called Samuel Hall ❧ Currelly Gallery.

Charles Currelly (1876–1956), the first director of the Royal Ontario Museum of Archaeology, in his memoir, *I Brought the Ages Home* (1956), suggested a colourful explanation for the ROM's master plan that relied heavily on his having been in the right place at the right time. He describes a chance meeting in a railway carriage near London with noted English architect Sir Aston Webb (1849–1930). The ROM was in the earliest stages of planning, and Webb was completing an addition to the Victoria and Albert Museum in London. Webb obligingly sketched the bisected rectangle—the "double quadrangle," as Currelly later referred to it—saying it was the perfect museum layout. Currelly sent the sketch via Sir Byron Edmund Walker (the first chair of the ROM Board of Trustees) to the ROM's architects back in Toronto.

Given the influence of both Durand and the Beaux Arts style, few would have disagreed with Webb's advice. It is unlikely, however, that Darling and Pearson were much influenced by the sketches of their noted but distant colleague. In fact, it would have been a radical development if this colonial but sophisticated firm had thought of doing things much differently. This was not a mediocre firm. A native Ontarian, Frank Darling (1850–1923) was trained as an architect in England and began to practice his profession in Toronto in 1873. He was a member of the Royal Canadian Academy of Arts (1886), president of the Ontario Association of Architects (1895), and director of the Toronto Guild of Civic Art (1907). John Andrew Pearson (1867–1940) also took his architectural training in England, where he was born the son and grandson of eminent architects. He came to Canada in 1888. The two formed their partnership in 1893. Pearson's most famous commission, perhaps, was as co-architect, with Jean-Omer Marchand, for the new Centre Block of the Parliament Buildings in Ottawa (1916), the original having been destroyed by fire. Darling was also the first honorary president of the Toronto Beaux Arts Club, and in 1915 he became the first Canadian to win the Royal Institute of British Architects Gold Medal. If Darling and Pearson did receive Webb's sketch—Currelly says they were given Webb's drawings and measurements "when they were appointed"—rather than inspiring their design, it more likely served to confirm the suitability of the concept they already had in mind.

As well, when Currelly sent Webb's drawings to Canada in the spring of 1908 (and who knows how long they took to get to Canada via Sir Edmund), planning had been underway for some time. In May 1908, for example, Currelly responded to what he heard were changes to the museum plan he had probably seen in the fall of 1907, one he thought "nearly perfect." It could be assumed, then, that while the specific components and façade treatments may have continued to evolve after 1907, a diagrammatic sketch and some simple dimensions received six to ten months later would not likely have caused a "nearly perfect" plan to change radically, and certainly not the basic footprint to be altered.

The ROM built the first part of the Darling and Pearson plan in 1910–1912 (opened 1914), and continued to be influenced by it when the second part was added in 1931–1933. The T-shaped addition designed by architects Chapman and Oxley created an H-shaped building, but the addition did not include galleries to complete the double quadrangle on the north and south sides. Without galleries to the north and south, there was no perimeter promenade or route as illustrated in the original design of two decades previous.

After the 1933 addition, the master plan was abandoned. The open courtyards were re-imagined as building sites: the 1978–1984 renovation by Moffat Moffat & Kinoshita filled the south courtyard with a massive curatorial building and the north courtyard with galleries terracing down to Bloor Street. The galleries were connected to the existing building by an atrium. However, the atrium was not conceptualized as a courtyard, and the new galleries did not otherwise connect to the existing galleries to the east and west, and hence did not create a perimeter route as envisioned by the original master plan. Abandoning the ROM's classic Beaux Arts plan was a dismissal of what may have seemed an outdated organizational concept when planning was underway in the 1970s.

In 1984, the key axis of the ROM—from the front entrance on Queen's Park, through the Rotunda and the present Samuel Hall ❧ Currelly Gallery, originally named the Armour Court, to a bay window overlooking the park-like Philosophers' Walk—was blocked by a new mechanical room, an exit staircase added to the west of it, and the Mankind Discovering Gallery. Interrupting a processional route such as this in a Beaux Arts–inspired building, where continuous sequence is essential, severely impairs the organizational structure.

But it was not the 1978–1984 renovation that first impaired this essential vista. In the 1960s, this axis continued beyond the Rotunda through only a portion of the Armour Court, where it was truncated by a partially enclosed gallery area for the display of the Lord Lee of Fareham Collection of antique silver and precious objects. Sightlines continued from there through a pierced metal screen, the remains of a gate from a Spanish church, to the bay window beyond, the termination of the original axis.

While the axis was still visually intact, visitors were now required to take a more circuitous route to traverse it. With the installation in the 1960s of the gallery of Central European Baroque, the bay window terminating the Samuel Hall ❧ Currelly Gallery axis was covered to prevent light from damaging artifacts and to provide more display area. The end of this lyrical axis with its view onto Philosophers' Walk was not to be revealed again for 40 years.

While filling in the open courtyards could be interpreted as merely expedient, it nonetheless demonstrated that the ROM's original architectural direction, the perimeter promenade as per the Darling and Pearson plan, had been abandoned. It was not a complete rejection of the original approach as it did not subvert the circulation plan and it preserved the original buildings. The subsequent imposition of a mechanical room in the Lee Collection display area during the 1978–1984 renovation was, on the contrary, an unequivocal statement that the Beaux Arts layout of the ROM was rejected as a basis for visitor circulation and gallery organization and display. It's not necessarily that the curators or designers specifically wanted it there, but that it could be placed there at all demonstrated that maintenance of the axis was unimportant. It was a more strident indication than the building of the Queen Elizabeth II Terrace Galleries and the curatorial centre in what were once the ROM's courtyards that the Beaux Arts architectural logic was now unpersuasive.

Abandoning the ROM's classic Beaux Arts plan was a dismissal of what may have seemed an outdated organizational concept when planning was underway in the 1970s

Does reorganizing a museum's content mean that axial relationships and traditional gallery layouts—ones associated with institutional order— are rejected?

The curatorial focus had shifted from display to education (as will be discussed later), and the building had changed in response. Windows were covered and many large galleries were sub-divided with the intent to create a more ideal pedagogical environment. Inside, the result was a visual jumble, a series of similar, dark, often enclosed spaces with little connection to the architecture, where objects often appeared to be overwhelmed by their backdrops. The building was difficult to comprehend as a total experience and hence to navigate. The display-organization diagrams of museum planners of the time had been literally realized with little sense of the building's being much more than an exterior shell to house introverted displays. It is no wonder that many people came away from the ROM with a fragmented sense of their visit.

Does reorganizing a museum's content mean that axial relationships and traditional gallery layouts—ones associated with institutional order—are rejected? In the 1970s and 1980s, perhaps symmetry and order became synonymous with old and authoritarian, echoes of palace-based planning perceived by museum executives as offensive to a mass audience. New and popular were symbolized by informal, and presumably less intimidating, smaller spaces, many with trend-of-the-moment diagonal walls and meandering paths.

Daniel Libeskind's renovation sweeps all of this away, restoring the ROM's original central axis and signalling a return to the Beaux Arts DNA of the building. In Libeskind's retrieval, the basic volumes of the heritage building are reminiscent of their original configuration, while the spaces themselves have been made contemporary and pristine. The spirit of the original spaces has been recaptured.

As well, Durand's influence re-emerges in the ROM's 2007 addition with the idea of a promenade: visitors walk through a series of carefully modulated spaces and come full circle to where they began. (At the École des Beaux Arts, the promenade—"la marche"—was essential to the organization of larger projects.) While the 2007 ROM is not symmetrical, many of its gallery routes are. If one imagines the Hyacinth Gloria Chen Crystal Court as a courtyard, and the Michael Lee-Chin Crystal as the north side of the "double quadrangle," the plan is very close to realizing the original Darling and Pearson conception. The only thing missing is a connection linking the dangling south wings of the historic buildings.

This new promenade restores an inherent navigational logic to which most visitors respond. Symmetry and balance help visitors comprehend a building even if they have never seen it before. This kind of plan is comforting because it is familiar. Our innate pattern-recognition ability has been culturally reinforced by exposure to the palaces that became museums and to a multitude of other public buildings with similar formats. In the ROM, major artifacts also serve as landmarks, reinforcing the use of axial arrangements for orientation. For example, the 6th-century Amitabha marble Buddha in the bay window and the 11th-century earthenware Luohan in front of it are both on axis with the east-west vista on the ground floor through Samuel Hall ❧ Currelly Gallery. Windows are not only architectural features; they have become navigational aids as well. Many visitors, consciously or unconsciously, use sunlight and the exterior landmarks visible through them to help orient themselves in the galleries.

In this gesture, the most recent renovations and addition allow visitors more freedom. What looked on the surface to be casual, comfortable, and friendly in the 1984 ROM iteration was revealed as disguised tyranny.

The highly manipulative warren of small dark spaces offered visitors less freedom for discovery by keeping them dependent on signage for navigation. A building with a readily perceived order is liberating.

The Gallery
Open Plan—Partially Defined—The Promenade

"The plan is the generator," said architect Le Corbusier, one of the seminal figures in 20th-century modern architecture. For museums today there are, broadly speaking, three plan approaches generating the architecture of galleries. The most contemporary might be called the *open plan* or flexible space. While usually associated with temporary exhibits, this kind of space is also used for permanent displays. "Flexible" is usually a euphemism for galleries with little visible architecture or, as some might say, personality. They are warehouse-like volumes in which display cases and fragments of walls become architecturally significant in an otherwise barren landscape. Such galleries typically do not have windows or skylights. These would limit their reconfiguration and let in too much light for many artifacts; artificial lighting can be more easily regulated.

The Centre Pompidou in Paris (1972–1977, Piano and Rogers) is an example of a series of flexible spaces in which large, open, sub-dividable areas are stacked on top of one another and connected by escalators that snake up the building's exterior. It is a highrise warehouse for temporary exhibits.

In the second plan approach, gallery spaces are *partially defined*—while the path is suggested, there is no obvious route a visitor should (or must) take to view objects. While circulation routes relative to galleries imply a hierarchy, and content may imply a viewing sequence, the route is for the visitor to determine. This space might be an atrium with rooms opening on to it, but more typically it is a grid of galleries with many doors and a multitude of possible paths. At its most complex, this approach is a maze in which visitors wander through a sea of walls, areas flow into one another, and rooms are not clearly discernible.

The Kimbell Art Museum in Fort Worth, Texas (1966–1972), designed by Louis Kahn (1901–1974), with its repeating vaulted spaces, is a masterful application of the partially defined approach. It is understandable simultaneously as one large gallery and as a series of more intimate spaces comfortable to the visitor and appropriately scaled to the works on display.

The third approach, the *promenade*, determines the routes for visitors to follow. Spaces are comprehended as rooms, or rooms and corridors. This approach can produce an informal collection of rooms or a more formal, classical series of galleries enfilade. This spatial concept is a direct descendant of palace-inspired museums.

The ROM has employed all three approaches since 1914. The original master plan, as shown in the illuminated manuscript presented to the Duke of Connaught, suggested each wing as a large, open gallery with minimum subdivision, a series of contiguous flexible spaces.

After the renovation of 2005, the wing built corresponding to this plan—the original 1914 building along Philosophers' Walk—returned to this open concept. The Herman Herzog Levy Gallery is the only significant element defining the space other than the glazed display cases. In the 1933 building, the new Daphne Cockwell

Kimbell Art Museum, Fort Worth, Texas, designed by Louis Kahn, 1972.

Guggenheim Museum, New York, designed by Frank Lloyd Wright, 1959.

Gallery of Canada: First Peoples and the Sigmund Samuel Gallery of Canada have similarly open architectural concepts, which can, however, be obscured by the density of displays.

In the architectural drawings and photographs of the 1914 ROM, as originally built, gallery spaces are more defined than in the illuminated manuscript. While there is a sense of rooms, however, there are few pre-determined routes—similar to the second approach described. The spaces were much like the galleries of the Victoria and Albert Museum in London of the same period, where viewers could walk up one side of a wing, turn, come back through a parallel series of galleries, and return to where they began. But the ROM layout, unlike many of the Victoria and Albert galleries, allowed options rather than a single predetermined path by providing additional doorways between rooms. Nevertheless, the appearance of these galleries when completed was strikingly similar to the Victoria and Albert galleries of this time, and the ROM's display cases appear to be replicas of those in London.

When the firm of Chapman and Oxley designed the 1933 ROM addition, administratively the ROM was five separate museums. The Royal Ontario Museums of Palaeontology, Mineralogy, Zoology, and Geology each had a separate gallery in the new building facing Queen's Park, while Archaeology expanded to fill the original 1914 structure. Each curatorial fiefdom in the new wing had its own entrance from the Rotunda, a designated display area, a director's office, a library, and areas for preparation. These new galleries were either a single open space, or an open space with work areas on the perimeter walls, or a gallery sub-divided by a single wall down the middle, creating two relatively long, narrow gallery spaces and forming a promenade for visitors. Other than this promenade gallery, the galleries were essentially flexible spaces, but not quite warehouse-like because the interiors had considerable architectural character.

Forty-five years would pass before the next major expansion. During that time the original wing and much of the 1933 galleries were converted into smaller galleries, some with curved and angled walls—what might be called *organic* in style. In most instances, there was only one way to walk through them. The promenade, and often it was a twisted one, became the norm.

The 1978–1984 renovation added galleries stacked in three levels along Bloor Street that opened onto an atrium. Escalators in the atrium connected the gallery floors. Given the characterless nature of the rooms, this arrangement could be considered a warehouse approach. The ground-floor space for the Chinese collection was open, but it was filled with displays to be viewed in a specified, if confusing, sequence, in cases that mostly appeared as walls and formed routes.

This tidy typology of three museum gallery approaches is complicated, of course, by the reality of museums. Museums often combine flexible gallery space, usually for temporary exhibits, with route-driven galleries for permanent exhibits. Administration areas may be no different from standard commercial office space. In addition, behind-the-scenes spaces, for instance, for preparation or storage, have special requirements. Restaurants, retail, auditoriums, and classrooms all have idiosyncratic architecture corresponding to commercial kitchens, stores, theatres, and schools rather than anything intrinsic to a museum.

A further complication is that the appearance of galleries, especially at first glance, may disguise their underlying intent and lead to misinterpretation. For instance, a museum such as the Guggenheim in New York, designed by Frank Lloyd Wright (1867–1959) and completed in 1959, can be considered a Beaux Arts progeny even though it might have seemed like a bold new scheme with no precedents other than perhaps a spiral parking-garage ramp. In her book *New American Art Museums* (1982), Helen Searing saw the Guggenheim's atrium as a courtyard and the spiral ramp as a series of display spaces along its perimeter not dissimilar to the galleries along corridors in the classic Beaux Arts formulation. In other words, it's the ultimate promenade.

Form Symbolizes Function

Museum buildings in various ages correspond to the purposes they are expected to accommodate, including symbolic ones. Museums of the 19th century were storehouses of precious objects tended by connoisseurs. The museum was a place where things were collected, stored, and displayed, and where collecting—not display—was the priority. Very little information beyond basic labelling was given. Some visitors were knowledgeable about what they were looking at; those who were not had few expectations beyond having the opportunity to gawk in reverential silence. Mere exposure to objects was considered edifying. Museums offered few amenities for visitors, and there was little space, either offices or workrooms, for the keepers of the collections.

New Yorker writer and social commentator Adam Gopnik has described this period as the "museum as mausoleum." The architecture was essentially a symbolic housing for "dead" objects. There was little concern that artifacts and specimens engage the visitor or be displayed in a dramatic fashion. They were not expected to do anything; their purpose was to be collected.

With collection as the primary purpose, museum plans were based on abstract principles of architecture, such as those articulated by Durand; they were not driven by the needs of visitors or many functional requirements. Premised on the pre–20th-century idea that museums, like churches, government buildings, prisons, and so on, had a correct symbolic form, the purpose of museum design was to find this ideal form, not to create a functional structure *per se*.

Conversely, modern architecture believed that function determined form, and form would vary according to the understanding of functional needs. Buildings were symbolic only inadvertently or as a secondary consideration.

The eclectic façade treatment of the ROM's 1914 building exemplifies the pre–20th-century approach in which symbolism was of paramount importance. It was an agglomeration of historic components that mirrored the idea of the museum as gathering disparate pieces of history together.

The ROM's first building also made a significant symbolic distinction between the museum, where objects were collected and displayed, and the offices, where administration took place. While their functions suggest that these spaces should be designed differently—exhibition hall versus office—this difference was expressed well beyond what any functional requirement demanded. The offices were designed to look like a separate building, one added to the Museum as an afterthought, even though it was always part of the concept.

The offices were designed to look like a separate building, one added to the Museum as an afterthought, even though it was always part of the concept

Compared to the exterior, the interior of the 1914 building was modern in terms of its lack of symbolism

It mimics a tower-style office building of the period, very distinct from the Museum proper. You can't mistake its purpose. It's as if the sacred aspect of the Museum required protection from the profane administration of it. (The 1914 office component was abbreviated as a budget economy; its top two floors were not added until 1937.)

Compared to the exterior, the interior of the 1914 building was modern in terms of its lack of symbolism. Its architecture was more functionally derived. The galleries were open spaces that could hold large glass cases and facilitate easy circulation around them. It wasn't only this lack of symbolism that made the 1914 building look somewhat modern; its large, industrial-looking windows were hallmarks of the new engineering-driven style.

Form Follows Function

A shift in emphasis from collecting to display after World War I brought about changes to museum architecture. Curators became concerned with displaying artifacts in ways that would engage viewers. This was a departure from the previous approach of collecting, studying, conserving, and permitting objects to be viewed.

The need to build the 1933 addition to the ROM was communicated in terms of the number of artifacts the Museum now had and the additional gallery space needed for them. This focus on display also prompted curators to demand better work areas and more storage space. As well, space for educational facilities, such as an auditorium, were part of this new focus on the viewer. The space required to support display was a new functional demand and it began to have an impact on the architecture of museums, including the ROM. Hence, while interest in displaying artifacts (as well as having more to display) manifested itself in new galleries in 1933, it also created offices, preparation areas, and libraries that were not prominent components of a museum before this time.

For some museums this shift was in tandem with changes in staffing: no more amateurs. Curators with appropriate degrees and higher curatorial standards became the goal. At the ROM and elsewhere, it was indicative of the move from curator/collector to curator/scholar. The ROM was part of the University of Toronto until 1968, a connection that reinforced the move to greater academic accreditation.

While the public face of the 1984 addition was the Terrace Galleries, the magnitude of the curatorial centre addition was equally impressive. It represented a further emphasis on curatorial needs, including onsite storage for the ROM's then continually expanding collections and research activities. The back and front of the house received equal attention.

The changes to galleries in the 1970s, and very noticeable in the 1984 renovation, demonstrate another shift in emphasis, from the display of objects with little explanation to the presentation of objects in a narrative, often an overtly educational one. Museology of the time introduced interpretive planning. This resulted in a more collective decision-making process with curators as the subject experts, working together with educators and designers to communicate with visitors. Objects were not necessarily viewed in galleries any longer, but in controlled *black box* environments where the architecture of the space was seldom important. For many, there was a change in the role of the curator from scholar to educator.

The 2007 Michael Lee-Chin Crystal addition, in terms of the priority given to artifact display, represents another functional shift. It's all about galleries. Curatorial spaces have not been added or renovated, and additional storage is off site. The prime function addressed in 2007 is the visitor and the totality of visitor experience, one that goes beyond viewing artifacts. The curator's role as it impacts Museum visitors is less overtly as an educator. Curators revert somewhat to the role of the curator/scholar, more like that of 1933 than 1984.

Similarly, the ROM's 2007 Crystal galleries appear like the 1914 galleries—large rooms full of objects in cases. The function of the gallery (at least on the surface) is back to where it started, a temple for objects. Of course, there is much more going on behind the scenes to support what is in the gallery and much more architecture outside the gallery proper aimed solely at making the visitor comfortable, and his or her visit lucrative—via retail or restaurants—for the Museum.

The ROM's 2007 Crystal exterior reverts to a level of interest in symbolic form comparable to that of the 1914 ROM. The overall impression is of a contemporary structure, stridently so in juxtaposition to what remains visible of the historic buildings. Just as the collection of historic elements decorating the surface of the 1914 building signalled that it was a repository of history, so the bold and idiosyncratic language of the Crystal communicates that while the Museum may house the past, it is a progressive and forward-looking institution.

The functions housed by the new ROM building were accommodated within an over-arching concept but were not the basis of it. The crystal sketch came first, with an understanding of what was to be housed; the architecture was not dependent on detailed summaries of gallery requirements or in-depth analysis of technical or circulation requirements. Form did not conceive function; form accommodated function. Windows were not primarily determined by practical or specific interior considerations. Much of their placement was determined by a process that was artistic. Even when they are consciously massed to give a sense of a light-filled building, their ability to be symbolic of a transparent institution and their ability to allow light into the building are equally important.

Regardless of what else the Crystal may represent, its exterior symbolizes change over continuity. The ROM wants to make it obvious that it's looking forward, not back.

Visitors Change the Museum

The first museums did not have to cope with masses of visitors. In the 1800s, most people were on the job when museums were open. Visiting a museum was not intended for everyone, although the middle classes were thought to become better citizens when they visited—on their day off. Crowd control was not an issue. Surges of visitors became a regular occurrence only with the advent of blockbuster special exhibits in the late 20th century. And that other source of visitors, hordes of boisterous students disgorging from buses, is a phenomenon that began in the 1930s but did not have noticeable impact until the 1950s.

Today, people make assumptions about the function of a museum well beyond their expectation of seeing interesting artifacts and specimens. They expect to be comfortable and engaged if not entertained as they learn something. We take it for granted that museums offer services to the visitor, the most obvious being restrooms

Regardless of what else the Crystal may represent, its exterior symbolizes change over continuity

In today's museums, at least those without significant government funding or massive endowments, the spaces that generate revenue are imperative

and a coat check, but now also including a range of restaurants and retail experiences. The ground-floor plans of new museums, in particular, demonstrate the complex number of visitor-oriented functions that shape the architecture, often taking precedence over an architect's stylistic vision and certainly overriding an idealized museum concept like that of Durand.

Enhanced Expectations

The considerable square footage needed for visitor-service functions, and the limited number of positions in which they can be placed to work effectively, means that they have a significant impact on museum planning. Retail space, for example, is typically on the ground floor with a separate, direct street entrance; restaurants are related to windows and outdoor spaces; educational areas, including classrooms, auditoriums, libraries, and meeting rooms, usually need ground-floor locations or direct access to where school buses unload; and shipping docks large enough to handle mammoth travelling exhibits are never inconsequential planning issues and can coerce a floor plan to accommodate them. As well, expanding spaces for offices related to fundraising and outreach shape the physical reality of the museum, as do the traditional requirements for preparation areas, curatorial offices, and on-site storage.

What wins the battle for prime real estate? In today's museums, at least those without significant government funding or massive endowments, the spaces that generate revenue are imperative. Profits from retail and hospitality services, including the rental of museum spaces for private functions, are important to museums' operating budgets. This is quite a change from the 1950s and 1960s, when boutiques in museum lobbies specialized in postcards and were run by volunteers, and tea shops offered basic refreshments.

The ground floor of the 2007 ROM represents the functionality of a modern museum and is similar operationally to the Museum of Modern Art (MoMA) in New York as reconfigured by Yoshio Taniguchi in 2005. Both institutions, for instance, give strategically placed space to retail use. Their stores have separate street access, allowing visitors to shop without entering the museum or when the museum is closed. Other less obvious similarities between the ROM and MoMA (and most other newer museums) include streamlined ticket purchase, coat check, and storage for all the things that post-9/11 security doesn't let a visitor take into the museum. The main floor is about crowd processing.

Both museums give pride of place to restaurants and bars, the ROM's in its penthouse overlooking the downtown skyline and the MoMA's adjacent to its elegant sculpture garden. Contemporary versions of the cafeteria are found in less stellar spaces—on the ROM's 1B or lower level, and down a hall on the second level of MoMA. The ROM has also recycled the 1933 Rotunda as rental space for special events along with Samuel Hall✿Currelly Gallery, the Hyacinth Gloria Chen Crystal Court, the RBC Foundation Glass Room on top of the Rotunda, the John David and Signy Eaton Court adjacent to the European Gallery, and the ROM Gallery of Chinese Architecture.

The elegant rooftop Crystal 5 Restaurant Lounge (C5) is quite a change from one of the ROM's first attempts at on-site hospitality, the modest 1933 tearoom and the Members' Lounge built on the west side of the Queen's Park Wing overlooking what was then the Chinese Sculpture Garden in 1970. (This original Members' Lounge was demolished to make way for the 1984 Terrace Galleries.) The new Members' Lounge was sited in the penthouse of the Terrace Galleries. In 1994 it was reinvented with a superstar chef, no longer just for members and their guests: Jamie Kennedy at the ROM was the first step towards fine dining at the ROM.

Revenue-generating spaces aside, pride of place at the ROM is given to its most important collections. The ROM holds the country's best collection of early Canadiana and some of the oldest artifacts in Canada relating to the First Peoples; one of the world's most important Chinese collections, including the largest collection of Chinese architectural artifacts outside China, three of the world's best-preserved temple wall paintings from the Yuan Dynasty, and the spectacular Chinese tomb complex; and the largest collection of Japanese art in Canada. All these are showcased on the ground floor of the Museum.

Blockbuster Impact

The importance of temporary exhibitions in the life of museums has grown, particularly during the last fifty years. Accordingly, the space for this function has increasingly influenced the way museums are designed. The static display of artifacts, varying only in that new items may be added to the permanent collection and others put into storage, has been eclipsed by the ability of temporary shows (travelling or originated by an institution) to attract large numbers of visitors. Novelty is provided by what has come to be known as the *blockbuster*—an important, must-see, highly promoted temporary exhibit.

The blockbuster exhibition originated with a change in the museum's focus, as previously noted, from collecting/conserving artifacts to displaying them. Temporary exhibits allow for the thematic display of works in a museum's permanent collection in a manner that reveals a thesis about them. Alternatively, a temporary exhibit can bring artifacts into the museum from other institutions and private lenders, to permit new and interesting associations with objects in the permanent collection or to illustrate topical themes.

With higher costs, dwindling public-sector support, or support linked to attendance, driving traffic to a museum became essential and the special exhibition a way to bolster attendance. The emphasis on temporary exhibits, especially the money-making blockbuster show, is about expanding the audiences of an institution, as well as generating revenue. If the permanent collection has become boring, then re-energize it—augment it with a temporary exhibition, giving past visitors a new reason to visit the institution. The temporary exhibition is an essential way to generate repeat visits.

Likewise, a temporary exhibition might entice people who have never set foot in the museum to come for a visit, and then ignite their interest in the permanent collection. Media attention is more easily generated when there is something new to report, and temporary exhibitions provide this, especially if they can be described in superlative terms—the oldest, most expensive, best, or rarest—and never before seen in a particular city, country, or continent. The temporary show has also become a way to broaden appeal to the travelling public. This is

Revenue-generating spaces aside, pride of place at the ROM is given to its most important collections.

FORM AND STRUCTURE

When the ROM's Michael Lee-Chin Crystal addition began to rise, its structure of rusting steel looked—for a while—to be the world's largest Anthony Caro sculpture. Appearing massive yet agile with unexpected twists and turns, and astounding joinery, it provided dynamic images that changed with the movement of the sun. The Spirit House, in particular, was a structural vortex at the metaphorical and engineering core of the building. It is where the building's "crystal" components overlap and form a negative space, at least in concept, a void. This void, which initially suggested itself as an atrium (albeit a twisty one), in the finished building has become a mysterious crevice, a fissure in a mountain, which is only briefly penetrated as a person goes between galleries.

As the concrete floors were poured, and more interstitial matter added, the lyricism receded. The connection of the structure to the spaces being created ebbed away as well.

As Daniel Libeskind explains, the Michael Lee-Chin Crystal is not a building inspired by an engineering logic, a new way of building, or new materials; rather, technology's role has been to facilitate the realization of the spaces he imagined. In other words, engineering is beside the point. "The architecture comes first, not the steel," he says. (Daniel Libeskind also does not believe that technology, such as computer-aided design, promotes creativity— it makes for better renderings and models, but does not help architects to create.)

When a space is exceptional, and the underpinning unseen but an engineering tour de force, the illusory quality of the space triumphs. When we do not understand how a building is constructed, it remains, like a stage set, fantastical for us. The ROM's Crystal is like this. Buildings seem less illusory when they are conventional, and we assume we know how they stand up or, when remarkable, if the architects give us clues about how they are built. Buildings by architects Norman Foster and Santiago Calatrava, for example, can appear to defy gravity but they always seem like engineering feats rather than feats without visible engineering.

The interior spaces of the Crystal, in particular, now that they have been covered in drywall, bear little relation to the lean, hard steel-structured jungle they once were. In fact, the remnants of the steel frame's angularity disappear in the completed interior as they are softened by the intervening floors and windows, and by the horizontality of the experience of being inside the building rather than looking at it as a skeleton of steel girders.

The inside of the Crystal is a series of volumes, what appear to be carved-out spaces rather than the soaring vaults that the steel structure may have suggested. These spaces are often manipulated to give an exhilarating sense of compression and release. Passages between galleries have thickness to them—it's like going between rooms in a fortress-like castle with massively thick walls. You are in spaces and then clearly between spaces. You move from the tension of a passage to the release of a large, open gallery space.

When parts of the Crystal's structure are perceived from inside the Museum, such as when the drywall-clad beams traverse window openings or come to ground in the temporary exhibition space, their engineering origins are not apparent. What are these beams holding up? What could they support?

Space without a sense of how it was made seems unreal, but it is not necessarily unpleasant. In the Crystal, the result is poetic space, space where there is an artificial thickness to walls and where any vestiges of the structure appear random and playful. In other words, the Crystal is an artwork.

This sense of joyful disorientation is experienced in the entry hall and retail area. Here the floor slopes up from the street to Samuel Hall & Currelly Gallery, the walls are angled, the vista unexpected, the windows deconstructed with beams flying through them, and the ceiling heights varied. Since any logic associated with conventional engineering is difficult to find, we cease to look for it.

The future of building for Daniel Libeskind relies not on new materials and construction techniques, but on new visions. The new can be created through the oldest of means. The attitude is not exactly *who cares how it's built,* but the means are all about the realization of the end product, not the means themselves. As Libeskind says, "In music you want to hear the music, not the notes."

Libeskind is a Romantic designer. The vision is paramount and the engineering practicalities are trivial by comparison. ■

important because most museums, including the ROM, are tourist attractions, relying in varying degrees on revenue from this audience. More than ever, the temporary exhibition space is where the pizzazz of the museum is to be found, the one spot where visitors can expect to be entertained.

A temporary exhibit space, one capable of accommodating exhibitions with large-scale items, occupies a relatively large floor area in a museum, but it also has other practical requirements determining where it can be placed. For instance, as noted, a temporary gallery must relate well to shipping and receiving, large freight elevators, and workshop spaces.

Canada Collects: Treasures from Across the Nation, a ROM temporary exhibition in Garfield Weston Exhibition Hall, 2007.

Temporary exhibition areas added to museums are often conceptualized as freestanding because of their bulk. What became the ROM's first temporary exhibition area—the Garden Court—was a separate structure connected by a short hall to what is now Samuel Hall✿Currelly Gallery. Originally built as part of the 1933 addition to house the Chinese tomb complex, its virtues as an exhibition hall became more apparent as the need for temporary exhibition space became more pressing. The Chinese tomb complex migrated to an exterior garden facing Bloor Street in 1959 and the Garden Court began to be used for changing exhibitions. For museums on more constrained properties, the roof or the basement become the only options. For the 2005 renovation of MoMA, the temporary exhibition spaces went to the top floor; for the ROM in 2006, Garfield Weston Exhibition Hall, the space for major temporary exhibitions, moved from the ground floor to the second level below grade.

In the ROM's Michael Lee-Chin Crystal addition, this space has grown to approximately 19,000 square feet, an increase of more than 10,000 square feet over its previous incarnation. This makes it the largest museum exhibition space in Canada and one of the largest cultural exhibit halls in North America. It is accessible by a fairly direct route from the main entrance, through the main lobby and down the stairs or the elevator. The space has many of the attributes expected of modern temporary exhibition spaces, including 16-foot ceilings, neutral décor, and complex environmental-control systems.

In a deviation from the current orthodoxy of temporary exhibition spaces, however, the space is not regularly shaped or column-free. It is therefore not a completely flexible space. Daniel Libeskind says the ROM's new temporary exhibit hall was initially planned as a big, empty box. Then, when greater cost efficiency dictated that the columns should terminate on the temporary exhibit level instead of the floor above—where beams might have carried the load and spanned the exhibition space to leave it free of columns—the form of the temporary exhibition space changed. No longer a big, blank box, the room now contains drywall-clad steel columns (at varied angles), as well as the base of the stairs and elevator shaft and the lowest level of the Spirit House. Daniel Libeskind believes that this exhibit space is preferable to the more standard version of a blockbuster hall he originally conceived. Why? Because it adds to an exhibition rather than disappearing when a show is installed. "Why should we assume that architecture can't add to an exhibition," he says. "Why must an exhibition travel from one anonymous box to another?"

Like the galleries on the floors above, this is not a neutral background that transforms itself for each new exhibit. Even if a show is temporary, an interloper into the domestic bliss of a museum's permanent inhabitants, it will conform, be influenced by, or be potentially enriched by the new circumstances of its display. And it

The ROM began in 1914 with galleries lit by large, two-storey windows with translucent glass, smaller, transparent windows, and translucent skylights

will not look or feel the same here as it did in other venues. This is a significant departure from what most museums expect of the blockbuster exhibition space.

That said, this kind of idiosyncratic exhibition space makes demands on the travelling exhibit, those installing it, and viewers as well. It will likely complicate the installation of most shows even as it enlivens them.

Light and Windows

Natural light in a museum presents a conundrum. Some objects degrade rapidly in sunlight regardless of how natural light is filtered or otherwise treated. And, like the argument about schools in the 1960s, the idea that views via windows distract visitors from the contemplation of objects or the audio-visual presentations accompanying them still has currency. How do you reconcile a viewer's need for daylight and variations in light level to avoid museum fatigue (or simply to see objects in varied and exciting conditions) with the need to protect objects from light damage and the need to present them in didactic scenes where darkness may be preferable for the information to be communicated?

Initially, galleries in retrofitted palaces relied on light through windows; candles at night were an exceptional circumstance for the viewing of artifacts. The Louvre's galleries were the first to experiment with light entering from above through skylights, adding a new variable to how galleries could be illuminated. Skylights also provided natural light without *wasting* walls that could be used for display.

Because the first galleries were dependent on natural light, J. N. L. Durand's ideal museum plan allowed for considerable perimeter area relative to the space enclosed. This configuration maximized the possible number of windows, and therefore the amount of natural lighting as well as natural ventilation. Durand's ideal museum did not indicate large windows on the façade, or skylights, but rather large clerestory windows, windows running along the tops of galleries. Natural ventilation presented environmental concerns, even for the first museums to adopt Durand's model, but there was no option. Until air conditioning was available, windows and ventilation were synonymous.

Since natural lighting from windows, even clerestory windows, was never easy to modulate and reconcile with wall space needed for display, skylights become the preferred option for the use of daylight. The Dulwich Gallery, designed by Sir John Soane (1753–1837) and built near London between 1811 and 1814, was the first freestanding museum to adopt the long-gallery-illuminated-from-above approach.

Candles were not an option for lighting vast gallery spaces because they were a fire hazard, expensive, produced excessive heat, and required maintenance. The advent of gaslight early in the 19th century was the first opportunity for a practical mix of artificial and natural light. Gaslight also suggested the possibility that galleries could be lit by artificial means alone.

The ROM began in 1914 with galleries lit by large, two-storey windows with translucent glass, smaller, transparent windows, and translucent skylights for the third-floor galleries. (The skylights were removed during renovations in 1970s.) Electric light was provided in all galleries via suspended globe fixtures. While the lighting of the galleries was one of the most modern things about them when they were built, today the fixtures appear

Victorian, and rather dated, compared to the classic and timeless approach of the galleries and their displays.

In the 1933 addition, windows on the first and second floors were designed to provide natural light, although they were smaller and began higher from the floor than those in the 1914 building to allow more useable wall area. On the third floor of the 1933 addition along Queen's Park, smaller windows ran along the outside walls of the galleries, and there was a double row of clerestories on either side of a raised, peaked roof running down the centre of the galleries.

Skylights on the sloping roof of the Centre Block (the east-west connection to the 1914 wing) top-lit the glazed ceilings of the third-floor gallery below. The second-floor galleries of the Centre Block had large, high windows. In the Glass Room, over top of the Rotunda, there were clerestories on all sides of the ceiling. Throughout the 1933 addition, artificial light was provided by fixtures that diffused light over a 30-foot by 20-foot bay, producing a much subtler light than the fixtures used in 1914. These spun-aluminium fixtures, no longer in place, were Art Deco in style and related to railing and molding interior treatments in the same style.

Natural light remained important even though new galleries could be completely artificially lit. According to ROM mythology, Sir Adam Beck (1857–1925), the founder and first chairman of Ontario's fledgling Hydro-Electric Power Commission, lobbied against skylights even in the 1914 building. In his memoirs, Charles Currelly recounted visiting museums in the United States with "Mr. Chapman" of Chapman and Oxley (the architects for the 1933 addition). Time and again the merits of artificial light were put to them, but Currelly remained steadfast: natural light was always better.

Skylights in the 1914 and 1933 wings, even though they were still valued as light sources, disappeared likely because of maintenance as much as the desire to limit incoming light. Windows in both wings began to be covered on the interior, principally during gallery renovations in the 1970s, not only because it was now recognized that many artifacts required darkness, but to free up the walls for additional exhibit space. Not until the 1978–1984 expansion were galleries constructed with the assumption of little or no natural light, although beginning in the 1950s, modifications to galleries had begun to create windowless exhibit spaces such as those for geology in 1957, mineralogy in 1967, and vertebrate paleontology in 1974.

Perhaps the ROM made only limited use of skylights in both the 1914 building and the 1933 addition because of the greater economy of building galleries on top of one another. A museum all on one floor would have allowed for extensive use of skylights, whereas the multi-storey museum that was built ensured a need for electrical lights.

The design architect of the 1984 renovation, Gene Kinoshita, believed natural light had an important role in a museum and often commented on its ability to counteract museum fatigue. As built, the Terrace Galleries had some natural light from the north along the Bloor Street perimeter on the second and third floors. On the ground-floor gallery fronting Bloor Street there were skylights and windows along Bloor Street. The Chinese tomb complex was installed here. It was to be Kinoshita's new atrium, however, that would illustrate his concept of how natural light could refresh and invigorate museum visitors. The atrium was flooded with light from skylights. Kinoshita's concept assumed that as visitors went between floors they would be re-energized in this

Currelly remained steadfast: natural light was always better

Daniel Libeskind's
renovation of the
1914 galleries has
restored light to them

space. Plans for an atrium garden to accentuate this oasis of light unfortunately had to be scrapped, although the planters had already been built and the plants installed when it was realized that they would harbour insects, which could migrate to the collections and damage them. Without this planting, the atrium was a light-filled but harsh space, not one where the public was likely to linger.

Crystal Light

Daniel Libeskind's first design had approximately 50 per cent of its surface covered by either glass or another translucent material. This first scheme was conceptual; the cladding was an idea, not a specified reality. The completed building's surface is approximately 20 per cent glazing, or windows. How did this change occur? Since light, even when diffused through translucent glass, may still have damaging effects, the translucent portions were deleted when the "new language" of the Michael Lee-Chin Crystal's revised skin was developed to better cope with Canadian weather conditions. This change to the arrangement of windows in the new building, however minor, altered the perception of the Crystal for many, from crystal clear to metallic and opaque. The Crystal Palace image of the initial model was arresting. Everyone loves light, and many were unhappy that the ROM was seemingly to be less light-filled.

In many areas of the ROM there is more light than expected. Daniel Libeskind's renovation of the 1914 galleries has restored light to them. It's not only that windows that were covered are revealed. Where many windows were originally translucent, they are now transparent. The impression of light-filled galleries is enhanced by the open-display concept. Displays are often islands floating in the gallery, and there is a proliferation of large, all-glass display cases. Particularly in the Joey and Toby Tanenbaum Gallery of China, multiple glass display cases appear, when natural light streams through them, like tanks housing exotic specimens in a vast aquarium.

There is natural light throughout the ROM. Light-sensitive objects are positioned away from sunlight, while light-tolerant objects, such as the dinosaur skeletons, are practically in the window. Some collections, such as textiles, require that their galleries have less glazing than initial schemes proposed because the majority of the collection can never be exposed to direct sunlight. (Some wondered why a textile gallery in the Crystal would have any windows at all.)

The Crystal addition, however, is circumspect in its use of light. The roof of Hyacinth Gloria Chen Crystal Court—an atrium—is pierced by two intriguing crystal shards that—while skylights—are more sculptural than illuminating. Light reaches entry and retail spaces through the glazing on the Bloor Street façade but does not penetrate very deeply. Windows in galleries provide diversion more than lighting *per se*, but they do offer relief from museum fatigue caused by standardized levels of artificial light. (Most gallery windows have screens, many retractable, to adjust light to appropriate levels.)

The Spirit House atrium that separates the two stacks of new Crystal galleries is surprising to some because it seems like a space that would naturally be topped by a skylight, but it is not. Artificial light is used here to increase the drama of the only space in the Museum that goes from the roof to the temporary exhibit space two levels below grade.

Windows should be equated not only with light at the ROM. Many of the Crystal's windows, or *apertures* as they are sometimes called because of their remarkable shape and depth, contribute to the sense that the galleries are spaces unlike any that visitors have ever experienced before. They are valued as part of the drama of the architecture, in addition to their ability to illuminate.

Many windows in the Crystal galleries are ones you can walk into; the glass is on the outside face, and the wall thickness is such that you feel you step outside the gallery when you're in this new-age bay window. (A typical wall, measured from the exterior of the skin to the interior drywall surface, is approximately four feet thick.) When you're in this space, you relate to the outside, rather than to the gallery, and this experience gives the sense of leaving the gallery, briefly, and being connected to the real world rather than the artificial one of the gallery. This in-and-out sense along the perimeter of the gallery relieves museum fatigue. The depth of the windows also helps to control light by limiting the amount that spills into the galleries.

The use of windows to frame views from inside the Crystal produces a Cubist-like, sculptural layering when you look out through them. The windows were not designed to be anonymous or invisible. They state unequivocally that the views being presented are calculated. They are active participants in what is being viewed—asymmetrical windows especially make you aware of the architect's intention, his choice of vista. Seeing is made to be an active, not passive, experience. A window in the elevator hall, for instance, looks to the angular skylights of the Gloria Chen Court and then to the peak of the restaurant roof in the distance. It's a three-dimensional collage.

These contrived vignettes are to be savoured. On the third floor, for example, two windows look onto the Gloria Chen Court. One is composed with the skylight shards in the view. The second requires an adult viewer to stoop in order to look down into the atrium. Rather than a view, it offers a collision of ceiling and balustrade. Like having to climb to the top of a hill for that special moment, the Crystal requires you to make an effort, then rewards you.

When Libeskind's designers worked with projections of his drawings on models to begin to determine the disposition of windows, they also imagined how light might project through the model as if the model were a crystal. Consequently, the language of the façade penetrates inside the building to the door openings, the balustrades, the openings to the bridges, and the bridges themselves.

The glazing as seen from street level, especially at night, gives the building a transparent quality. Some of the collections are on display to pedestrians on Bloor Street, a tease for the treasures within. The window openings often expose steel girders running through them, providing powerful glimpses of the structural underpinnings of the building. Another tantalizing moment for the pedestrian.

In retrofitted-palace museums and their Beaux Arts descendants, the pattern of windows or window placement had little to do with the interior contents and more to do with achieving an elegant and rhythmical façade. In other words, while windows were required to light the interior, their design seldom referred to specific interior considerations and was subordinated to the creation of a harmonious façade. Similarly, as noted, the window patterns for the Crystal began as the arbitrary projection of a drawing from Libeskind's

The use of windows to frame views from inside the Crystal produces a Cubist-like, sculptural layering when you look out through them. The windows were not designed to be anonymous or invisible

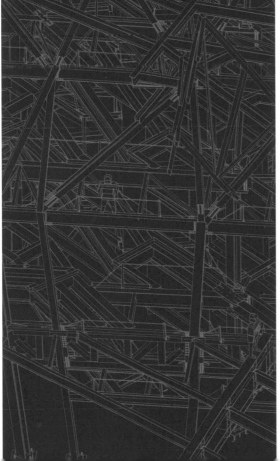

Chamber Works artwork series onto the skin of a model of the Crystal. Over time the windows were refined to respond to the functional needs of the spaces within. There is no pretense that window placement is completely rational, but there is a recognition that windows ultimately serve a purpose other than stylistic. The window pattern is a good example of reconciliation of the abstract and the tangible, the collision of an artist's vision with practical purposes.

Addition and Renovations

The Libeskind renovation reveals the serene, elegant proportions of the ROM's historic wings, in stark contrast to the previous renovations that produced a warren of galleries. The sequence of rooms in the 1914 wing has not been literally restored, but the classic Beaux Arts proportions have been liberated. Exposed mechanicals, light wood floors, a white colour palette, and exhibit cases with geometry purposefully at odds with the rectilinear grandeur of the historic spaces combine to create a contemporary but classic ambiance that links the original buildings to the Michael Lee-Chin Crystal addition without obscuring their distinctness.

The Crystal addition is more controversial than the back-to-basics approach of the renovation. To design an addition to the ROM by recreating its historical style or a contemporary version of it, according to Daniel Libeskind, would be to parody the existing structure. Even if he had wanted to take this approach, he would have to have chosen which era to mimic because the ROM is an agglomeration of styles.

Designing an addition to a historic building has always been a challenge for architects. Sir Aston Webb, when he spoke with Charles Currelly about the not-yet-built ROM, expressed his frustrating experience with his addition to the Victoria and Albert Museum. According to Currelly's memoirs, Webb said "that there were many difficulties in working with an older building, and that it would be an easier proposition to start a new one, taking advantage of modern knowledge of lighting and design." Webb's sentiment is echoed in Libeskind's belief that the only time to which you can be true is your own—at least when it comes to creating authentic architecture.

There is also a misperception that the ROM's 1914 and 1933 wings form a harmonious whole and that Libeskind's addition is the only incongruous component (or at least the only one visible from the outside). Although from the vantage point of the 21st century the 1933 building appears to most to be an appropriate addition to the 1914 structure, it was not considered harmonious when it was built. In *Construction*, a journal for architects and contractors, a regular contributor who wrote under the pseudonym Sinaiticus commented in November 1932: "Although no attempt has been made to harmonize the new with the old, nevertheless the addition is a most successful piece of work."

Libeskind is not a sentimental architect. He does not see old buildings, even a historically important one such as the ROM, as requiring a "nice" addition. In its time, the earlier ROM was a potent statement and so is Libeskind's addition to it, in its time. Like Dutch architect Rem Koolhaas, Libeskind does not pretend that life is anything but complicated; Libeskind may also be saying that life in 1914 was no less complex or painful than it is today, so let's not get nostalgic about a building (and a design style) that was grappling with its own epoch demons.

Perhaps because of this, Libeskind's approach to the ROM addition is not called *sensitive*, not like, for instance, the post-modern approach by Venturi, Rauch & Scott Brown for the Sainsbury Wing of the National Gallery in London. Their 1987 addition to the historic National Gallery used proportions and materials that fit with the original structure, although it is still perceivable as a contemporary addition rather than a parody.

It's that other Venturi and Scott Brown addition, the one to the Allen Memorial Art Museum, at Oberlin College in Oberlin, Ohio (1977), that mirrors the Libeskind ROM concept: that the best way to reveal an existing building's qualities, and to honour them, Libeskind would argue, is to build an addition that challenges them or at least does not pander. To copy an existing structure, to be compatible in an obvious manner is subtle ridicule, not reverence. With the Venturi and Scott Brown project in Oberlin, there are some tenuous links between the Tuscan Renaissance building and its checkerboard-patterned addition. The architects point out that the bold pattern corresponds to the rather more demure red outline highlighting what looks like panelling on the historic building's exterior, but it's more different than the same. Libeskind calls this kind of juxtaposition a "conversation" between a historic building and its addition, although others might say it's more of an "argument."

At the ROM, the most poignant image of the conversation between the old and the new is found on the north elevation of the 1914 building. Here, the delicate line of a Venetian-style window is forcefully obscured by the west Crystal in a self-consciously abrupt manner. Again, for some it is a powerful, exhilarating moment, while others find it more a rude confrontation.

For Daniel Libeskind, the Crystal is responsive to the historic ROM buildings. There is a space around the Crystal's exterior such that it does not quite touch the historic buildings. This space is practical because it creates rain gutters, but it invites a more lyrical interpretation as well. The image is one of buildings that were locked in a tight embrace and then recoiled from too much intimacy. Since the floor levels of the Crystal and the historic buildings relate on the interior, this lack of integration is visual and apparent only on the exterior.

A more magisterial rapprochement between old and new is visible inside. The slanted wall of the Crystal, poised with a slight bow as it touches the floor of the Gloria Chen Court, is separated by the solemnity of the Gloria Chen Court from the exposed wall of the 1933 Centre Block. The historic sobriety of the old is matched by the Crystal's more subdued interior face. The spaces between the Crystal and the 1914 and 1933 buildings— the areas running north-south to either side of the Crystal—are some of the most powerful in the building: there's the new, the old, and a third component, the spaces created between, balancing points between past and present.

In years to come, will the Crystal addition become an intrinsic part of the whole we know as the ROM, just as the 1914 and 1933 portions seem compatible if not indistinguishable today? Or with the passing of time will the Crystal become even more of a stranger to the historic ROM, one of those symbols of an epoch that make you wonder, *what was the architect thinking?*

Civic Context

As soon as the ROM opened in 1914, donations of artifacts and specimens to the new museum accelerated. The Museum, according to the press of the time, represented a sign of maturity for Toronto, a place of pride,

Sainsbury Wing, National Gallery, London, designed by Venturi, Rauch & Scott Brown, 1987.

A museum should be a place in the middle of the action, transparent, accessible, and demanding engagement

and this encouraged donations from local citizens. It has remained an important part of the civic context ever since, both as a building and as an institution. This local pride has been bolstered by the ROM's international reputation.

The City of Toronto needs cultural monuments as most cities do, to create an aura of civic dignity and to act as a magnet for tourists. Of course, cultural institutions are more than tourist attractions. Best-selling author Richard Florida, well known for developing the concept of the creative class and its ramifications in urban regeneration, posits that the city of the future depends on creativity, and it must therefore attract and keep creative residents. To that end, institutions such as the ROM are part of an environment needed to entice that fickle, mobile category of resident, the knowledge worker. If a cultural civic environment is a basic requirement for the success of a contemporary city, then its major cultural institutions should be vital components of that success. But the ROM in its pre-Libeskind iteration didn't seem like a *player* in Toronto's future. What has changed?

Daniel Libeskind's approach positions the Museum as an institution with a multi-faceted role, far beyond conserving, researching, interpreting, and displaying artifacts. Specifically, Libeskind believes that a museum building must also contribute to the urban fabric and be a generator of civic energy. It cannot be a warehouse inconspicuously positioned on the periphery of a town, or a metaphorical fortress, downtown but unapproachable. Instead, a museum should be a place in the middle of the action, transparent, accessible, and demanding engagement. The responsibilities of a museum today might begin with the artifacts it houses, but many other imperatives contribute to shape its form, as well as its function. The bold move of the Michael Lee-Chin Crystal puts the ROM on the civic and cultural map—from the vista down Bloor Street to the collection itself, the Crystal addition makes the ROM part of the city again.

At a more prosaic level, the new ROM offers much to Toronto's urban fabric. The ROM's new Bloor Street Plaza is a generous space and it continues, metaphorically speaking, inside the building as it gradually slopes through the lobby right to the existing Samuel Hall ❀ Currelly Gallery. The ROM's ground-level public spaces are urban in character, a townhall setting, and the façade, particularly at night, is transparent, revealing spectacular objects from the collections, the sight of which enriches the experience and character of the city.

Daniel Libeskind's vision was imagined for an urban density that its immediate neigbourhood did not yet have. Assume intensification along Bloor Street and the Crystal appears more civic-minded. As well, the aluminum skin, with its light-reflecting properties, reflects the Crystal's environment even as it mirrors the movement of the sun and changes in the weather. The appearance of the façade will modulate, giving many postcard-perfect images, more than most buildings in town. Few buildings should be landmarks; instead, like housing, they should remain context. A museum (or an opera house or a city hall) is the type of building that should stand out. The Crystal is a surprisingly delicate presence and a right-sized landmark for Toronto.

In this regard, Daniel Libeskind may have been influenced by Frank Lloyd Wright's Guggenheim Museum. Like the ROM's Crystal, the form of New York's Guggenheim breaks the rectilinear street façade. Both proclaim their specialness with a shape unlike any other in the city. And like the Guggenheim, the Crystal is architecture to which the contents it houses must conform (although the Guggenheim presents more constraints in how it dictates art is to be displayed). Both buildings are promenades. And both represent ideas about architecture that had been on their architects' minds long before a project that could materialize them came along.

Toronto was unsure of what it thought of the ROM's new packaging when the Crystal opened. Even as people admitted they hadn't visited for decades, or that the place was dreary, there was simultaneously a discomfort that the ROM was no longer the demure, dowdy, stolid thing it had been.

The prevailing attitude of Toronto citizens has swung in the 1990s from being primarily fear of the new and bold, to a tolerance of it and, sometimes, to a sense of pride in it, at least when the finished building is an unquestioned success. The concern that expensive cultural projects, such as the scheme for a new opera house that preceded the one completed in 2006, were unseemly because Toronto had homeless people to look after and other pressing social issues, has lessened. A riot of new buildings has proven that bold can be acceptable: the checkerboard Ontario College of Art and Design (OCAD) by British architect Will Alsop, of Alsop Architects, and the expansion to the Art Gallery of Ontario (AGO) by Frank Gehry have given Torontonians the confidence that the unexpected is not always a bad thing. It's a return of civic confidence that dwindled after the then-brash new Toronto City Hall by Viljo Revell (1910–1964) was completed in 1965.

But while more confident, the Toronto public's attitude, as the volumes of the Crystal began to materialize in their final form in the spring of 2007, was initially one of relief. The new ROM was not a skeleton of rusting steel, but the *niceness* of KPMB Architects' addition to the Royal Conservatory of Music next door on Bloor Street was still easier to accept than the out-of-the-ordinary ROM. The security of the usual, a vision of the city promoted by urban guru Jane Jacobs, extended not just to her vision of friendly, human-scale neighourhoods but into the public's imagination about public buildings as well. Low key was good for residential so it must be ideal for city halls, art galleries, and museums. The power of the unexpected, a trait of urbanity, is not incompatible with friendly residential. Toronto is learning to live with a new idea of what constitutes an appropriate urban mix.

"If the ROM needs money, why is it spending so much?" While the prevailing European attitude is that only the best is acceptable for the cultural institutions that represent a society, and in the United States grand cultural monuments are testaments to business success and therefore the bigger the better, in Canada we remain uncomfortable with bold, especially if it is expensive.

But attitudes about the cost of civic buildings are only part of understanding the reaction to the Crystal or at least to comments made prior to being inside. Unlike cities that relish architectural diversity, such as Barcelona, and welcome the avant garde, such as Paris, Toronto is still a conservative town. In the years leading up to the opening of the Crystal in 2007, reaction was mixed and often hostile. Is this negative reaction similar to the negative one that welcomed the Eiffel Tower in 1889? If so, then it suggests that the Crystal will become intrinsic to the Toronto psyche. While this may mean that it will lose some of its provocative edge (it has already stimulated many to think about the nature of architecture in the city), it will become one of the few unique elements, such as the CN Tower and the new City Hall, that visually symbolize Toronto.

Toronto is learning to live with a new idea of what constitutes an appropriate urban mix

> Does a museum cross some sort of moral line when it turns itself into an attraction?

Destination Architecture

Love it or hate it, tourists will not leave Toronto without visiting the Daniel Libeskind ROM. Beyond its significance as a cultural institution, the Museum is now branded because of its connection with a star architect. Even if they do not recall what they saw there, visitors will remember the Michael Lee-Chin Crystal. Most visitors can't remember what they see at the Louvre, except perhaps the Mona Lisa, so it may be that for the ROM the Crystal itself becomes the premier attraction.

The ROM by 2007 had shifted from presenting itself as an institution of high-minded if abstract purpose, to an institution intent on attracting visitors to its building and collections. The Crystal has become an icon of popular culture displaying contents of what used to be termed highbrow culture. This is how the ROM master plan (approved by its board in 2000) wanted it. The plan called for the construction of an "iconic" building, one that would capitalize on the ROM's high-profile location and become a unique, compelling destination for reasons beyond the contents it housed.

Does a museum cross some sort of moral line when it turns itself into an attraction?

Museums in the 19th century were supposed to improve public taste as part of their broader mandate to educate. This was how good citizens were molded. Today, if there is education, it is directed overtly only at children; otherwise, culture is typically presented as an attraction. Getting the viewer into the museum therefore becomes a primary concern.

For some museum directors, the idea that you could consciously create a destination is abhorrent. Glenn Lowry, director of New York's Museum of Modern Art, made the point that the MoMA's 2005 renovation was not about creating destination architecture. That people came to see the contents was all that mattered, and the rest—you couldn't be a serious person if your visit to MoMA had any other purpose than this. Ironically, most visitors are checking off the MoMA as one of the sites they must see as a tourist in New York.

Even those who dislike the Daniel Libeskind design can recognize the Crystal's power to attract both local visitors and tourists. It is destination architecture. Ever since Frank Gehry designed the Guggenheim Museum in Bilbao, Spain, the equation between memorable (of any kind) architecture and its potential to draw tourists has been paramount in the minds of civic boosters. Hence the term *Bilbao Effect* for a building such as the Bilbao Guggenheim or a public space such as Millennium Park in Chicago. By virtue of their architecture they attract visitors, generate economic benefits, and promote widespread change, presumably upgrading local neighbourhoods and the surrounding city. The motto is: "If you build it, they will come."

Temple, Agora, or Coliseum?

In the classic museum dichotomy of temple versus agora, the temple is the metaphor in which artifacts are displayed to be contemplated as beautiful objects. Other meanings of objects are suppressed; aesthetic considerations are paramount. The fewer objects displayed, the more precious they appear, and the more "sacred" the space in which they are displayed. Architecturally, the temple is a coded reminder of the pre-Christian city, classical ideals, and worship.

On the other hand, the agora or marketplace metaphor suggests that the meaning of objects in a historical context and their story-telling ability is what gives them value. It is their meaning, not their aesthetic value or beauty, that should determine how they are displayed. Like a market, the museum-as-agora offers choice, both in the objects to view and in the numerous ways they can be interpreted. In the temple, objects enthrall the viewer; in the agora, objects educate.

Today, there is a third metaphor—the coliseum. While the agora suggests engagement or an entertaining element to the experience, the coliseum goes one step further. It's all about entertainment. Nothing much is learned by a visit to the coliseum. A ticket purchaser wants stimulation but does not want to have to think too much in the process. The shift to the coliseum began with the best intentions. In the studies leading up to the construction of the 1984 Terrace Galleries, an approach to display called "storytelling" was described. Its intent was initially not to entertain but to connect objects to history and sociological issues that a contemporary audience should care about. It was didactic. However, as stories began to take precedence over the artifacts, the shift to the coliseum was underway. The coliseum period, when the experience overwhelmed, came to fruition at the ROM in the 1990s.

Where is the Daniel Libeskind ROM in this temple-agora-coliseum trio? The novelty of the Michael Lee-Chin Crystal architecture does have a bread-and-circuses aura to it, but, while designed to be enlivening, the building is not a site for passive entertainment. It could be said that it should be popular because it's built, to a degree, with public money, and it is, but it still requires the viewer to work—to choose paths and to make viewing decisions. The artifacts, except in few circumstances, are not given a theatrical setting. What looks like an attraction, a.k.a. coliseum, on the exterior, is a temple inside. The ROM is a place for the enjoyable contemplation of artifacts and specimens.

Museum as Metaphor

Museums are a building type with an affinity for metaphor. The metaphor of choice, as mentioned, is often the temple: steps, pillars, and a grand entrance hall much like the nave of a church prepare the viewer to venerate contents that, simply by being in this setting, appear important and deserving of preservation and adulation.

Because of their ability to create awe, museums are often referred to as secular cathedrals. While the objects enshrined can be diverse, when institutionally assembled they become icons of shared histories and values. For an example of a museum designed as a secular cathedral, one need look no further than the arched, church-like front entrance of the ROM's 1933 addition. The sculptures of ancient peoples and animals by Charles McKechnie that embellish the façade also establish a cathedral connection, one reinforced by the dome of the Rotunda and the grand processional of Samuel Hall✿Currelly Gallery.

New York Times art commentator Michael Kimmelman succinctly summed up the religious metaphor inherent in museums. Museums, he wrote, "are our new theaters of conscience, memorials to suffering, choreographed

Guggenheim Bilbao, Spain, designed by Frank Gehry, 1997.

Jay Pritzker Pavilion, Millennium Park, Chicago, designed by Frank Gehry, 2004.

Architects often use
metaphors to make
their otherwise abstract
creations comprehensible

places of ritual genuflection, where we go to contemplate our fallibility and maybe even weep a little while admiring the architecture."

As a metaphor, the term "crystal" for the ROM's addition is memorable and seems reasonable given the building's appearance. Despite some confusion about what kind of crystal it is—it's more a crystal shape than crystal clear—the metaphor is a powerful albeit literal one, repeated consistently. Unlike the temple metaphor, however, "crystal" is solely a way of describing the building's form.

The term "crystal" is more convenient than it is comprehensive, with little meaning beyond the sculptural shapes of the addition. It does not help us to understand the position that the Museum (or the architect) is taking about the display of artifacts. It does not suggest contemplation, egalitarianism, or any other political or social idea that a museum can represent. Nor does it suggest that the museum is a temple.

Architects often use metaphors to make their otherwise abstract creations comprehensible. It's easier to use a metaphor than to launch into a complicated theory about design when the *raison d'être* for a building is being given. In this way, strong metaphorical images help to win competitions because they can demonstrate clarity of approach, a vision, without much being said. Libeskind's original napkin sketches, for instance, were more persuasive than the less metaphorically potent competitors' schemes.

Does a strong metaphor equate with good architecture? Not always, but it helps to create a memorable architecture. If you're promoting architecture as a destination, a metaphor becomes an essential tool to communicate to potential tourists that a building, even if its contents may not interest them, is a *must see*.

Why a Crystal?

All of which begs the question, "Why a crystal?" Why not? It could represent the natural world the ROM showcases, just as the traditional 1914 and 1933 wings could symbolize the other side of the ROM's dual mandate, culture. Can this metaphor describe a building that has a distinct urban presence? Unquestionably. Does the application of the crystal imagery provide exhilarating interiors? An obvious yes. Does the metaphor generate forms suitable to house a complicated museum program? Yes, again. If nothing else, the metaphor is apt for communicating the building's form and useful in terms of the building it has generated.

What makes a metaphor good or bad? The Sydney Opera House becomes the sails of the boats surrounding its site, which juts into Sydney's harbour. While the metaphor has nothing to do with opera, it clarifies the design approach instantaneously, and certainly makes a contextual linkage to the site adjacent to a harbour almost always filled with . . . sailboats. It's good because it's obvious, even though it does not explain much more about the opera house than its apparent resemblance to a sailing ship.

The Flying Dutchman notwithstanding, the connection between an opera house and a sailing ship is tenuous, but the metaphor is a harmless one, and opera is possible although apparently not ideally presented in the building. The Guggenheim Museum in New York also has a strong visual metaphor—the spiral—but it is a problematic concept for the display of contemporary art. It succeeds because it still delivers a powerful experience for the visitor.

HOW TO DESCRIBE THE ROM'S HISTORIC FAÇADES?

Art historian Alan Gowans described the exterior of the 1914 ROM building as "a typical mixture of motifs from various times and places—Renaissance palaces, Romanesque abbeys, late Roman basilicas—assembled with a view to creating a visual metaphor of 'culture of all times and places' appropriate to the function of the Museum building." In other words, the Museum contains many fragments of earlier civilizations, so why not have its exterior reflect this. It certainly is an architectural style that stirs imaginations. The north façade has been referred to not only as Venetian, but as Gothic Venetian with Romanesque undertones. Historical pastiche is never easy to describe in words, especially if the result is pleasant.

Venetian or Gothic Venetian was an appropriately exotic style to use for a major museum. Darling and Pearson was the premier architectural firm in Canada—Darling also did the Bank of Montreal building in Toronto at Front and Yonge and the University of Toronto's Convocation Hall, and Pearson would be co-architect with Jean-Omer Marchand for the Centre Block of the Parliament Buildings in Ottawa after the fire of 1916. Each of these buildings was given a style appropriate to its use, a well-established Beaux Arts principle.

An alternative explanation for the 1914 façades suggests that their eclectic nature mirrors the complexity of, or fascination with, the British Commonwealth and the excitement of the exotic worlds being explored at the time. Another is that the overriding ambitions of British subjects—such as those in Canada—to appear sophisticated, and not "hicks" in some distant colony, was a top-of-mind concern for the designers. The mix of historic styles provided proof that Toronto was just as cosmopolitan as London. And while Toronto may have been the outback, Darling was a sophisticated architect who had trained in London and read the same journals as English architects. The ROM founders may have had something to prove, but Darling was likely designing according to his training and much like his peers, internationally, were doing.

Neo-Byzantine is a term occasionally used to describe the 1933 wing with the emphasis on "neo" as it has little in common with Byzantine architecture. The claim is sometimes made that neo-Byzantine at the ROM is really Gothic Revival.

Architect and historian Michael McClelland, a principal of ERA Architects in Toronto, has commented on Chapman's 1933 approach and its relation to Darling's 1914 approach:

Neo-Byzantine is probably closest to Chapman's approach. Art Deco was a fairly slick term then. We use it now but I don't think Chapman or John Lyle, a contemporary of Chapman's, thought they were doing Art Deco buildings even if we see the influence today. The foreignness of the Byzantine style would have had similar connotations to the Venetian for Darling—exotic and intellectual. An interesting comparison is Holy Blossom Temple in Toronto, also by Chapman, in the same style, for somewhat similar reasons. This style would be more appropriate than a classically derived one.

For many, the façade treatment is about trying to fit into the university aesthetic of the period, a parody of English university buildings typically found at Oxford or Cambridge, and these diverse styles often have elements of Gothic Revival. The fact is that the 1914 and 1933 façades are both jumbles of symbols and the anomaly of the Michael Lee-Chin Crystal addition is just one more element of the mix. ■

There is usually friction between a powerful metaphor and the practicality of what a building is to do

Buildings with no metaphoric poetry are an endangered species. Few will know how to remember them regardless of how well they function. Occasionally, a building may elicit an unfortunate metaphor inconsistent with its intent: a library that appears to be a fortress, a hospital that resembles a shopping mall, or a school that looks like a prison.

The most brilliant metaphors are ones that communicate a vision about both form and function. The Kimbell Art Museum in Fort Worth, Texas (1966–1972, Louis Kahn), combines a strong vision of built form with an equally beguiling idea of seeing art in intimate spaces. The metaphor of the ancient baths of Rome works well: viewing art, like bathing in ancient Rome, combines intimate private activities with a large, shared public context.

There is usually friction between a powerful metaphor and the practicality of what a building is to do. For instance, even buildings that don't seem very metaphorically driven, such as the National Gallery in Berlin (1962–1968) designed by Ludwig Mies van der Rohe (1886–1969), can be prisoners of an image. There is tension between his temple-on-a-podium approach and the reality of housing the National Gallery. The realization of Mies van der Rohe's metaphor created a soaring, glassy pavilion that is not well suited to being a temporary exhibit space; and the opaque plinth it sits on offers no natural light for the permanent collection, which is relegated to rather cramped quarters. Yet, because of the poetry of its metaphor, the building has captured the public's imagination and is an admired Berlin institution.

Ducks and Sheds

In their groundbreaking 1972 book *Learning from Las Vegas*, Robert Venturi, Denise Scott Brown, and Steven Izenour describe two types of buildings—ducks and decorated sheds: "The duck is the special building that is the symbol," whereas "the decorated shed is the conventional building that applies symbols." With a duck, "space, structure and programs" are subsumed in an "overall symbolic form." The duck nomenclature comes from an image of a roadside diner that was, literally, built to look like a duck in order to attract customers. In contrast, the decorated shed denotes a post-modern approach in which "space and structure are directly at the service of the program, and ornament is applied independently of them."

With this conceptualization, the Michael Lee-Chin Crystal is a duck pressed between two decorated sheds—the two historic wings. The various symbols in stone and brick—a diverse collection of symbols to be sure—are applied to ensure that we do not confuse the older structures with what otherwise might be warehouses or factory buildings. Is an exuberant duck best in the wild—essentially perceived as an autonomous, mostly free-standing, structure, as is the Denver Art Museum addition designed by Libeskind and opened in 2006? Or does a crystal duck, as Libeskind might say, energize the urban mix by its close proximity to sheds?

Metaphor or Personal Vision?

Museums are made for metaphor because they strive to be special places that represent what a society is tenaciously preserving. A metaphor is a natural way to communicate the essence of what is unique. The ROM is indisputably a unique container, perfect for housing singular objects in a world of mass production and conformity. But the crystal metaphor may have obscured this notion: the point of the Libeskind addition was to create a singular space (symbolizing the housing of the rare and precious), not to build a "crystal" *per se*. In other words, the purpose has always been to build a remarkable museum, not an odd structure that happens to look like a crystal. The crystal metaphor may have also overwhelmed the fact that the structure is driven by a visionary architect.

The ROM's addition may be more Libeskind-like than crystalline. Libeskind says the crystal metaphor for the ROM came from his sighting of a crystal in one of the displays when he first toured the Museum. He likens his crystalline addition to the Denver Art Museum to the jagged peaks of the Rocky Mountains, which he saw from the plane as he arrived in Denver. The spiral imagery of his proposal for an addition to the Victoria and Albert Museum in London (this design was not built) has a crystalline ambiance to it as well. He often remarks on the miracle of crystals. It may be that he takes his general crystalline concept and gives it a local interpretation.

But the roots of Libeskind's design transcend his interest in crystals. In his artwork, much of it now at the Getty Center in Los Angeles, there are glimpses of ROM-like spaces and a conceptualization of space that permeates many of his projects. (Libeskind calls this artwork "architecture"; the difference between it and his buildings—other than scale—is that buildings are "architecture with programs.") As well, Libeskind's writings about architecture, ten or more years before the Crystal's design, suggest that crystalline forms and idiosyncratic spaces have been on the architect's mind—consciously or unconsciously—for a long time. Crystals are the way he has chosen to represent a complicated and deeply thoughtful view of architectural space.

Libeskind's approach to design is a personal one and his buildings are an expression of it. Much like any artist's work, Libeskind's is more understandable as art when directly experienced rather than when expressed through commentary or metaphorical summation. The same might be said of Frank Gehry's architecture. These architects do not represent a style beyond their own, in other words, a trend.

Characterizing a building in terms of a metaphor at all is perhaps missing the point with the 21st-century artist/architect. Metaphors, while they are useful for describing many buildings before they are built, are often forgotten after the fact. People don't talk about Toronto's "new" City Hall, for example, as the clamshell of democracy (hard on the outside, soft with windows on the inside) protecting a pearl—the council chamber inside the shell—symbolizing democracy, but they once did. The form demanded an explanation and this was the metaphor that worked. Like the clamshell-and-pearl metaphor, the ROM's crystal metaphor may fade as the building once again becomes simply the ROM. The addition had to become a "crystal" so that we could understand it, or accept it, but in time it will be more obviously an architect's signature creation, one beyond metaphor.

A delightful aspect of metaphors (at least, successful ones) is that they can be interpreted in many ways. Literal metaphors—the building is a sailboat, not merely suggestive of one—cannot intrigue the sophisticated viewer. It is what it is, no further thought is required. Libeskind's crystal metaphor stimulates speculation.

Distinguished essayist and novelist John Ralston Saul remarked at the opening of *A Season of Canada* at the ROM in October 2007 that Libeskind's Crystal evoked the power of the Canadian landscape. You could imagine it as a Lawren Harris painting of a majestic mountain or iceberg. Rather than taking its cue from the

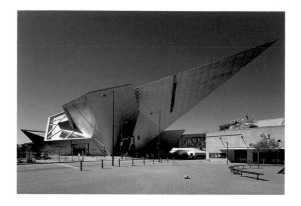

Frederic C. Hamilton Building, Denver Art Museum, Denver, Colorado, Studio Daniel Libeskind, 2006.

Lawren S. Harris, *Mt. Lefroy*, 1930.

architecture of its colonial past, rectangular and rigid, Toronto has broken free, inspired by something truly Canadian—the beauty of our natural environment—to build an addition to the ROM.

While the crystal metaphor may give an imaginative explanation for the ROM's new addition of the "sails-on-boats-in-the-harbour" variety, that a building is rationalized as an architect's personal vision is not valid for many. Some commentators maintain that the Crystal is too similar to other Daniel Libeskind buildings, suggesting that it therefore cannot fit the ROM's particular needs, or that the Museum was getting a second-hand building, the same old thing recycled.

Of course, the reverse causes problems too. With Frank Gehry's addition to the AGO, for instance, the concern was that it did not look enough like a typical Gehry building or at least his best-known curvy, titanium-clad creations of the last few years. "Why pay all this for a star architect and then get something anyone can produce? Where's our Bilbao?" While a grand metaphor explains, an architect's personal vision is, for some, mere hubris, and the client no more than a handmaiden in the service of a celebrity genius. In time, a building that survives is neither a metaphor nor a personal vision but a symbol embraced by the people of the city and the wider culture, a tangible reminder of who they are, were, or want to be.

Neutrality

The renovated palaces that became the first museums did not have neutral backgrounds for their collections. Architecturally, these early museums retained their original residential character, although rooms were often contrived to show particular collections to their best advantage, especially when the decision had been made to give public access to them. That said, little of the decoration of these galleries, even when the intent was to give a worthy setting for objects, was subservient to the artifacts on display. The carved, gilded, marbled, or otherwise garishly festooned walls, floors, and ceilings, not to mention furnishings, were not secondary to the art; rather, they were a rich component of the total package in which the artworks were the jewels. The environment was intended to be sympathetic or appropriate but never neutral.

But the settings for artifacts soon began to recede. The museums built in the 19th century, while often patterned on palaces, were usually more moderately decorated; colours were more sober and detailing restrained, especially if the building had a classical inspiration. There were exceptions in public areas, and some galleries, particularly those given by individuals as memorials to their collecting acuity, could be lavish, perhaps recreating the former residential environment that had housed the artifacts.

For London's Great Exhibition of 1851, Joseph Paxton (1803–1865) designed one of the first neutral buildings ever constructed for display. The Crystal Palace, while not so neutral-looking today, was "neutral" in the context of its time. Although it was rich with ironwork detail, it did not have applied decoration. It was modern because it was stripped back to its skeleton and the luminosity of its glass skin. It was transparent and could be conceptualized as a monumental greenhouse. Inside, it had few permanent spaces but was a shell adaptable to a variety of contents.

Buildings such as the Crystal Palace and the iron and steel railway stations of the late 19th century (or at least their train sheds—the façades were often contrived as temples or palaces) were sources of inspiration for modern architecture. Neutrality began in earnest with modern architecture at the turn of the 20th century and became the predominant style for new museums and additions to existing institutions. By the mid-20th century, most new museums (and the renovations of many existing galleries) adopted the all-white and minimal look. If you were creating a diorama for modern art, it would be a white box. Not only do we expect to see such art in this type of environment, but some modern works might not be recognized as art in any other environment.

The Isolated Object

> Nowhere does the triumph of the aesthetic museum reveal itself more dramatically than in the history of art gallery design. Although fashions in wall colours, ceiling heights, lighting, and other details have over the years varied with changing museological trends, installation design has consistently and increasingly sought to isolate objects for the concentrated gaze of the aesthetic adept and to suppress as irrelevant other meanings the objects might have.

—Carol Duncan, *Civilizing Rituals: Inside Public Art Museums* (1995)

Neutrality gets mixed up in a modern museum. Some museums are modern and neutral on the exterior and equally so on the interior—an example is the Menil Collection in Houston, designed in stages by Renzo Piano in 1987 and 1995. Some are modern on the outside, neutral on the interior, and then, depending on the collection being housed, also theatrically historic. The Getty Center in Los Angeles designed by Richard Meier in 1997 is an acropolis-like group of buildings on a hillside. It mixes external modernity and much stark white internal modernity with some interior spaces that are given a traditional Metropolitan Museum look thought appropriate for Old Masters. Some new museums are anything but neutral on the outside but have galleries on the interior that are. For example, the San Francisco Museum of Modern Art (1995) designed by Mario Botta combines chutzpah—the architect's signature stripes and high style on the exterior and in the main public spaces—with much more sober, gallery spaces.

There is often an abrupt change in style between the contemporary appearance of a museum's exterior and the classic order of the galleries inside. Herzog & de Meuron's de Young Museum in San Francisco (2006) appears to be an irregularly shaped, hard-edged, copper-covered sculpture on the exterior. Once inside, the galleries are light, airy, and mostly enfilade. David Chipperfield's Figge Art Museum in Davenport, Iowa (2006), appears to be a translucent box on the outside, but the interior has a much more conventional arrangement of permanent galleries with a series of rooms connected by multiple axes.

Daniel Libeskind's ROM addition has a non-modern (but contemporary) exterior in harmony with its sculptural interior. Or if harmony is not the most apt word, one might say that the mood of the exterior continues on the interior, although the interior spaces have a more sensuous ambiance compared to the sleek but

Getty Center, Los Angeles, designed by Richard Meier, 1997.

San Francisco Museum of Modern Art, designed by Mario Botta, 1995.

Despite the Michael Lee-
Chin Crystal's sloping
walls and artfully
composed windows,
the gallery floors are one
of the least neutral aspects

prickly exterior. And while there is no strident use of colour, the gallery spaces, in particular, cannot be described as neutral. They announce themselves as volumes that house artifacts rather than as walls and floors to be understood only as background with no vitality of their own. Despite the Michael Lee-Chin Crystal's sloping walls and artfully composed windows, the gallery floors are one of the least neutral aspects. The stripe pattern formed by floor grates for air supply and conduits for wiring of all kinds barely registered on renderings and models. But when the building was complete, the floor spoke loudly, and will always interact with whatever is placed on it.

Beyond Neutral

For MoMA's 2005 renovation, Yoshio Taniguchi reworked the designs of his architect predecessors Philip Goodwin (1885–1958), Edward Durrell Stone (1902–1978), Philip Johnson (1906–2005), and Cesar Pelli. MoMA offers a comparison to the ROM. If less is more, then much less must be considered much more according to Taniguchi. His widely quoted remark about lots of money creating a beautiful building and even more money making it disappear, suggests that the best building, or museum, is one you do not see.

Neutral architecture in a museum context means that a building does not interfere with the appreciation of the artifacts. Many curators and architects believe that this is the best a building can do in relation to art or artifacts; there is no consideration of the idea that a building could enhance the experience of what it contains. Taniguchi's statement goes one further if it means that no perception of a building enhances the viewing of artifacts. Of course, few are likely to tell the MoMA that the emperor has no clothes and that they might have a building that has disappeared and taken its architecture with it. Architecture that disappears is banal, not subtle. Despite the power of its virile external form and its athletically agile interior, the new ROM is a subtle container for artifacts and specimens. It does not aspire to disappear.

Nor does the ROM aspire to be dispassionately corporate. While MoMA has a corporate ambiance because of its cool demeanour, the ROM wears its emotions on its proverbial sleeve. While MoMA has the guile of the art dealer, the ROM has the exuberance of the connoisseur smitten with a new acquisition.

Of course, MoMA is not devoid of architecture so much as it does not suggest a role for architecture as an important component in the visitor's experience. For the aesthetically alert (or perhaps the well indoctrinated who want to see the emperor dressed), the play of mass, void, and scale, and the use of light and views, isn't neutral. Regardless, it is perilously close to absent architecture. While the Michael Lee-Chin Crystal is equally subtle in its architectural vocabulary, its sculptural vigour and layered window details, in particular, give it much more architectural presence.

With Daniel Libeskind's design, despite the primacy of strong architecture, it is quite apparent that many objects of a diverse nature can be successfully displayed in the galleries. The new ROM is not a warehouse, but neither is it a custom environment relating to its content. Architecture determined by the specific artifact or artifacts it is to house is not be confused with a process—the one most comparable to Daniel Libeskind's at the ROM— through which the architecture meets a general criteria for what will be shown in it but also is driven by its own conceptual imperatives. The particulars of art or artifact display are reconciled with the spaces later. With this approach, architecture does not attempt to accommodate a curator's theatrical vision; rather, the arrangement of artifacts must accommodate the building. Here, an architectural vision is tantamount to gallery creation.

Non-neutral Accidentally

Many of the most beautiful and object-friendly museums in the world, for example, the Uffizi Gallery in Florence and the Tate Modern in London (Herzog & de Meuron, 1998–2000), were not purpose-built as museums. The former began in the 1500s as palatial administration offices and the latter as a power plant in 1947. But after their respective retrofits, both accommodate artifacts superbly. A less obvious example is the Kimbell Art Museum. While purpose-built as an art gallery, its forms were driven not by specific artifacts but by the more general needs of their display and the creation of a strong, almost archaic, form.

Many buildings can be repurposed to become successful galleries while not physically changing a great deal. This may be difficult to accept for those who assume that a gallery must be a purpose-built building, because it proves that a multitude of environments beyond the neutral box work well for display. Most awkward for some museum goers are spaces that are not rectilinear—whether repurposed or built new as galleries. Right angles and symmetry are rational, whereas odd-shaped spaces like those in the Michael Lee-Chin Crystal are difficult to reconcile as exhibition spaces when the expectation is square and orderly.

Greek temples or French palaces of the 16th century did not require practical explanations to justify their designs; that they could be used for practical purposes seemed to be explanation enough. Similarly, the transformation of old spaces for new uses suggests that there are successful alternatives to neutral for museums. The Crystal's shapes may be arbitrary, but they are no less so than those that resulted when turning a power plant into an art gallery. Elegant spaces that can be well lighted, and their temperature and humidity reasonably controlled, may be all that galleries really are, and perhaps this is an unvoiced intuition of Daniel Libeskind.

The Anxious Object

Is less museum better than more? An architect ponders many questions when designing a museum or gallery but none as fundamental as these: Does a museum with a strong architectural presence inhibit the presentation of artifacts relative to museum spaces that are seemingly invisible, a bland envelope for the objects they house? Should a building disappear or be the shell for a stage set for the display of artifacts and specimens? Does the more one notices a building translate to a reduced appreciation, or reverence, for what it enshrines? Does architecture make museum objects anxious? These questions usually relate to the impact of a building's interior architecture, but it can be argued that the stage for how objects are perceived is set not only by galleries but by the entire architectural experience of a building—exterior, interior, supporting public spaces.

Daniel Libeskind's ROM renovation and addition take an emphatic position in this debate. The Michael Lee-Chin Crystal declares unequivocally that the more potent the architecture, the more dynamic the relationship

Greek temples or French palaces of the 16th century did not require practical explanations to justify their designs

The retrieval of the ROM's historic galleries, compared to the Crystal addition, is a subtle but nonetheless definite statement about the renovation of heritage buildings

between artifacts and their environment, the richer the experience for the viewer of that artifact, and likely the more memorable his or her entire visit to the institution. To twist Robert Venturi's phrase, *less would create a bore*.

The retrieval of the ROM's historic galleries, compared to the Crystal addition, is a subtle but nonetheless definite statement about the renovation of heritage buildings. The exterior shells of the heritage buildings have been restored but their interior spaces have been gutted to reveal their basic volumes. These are now contemporary spaces reminiscent of their original configuration.

In terms of the exhibits, the prominence of the glass display cases produces a back-to-the-future quality, emphasizing a Proust-like retrieval of the past recalled to serve the present. Objects in imposing cases, meticulously organized in galleries with little interpretative scenery, are indeed similar to the many images from the 1914 ROM. Objects are housed by their gallery, but you are aware of the gallery.

In the Crystal addition objects are in a dialectic with their galleries—whether they want to be or not. Libeskind's building is an inhabited sculpture.

The opposite approach to that of both the renovated historic section and the Crystal is to have artifacts integrated into their environment, to purpose-build for each object or grouping of objects. The choice of object, the architecture, and the display system are contrived to produce a singular impression: a spatial arrangement, such as pairing a room's proportions with the shape of an artifact or group of artifacts or art objects; a historical setting for period furniture or paintings; a primeval scene as a background for dinosaur bones; or a multi-media extravaganza that puts artifacts on the periphery of a Disney-like world of narrative. At the extreme, a museum building can be a mere shell for the interpretive stage set that consumes objects with the intention of animating them for an otherwise uninterested viewer.

While the Michael Lee-Chin Crystal addition appears to be a bold departure, a brazenly contemporary gesture, aside from its controversial surface, it is a back-to-the-future approach. Objects at the ROM are housed in as classic a manner as when the ROM first opened. The galleries could be at the Louvre, but a Louvre built now, not centuries ago. They are grand spaces, the result of an aesthetic that can accommodate changing functions while providing a glorious envelope for whatever is housed or whoever is passing through. The ROM in 2007 is both newer and older than it has ever been. ∎

1914

Page 60: The corner of Avenue Road and Bloor Street, c. 1914. *Page 61*: View of the Museum from the southwest, c. 1914. The two-storey office building was eventually completed as four storeys in 1937.

1914: The Original ROM

When the Governor General of Canada, the Duke of Connaught, officially opened the Royal Ontario Museum on March 19, 1914, it was a celebration of a building *and* of a vision that had begun to coalesce a decade before.

The ROM was a joint venture between the University of Toronto and the Province of Ontario. Much of the impetus to create the new museum was the desire to consolidate the science collections of the various departments of the university in one location. This ambition coincided with the determination of Toronto's social elite, led by Sir Byron Edmund Walker (who became the first chair of the ROM board), to establish a museum of international caliber in the city. Given that the Toronto establishment of the time was a small, interconnected group, the interests of the province, the university, and higher society were, not surprisingly, shared. Walker was president of the Bank of Commerce and on the board of the university; another key ROM supporter, financier Sir Edmund Osler, was a prominent member of the provincial parliament. Other establishment supporters included Mrs. H. D. Warren and the Massey and Flavelle families. Donors from the outset have played a vital role in shaping the ROM.

In terms of the architecture, it was likely that those connected with the university played a direct role in its design. While Edmund Walker was part of the process that determined a site, there was never any doubt that it would be one conveniently located close to the university. When it came time to select an architect, a firm that had already undertaken significant commissions for the University—Darling and Pearson—was chosen.

As Lynne Teather notes in *The Royal Ontario Museum: A Prehistory, 1830 to 1914,* by 1905, four University of Toronto professors—Arthur Philemon Coleman (geology), William Arthur Parks (palaeontology), Thomas L. Walker (mineralogy), and Robert Ramsey Wright (biology/zoology) were active participants in the creation of the ROM from a conceptual and collections perspective. Coleman, Parks, and Walker became the directors of their respective museums within the ROM when it opened in 1914. Wright retired in 1912, to be replaced by Benjamin Arthur Bensley, who became the director of the Royal Ontario Museum of Natural History (later Zoology).

Henry Montgomery was another important earlier participant. He had been the curator of Trinity College's museum and then, from 1903 to 1907, was the curator of the University of Toronto Museum. Montgomery, an archaeologist, had held administrative, curatorial, and teaching positions at both the University of North Dakota and the University of Utah, and was thus well qualified to contribute to the discussion of what was needed for Toronto. His May 1906 *Report on U.S. Museums* was written after a tour of institutions that included the Metropolitan Museum of Art, the American Museum of Natural History, The United States National Museum, and the museums of Yale and Harvard universities. It was likely the foundation for the ROM's master plan subsequently begun by Darling and Pearson.

Montgomery's report came almost simultaneously with *The Report of the Royal Commission on the University of Toronto, 1906* (prompted by Walker), which addressed, among other things, the financing and administration of a new museum. It recommended building a museum as soon as possible and also suggested a site "in the University grounds adjacent to a public thoroughfare."

Convocation Hall, University of Toronto, designed by Darling and Pearson, 1906.

Summerhill Station, Toronto, designed by Darling and Pearson, 1916.

Should the museum be a permanent wing of the School of Science? On College Street or Bloor Street? These questions, along with the functional requirements of the museum, including the need for a lecture hall that did not materialize in the 1914 phase, were still being discussed.

Charles Currelly had become a central player in shaping the museum's architecture by this time. With Henry Montgomery soon to leave the university, and with the increasing interest in Currelly's exciting archeological finds in Egypt fuelled by his friends Sir Byron Edmund Walker and Nathaniel Burwash, Chancellor of Victoria College, Currelly's influence expanded. He became the authorized collector for the university in 1906 and was appointed director of the Royal Ontario Museum of Archaeology within the ROM in 1912. He would hold the position until his retirement in 1946.

A story Charles Currelly recounts in his autobiography suggests that noted English architect Sir Aston Webb may have had a hand in the design for the building. Currelly had been on an outing with the Royal Society, as a guest of one of its members:

> On the way home I sat with Sir Aston Webb in the train, who was just finishing up the great addition and the entrances to the Victoria and Albert Museum. . . . He said that there were many difficulties in working with an older building, and . . . had . . . evolved what he thought would be a perfect form of museum if one were starting a new one. He made me drawings and gave me measurements. . . . I sent the drawings and measurements to Sir Edmund Walker, who turned them over to Darling and Pearson, when their firm was appointed architects for our building. The galleries were to be thirty feet wide each side of a central wall, and the general form of one or more quadrangles. Mr. Darling had decided on a double quadrangle. I may say that after years of working and living in the building I would recommend the same structure still, as the most economical and practical form I know.

—Charles Currelly, *I Brought the Ages Home* (1956)

While Darling and Pearson created a master plan for a large museum reflecting both the prevalent Beaux Arts style and the museological spirit of the times, only one wing was to be constructed immediately. In the drawings that remain, the project's scope was further reduced primarily by eliminating the large lecture hall fronting Bloor Street and two floors of the office tower component. The front door was modest; a grand entrance was planned on Queen's Park.

In retrospect, the building of the first section of the ROM might seem enviably simple; at the turn of the last century it was not. There were many challenges to overcome. In 1909 the building's budget was finally approved: $400,000 (including display cases) to be equally shared by the Province of Ontario and the University of Toronto. Construction began in the fall of 1910 with the roof complete by December 1911; the Museum opened to the public in 1914. And it came in under budget, costing $390,567.

The ROM also materialized in a legislative sense as construction was being completed with the passing of

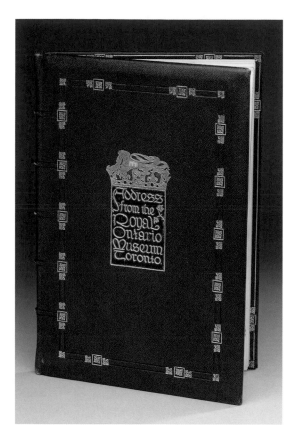

the *Royal Ontario Museum Act* on April 16, 1912. Over the next 18 months, the ROM's board of trustees enacted a series of bylaws that established five semi-independent constituent museums, all housed in the same structure, and each with its own director. Except for Currelly, all the directors were also professors at the University of Toronto.

The 1914 building has a feel of frugality. To use architect Robert Venturi's phrase, it looks like a "decorated shed." It was a Romanesque turn-of-the-century brick factory-like structure decorated with just enough cultural symbols, such as the Venetian-style windows, to communicate that it was a cultural building. Three galleries on top of each other, rather than everything on one floor, was an economical way to build and made good use of the site.

The completed building was a source of great pride for the community and spontaneous donations of artifacts began almost immediately. It was extraordinarily ambitious for a town of Toronto's size to have had such bold plans—and to have realized them. It was a pattern to be repeated with each major expansion of the Museum.

must r
highne
money
provin
sity of

this first section of th
the zeal of our collec
their separate devr

PLAN OF THE PROPOSED MUSEUM BUILDING

A FLOOR

the Chairman of the Board of Trustees of the

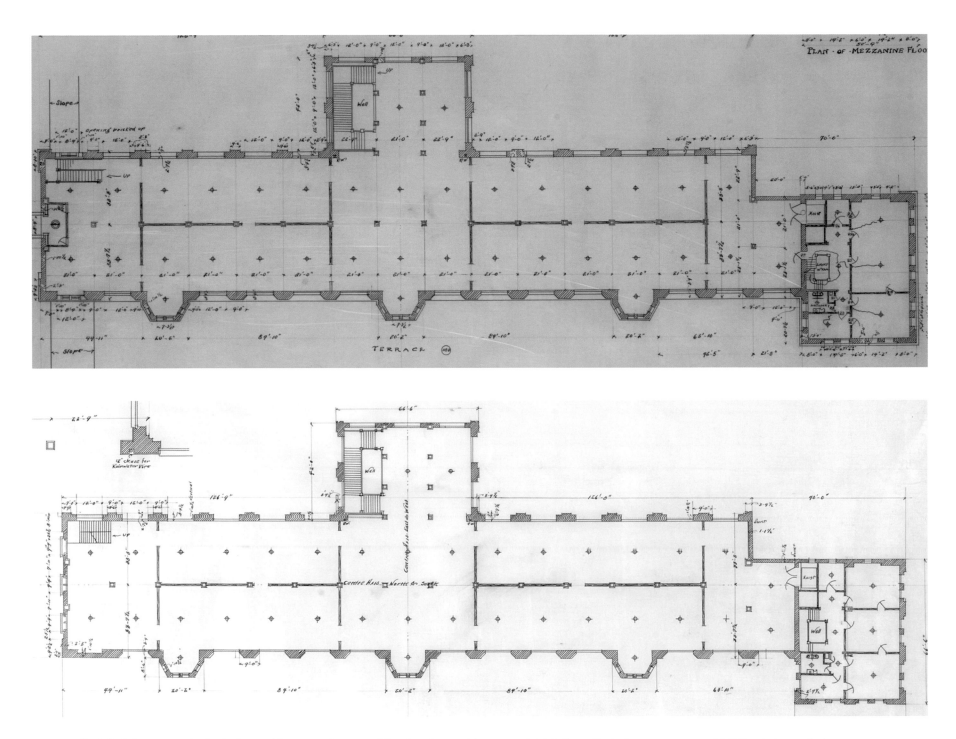

Page 66: The ROM's first master plan by Darling and Pearson is derivative of French architectural theoretician J. N. L. Durand's ideal museum concept of 1802, which uses the Louvre as its prototype. The master plan as shown here is from the Presentation Address to the Duke of Connaught. The 1914 building is represented in the upper portion of the plan. Page 67: The first-floor plan (top), and second-floor plan (bottom), as built, Darling and Pearson, 1910. Page 68: View of the 1914 ROM from Bloor Street with Philosophers' Walk winding down through the University of Toronto campus. From the 1914 Presentation Address. Page 69: View of the 1914 ROM from Philosophers' Walk soon after completion of the building and prior to landscaping.

held in the University buildings and elsewhere until the accumulation demanded the erection of a museum building.

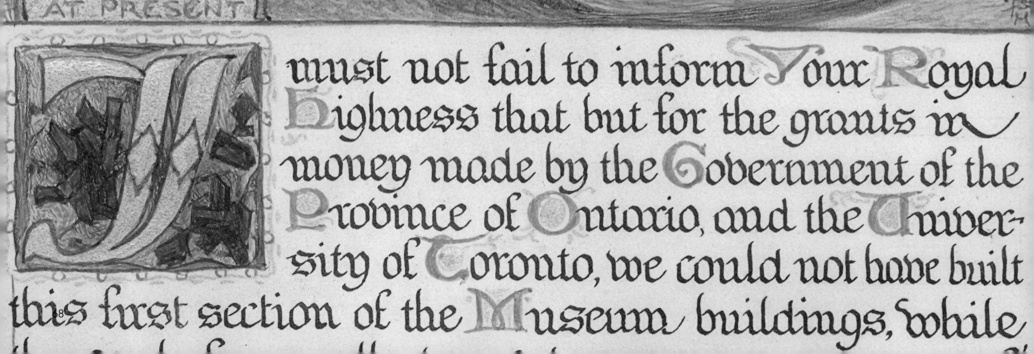

The Museum Building as at Present

W must not fail to inform Your Royal Highness that but for the grants in money made by the Government of the Province of Ontario, and the University of Toronto, we could not have built this first section of the Museum buildings, while

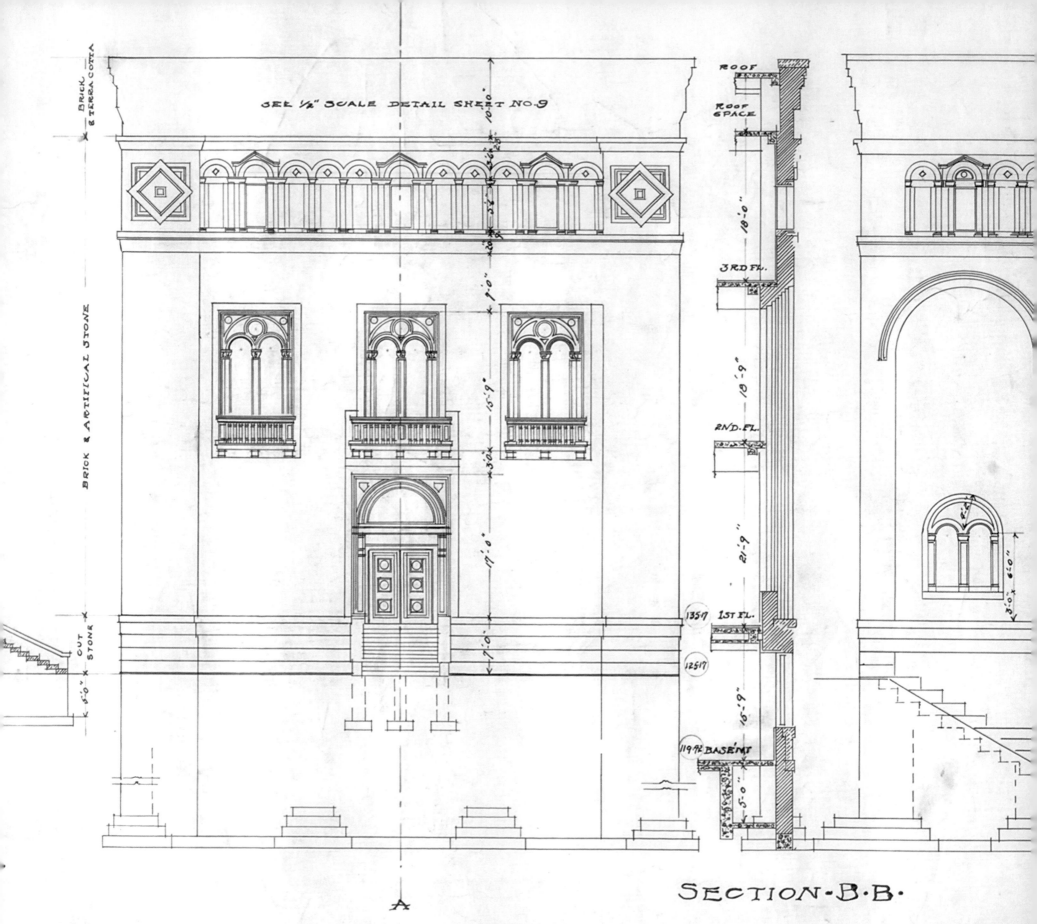

SEE 1/2" SCALE DETAIL SHEET NO. 9

BRICK & TERRA COTTA

BRICK & ARTIFICAL STONE

CUT STONE

10'-0"

2'-6"

8'-0"

7'-0"

15'-9"

3'-0"

17'-0"

7'-0"

ROOF

ROOF SPACE

18'-0"

3RD FL.

18'-9"

2ND. FL.

21'-9"

1351.7   1ST FL.

125.7

16'-9"

119.92   BASE'MT

5'-0"

6'-0"

3'-0"

A

NORTH ELEVATION

SECTION·B·B.

70

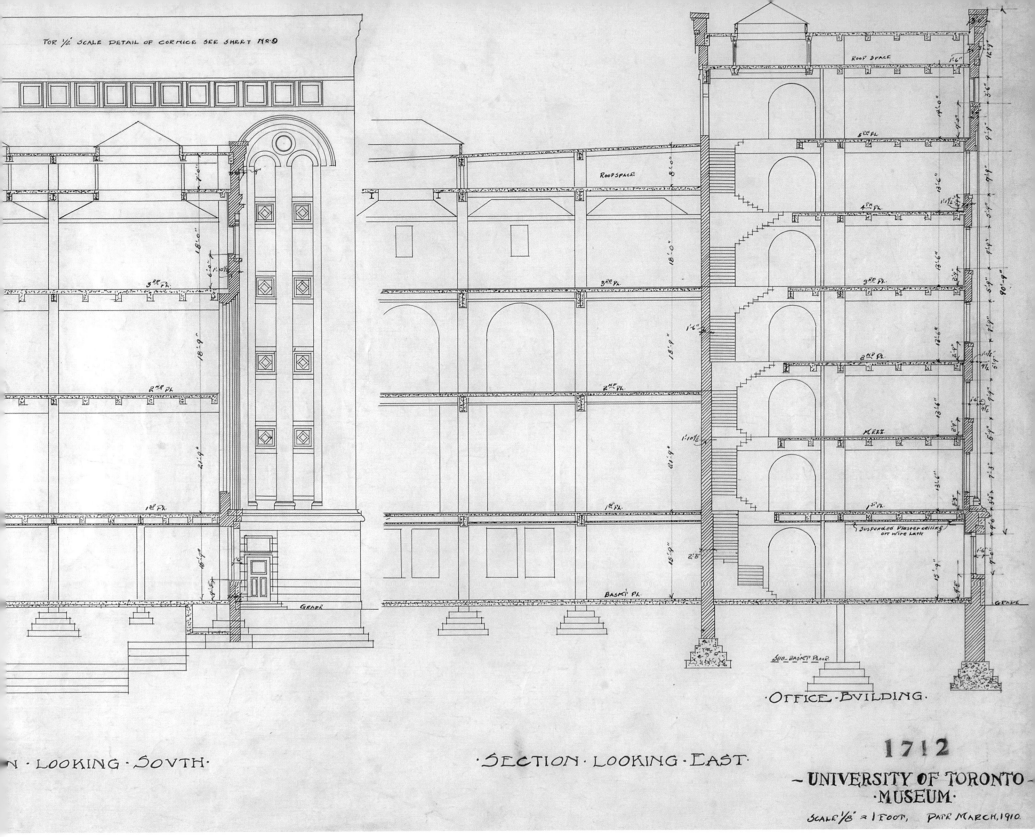

TOR 1/2 SCALE DETAIL OF CORNICE SEE SHEET N° 9

ROOF SPACE

OFFICE·BVILDING·

N·LOOKING·SOVTH·   ·SECTION·LOOKING·EAST·

1712
~UNIVERSITY OF TORONTO
·MUSEUM·
SCALE 1/8" = 1 FOOT.   DATE MARCH, 1910.

Page 70: Section drawings of the Bloor Street façade and main entrance, Darling and Pearson, 1910. Working drawings were simple on the assumption that most detail would be resolved on site during construction. *Page 71:* Section drawings through the galleries and office-building components, Darling and Pearson, 1910. There were originally skylights on the third-floor galleries (left). The office building (right) was eventually completed with four storeys (in addition to the basement) rather than six as shown in this section. *Page 72:* Detail of the office-building cornice from the working drawings, Darling and Pearson, 1910. *Page 73:* Similar cornice detail from the 1914 gallery building, photographed in 2006.

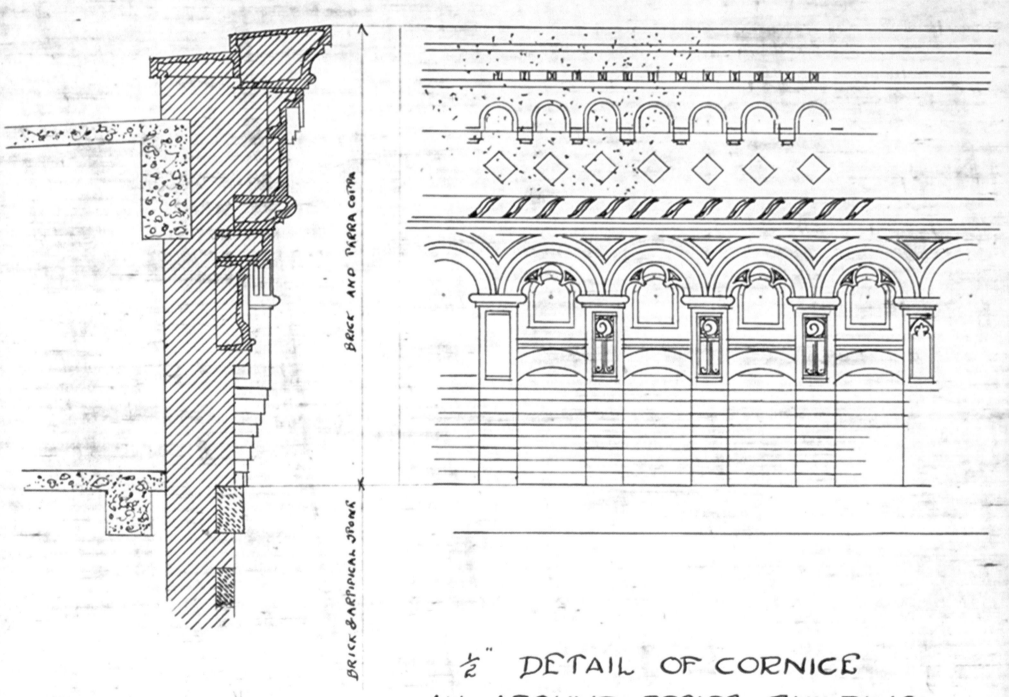

BRICK AND TERRA COTTA

BRICK & ARTIFICIAL STONE

½" DETAIL OF CORNICE
ALL AROUND OFFICE·BUILDING·

Page 74: Geology workroom in the basement, 1914. The windows look out to Philosophers' Walk to the west. *Page 75*: Chinese gallery, first floor, 1914. *Page 76*: European collection, east first floor, looking south, 1914. *Page 77*: European collection, west first floor, looking south, 1914.

Page 78: Archaeology gallery, second floor, 1914. *Page 79:* Mineralogy gallery, third floor, 1914. Skylights above.

1933

81

1933: Queen's Park Building and Centre Block

According to Lovat Dickson in *The Museum Makers*, by 1918 "the existing building had become so unbearably crowded that there was scarcely room to pass in the aisles, and the new acquisitions and gifts were piling up in storerooms elsewhere in the city." The Province asked the Museum to submit plans and estimates for an addition. Despite the overcrowding and the popularity of the Museum, the next phase of ROM building did not start in earnest until 1928. A report in that year by Professor B. A. Bensley, director of the Royal Ontario Museum of Zoology, summarized the needs of his department, but it also illustrates the shift from a focus on display to a concept similar to the ROM's philosophy in the 1980s.

> It is essential to get away from the idea that the museum consists solely or even mainly of a layout of space from an exhibition point of view and realize: (1) that extensive provision must be made for office, workroom and storage purposes: (2) that there must be tangible facilities for public instruction in the way of lecture amphitheatre and classrooms: (3) that gallery exhibition requirements as regards lighting, heating and wiring should be studied before and not after the final plans are drawn.
> —B. A. Bensley, *A Preliminary Statement Concerning the Needs of the Royal Ontario Museum of Zoology in Relation to the New Bloor Street Extension* (1928)

The Toronto firm of Chapman and Oxley was hired in 1929 to design the addition, which would more than double the size of the Museum. Alfred Chapman had studied at the École des Beaux Arts in Paris and his designs, including the recently completed Toronto Public Library on College Street, illustrate the Beaux Arts penchant for axial planning and symmetrical design. Chapman and Oxley continued to implement the Beaux Arts–inspired Darling and Pearson master plan of a double quadrangle by completing a wing along Queen's Park and connecting it to the existing Museum with the Centre Block, the ground floor of which is now called Samuel Hall ❧ Currelly Gallery. They suggested future additions that would provide the master plan's north wing along Bloor Street (the Bloor Street wing was the initial assumption for a phase-two expansion but not pursued) and a south wing to complete the double quadrangle at the south end.

The Chapman and Oxley addition gave the Museum a new main entrance on Queen's Park with a grand rotunda to celebrate it. In a deviation from the master plan, a special wing, called the Garden Court, was designed for the Chinese tomb complex—including the magnificent stone lions—which until then had been in storage and not previously displayed. The Garden Court was sited in the south courtyard and connected by a short hallway to the Armour Court Samuel Hall ❧ Currelly Gallery in the Centre Block. The plan suggested a matching building as a future addition in the north courtyard. (The Garden Court was transformed into a space for temporary exhibitions in 1959 and the Chinese tomb complex was moved outside to the north courtyard, the semi-enclosed space on the north side of the Museum along Bloor Street now occupied by the Michael Lee-Chin Crystal.)

Argyle House, 1930, at 100 Queen's Park, with the 1914 Museum visible in the background.

Demolition of Argyle House, 1930, to make way for the 1933 addition on Queen's Park.

Page 80: Toronto c. 1933: the Great Depression. *Page 81:* Architect's concept of the entrance to the 1933 building emphasizing its Art Deco influences while minimizing the more traditional stonework and Romanesque details. Drawing by G. K. Pokorny.

Eaton's Store, Toronto, a good example of the influence of the Art Deco style in Toronto, designed by Ross and Macdonald, 1930.

The arrangement of the five museums, or departments of the ROM, in the 1933 addition, was a political triumph. The four natural history museums were placed in the new building fronting Queen's Park, each having its own entrance off the Rotunda. Offices, libraries, and workspaces were provided in each museum department. Archaeology now took over the entire 1914 wing and most of the Centre Block. Ethnology galleries were installed in the basement of the Centre Block; the rest of the basements were used for shipping, storage, and preparation. A lecture theatre and a tearoom opening to a garden were added on the west side of the new building's north wing.

The basic forms of the 1933 addition are Art Deco in concept, most notably the long façade broken by a massive centre block and subtle projecting pavilions at each end. The exterior limestone cladding relates to the most prominent University of Toronto buildings, such as University College, which in turn were modelled on 19th-century university buildings at Oxford and Cambridge. There are some odd clashes of style, such as the Romanesque windows above the Art Deco–like rectangular windows on the main and second floors of the Queen's Park façade.

The detailing, including the carvings above the main entrance on Queen's Park, are Art Deco–inspired, while others on the façade appear almost ecclesiastical and Romanesque. There is a sense that the architects would have liked to be more fashionable and to have created an Art Deco building, but that their ultimate client, the University of Toronto, was more conservative and demanded a structure commensurate with its notion of a proper English university and one, particularly because it was a museum, with overt historic references.

A. S. Mathers, a prominent Toronto architect, gave a backhanded compliment in the *Journal of the Royal Architectural Institute of Canada* when the 1933 wing opened: "It is a fine performance on the part of the architects even though it is as I hope for this country a brilliant climax and finale to that great school of North American architecture founded by the late H. H. Richardson."

On the interior, there is a comparable mix of Romanesque forms, such as the arches of the Rotunda; Beaux Arts classicism, such as the stairs, gallery landings, and decorative moldings; and Art Deco details, such as the light fixtures and ornamental grilles. The interiors of the office building, the top two floors of which were added in 1937 and included the H. H. Mu Far Eastern Library, show a delicate Art Deco influence. (The H. H. Mu Library was relocated to the top floor of the curatorial centre in 1981.) The RBC Foundation Glass Room, above the Rotunda, is the most purely Art Deco space in the building, both in general form and in its details and fixtures.

The most remarkable aspect of the 1933 addition is perhaps not the design but the manner of its construction, which began in 1931. The Great Depression began in 1929 and, rather than defer construction, it spurred it on. The Museum extension became a make-work project to address massive unemployment. Every effort was made to make the project as labour intensive as possible. While machinery could have been used to dig the foundations, the job was instead done by hand, with pick and shovel. References are made to horse-drawn wagons as well, but photographs show trucks. There is a level of hand finishing and carving that might not have been considered except that it created more jobs, hence was preferable to a more modern approach that might have simplified the building's details. Interesting, because for the 1914 building "modern" labour-saving technology such as artificial stone and pre-cast terra cotta details had been used.

The Province of Ontario also stipulated that local materials be used. With this in mind, the exterior walls of the new wing, other than those that would enclose the courtyards and would not be visible from the street, were faced with Credit Valley and Queenston limestone: the base course from grade to the first floor window sill is Queenston limestone, as is the trim, and the remainder Credit Valley stone laid in rough ashlar of varied hues. Brick from the yards in the Don Valley to match the existing building were used for the inner courtyard walls. Marble from Bancroft, Ontario, was used for the interior decorative marble flooring and trim. Four thousand 12" x 18" sheets of glass mosaic tile were imported from Venice for the Rotunda. Connolly Marble Mosaic and Tile cut approximately a million individual small tiles in Toronto and installed them using locally resident Italian artisans. The ceiling mosaic took eight months to complete. The individual tiles (or tesserae) are backed with a coating of gold leaf, which gives the mosaics in the Rotunda a luminescent quality.

While many of the construction methods were antiquated, the building was technically up to date in many ways with state-of-the-art lighting and concealed steam heating aside from a few wall radiators in the basement. It was the largest installation of concealed radiation in Canada, supplied primarily from the central steam plant of the University of Toronto. All floors are concrete beam-and-slab construction with the exception of the floor of the Glass Room, which is made of thick slabs of glass supported by steel framing. The steel deck roof is carried on steel trusses and finished with a peaked copper covering.

The extension had its official opening on October 12, 1933, although a few galleries had been opened the previous year. Alterations to the existing building were completed by 1934; the addition to the office tower of its top two floors (planned but never built for the original building) was finished in 1937. The total budget was $1.8 million. The ROM was now the largest museum of the Commonwealth outside England.

In 2004, the north wing of the 1933 building was renamed the Hilary and Galen Weston Wing and the south wing was renamed the Weston Family Wing.

Bank of Commerce, Toronto, designed by Darling and Pearson and the New York firm of York and Sawyer, 1930.

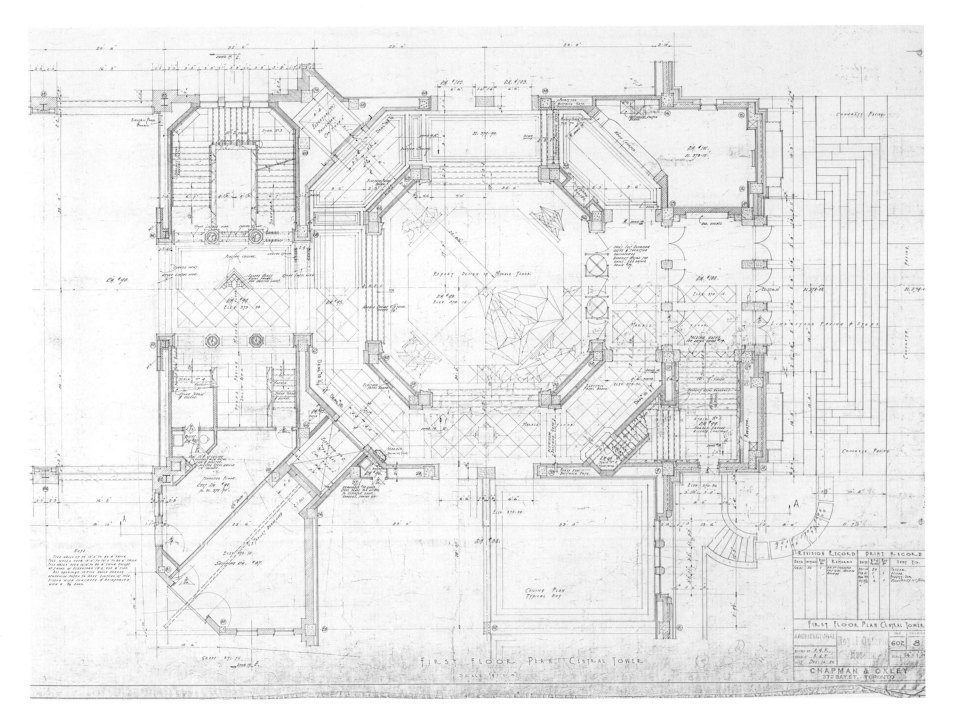

Plan of the first floor of the 1933 addition, showing the Rotunda and the Queen's Park entrance (top), Chapman and Oxley, c. 1930. This detailed plan clearly indicates the inlaid figures and patterning of the Rotunda's marble floor.

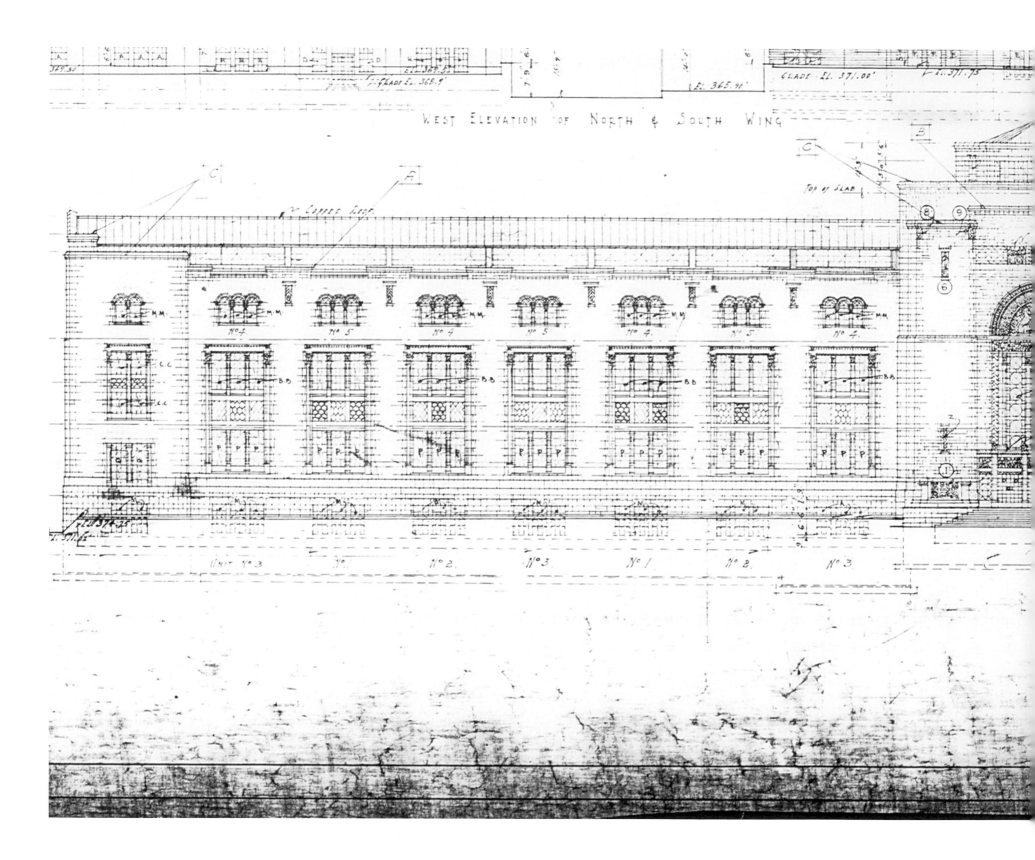

WEST ELEVATION OF NORTH & SOUTH WING

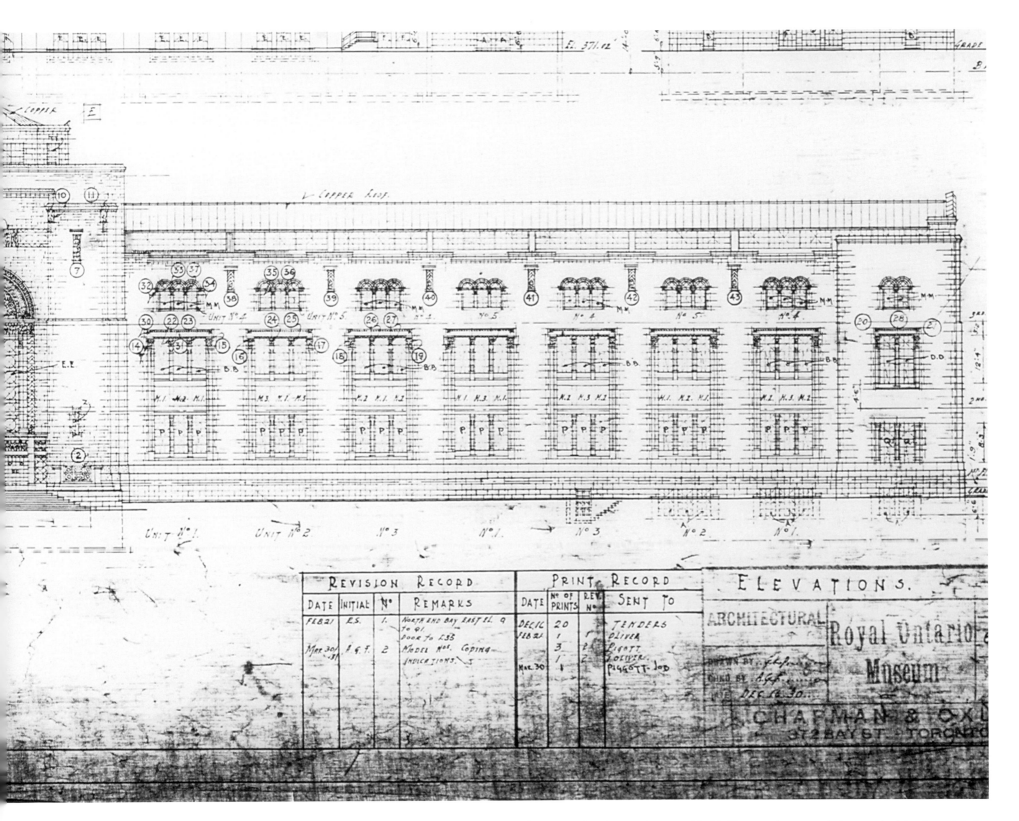

Pages 86–87: Elevation drawing of the façade of the 1933 addition along Queen's Park, Chapman and Oxley, 1930. *Pages 88–89:* Elevation drawing and photograph of the Queen's Park entrance, Chapman and Oxley, 1930. All the figural ornament, including elements in the tympanum, the semi-circular area above the main door, evolved as construction proceeded.

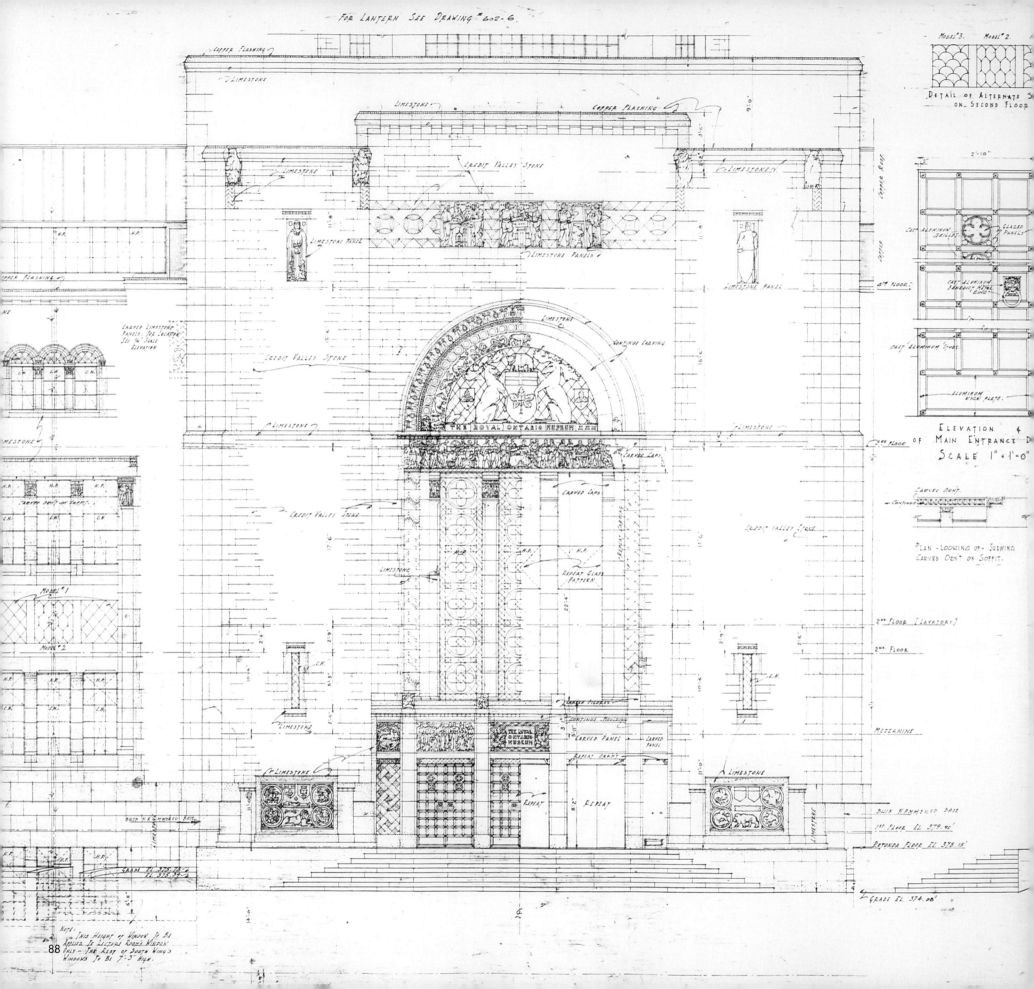

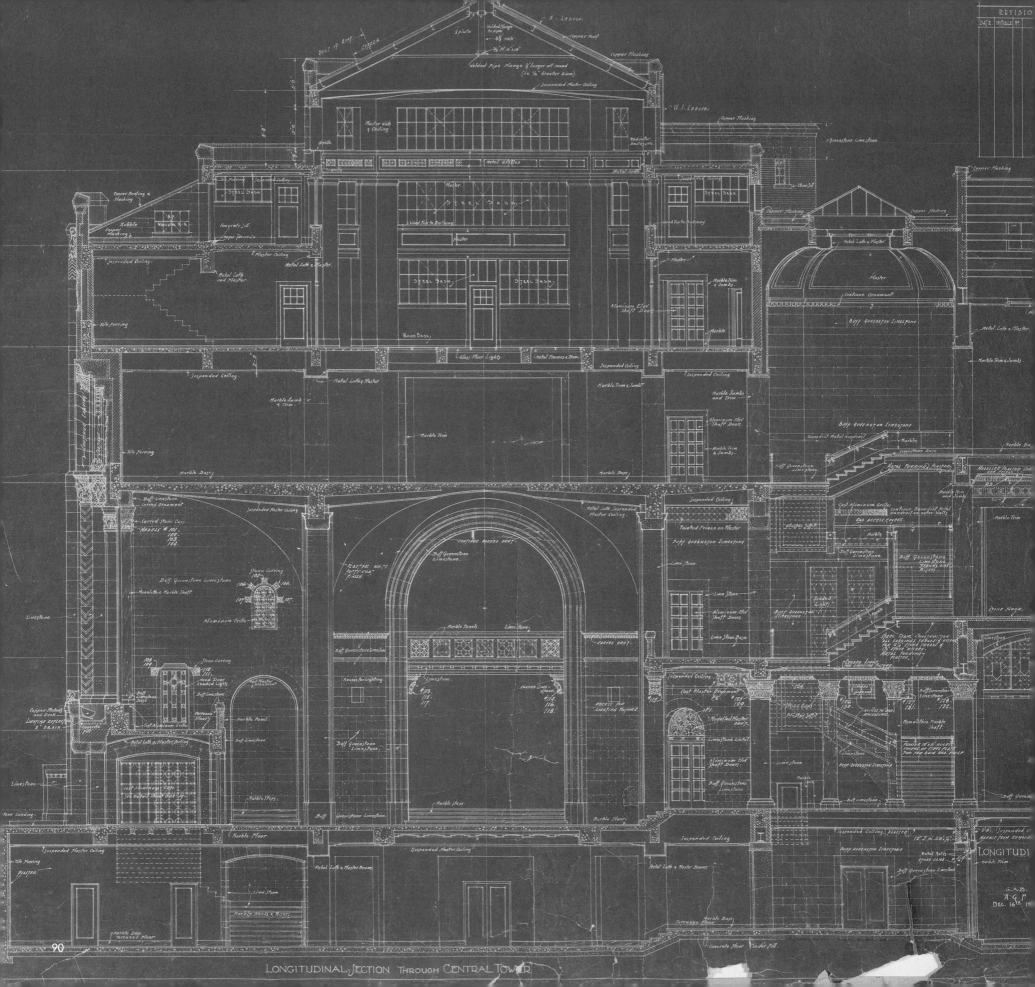

LONGITUDINAL SECTION THROUGH CENTRAL TOWER

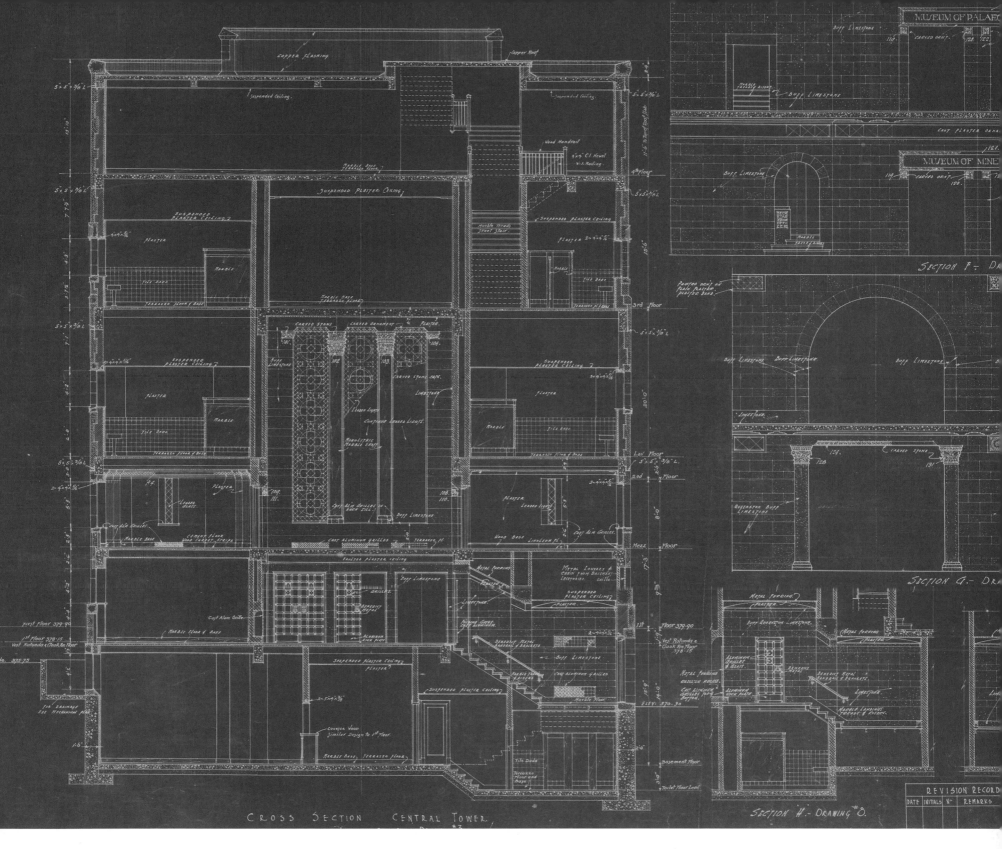

CROSS SECTION CENTRAL TOWER.

Page 90: A section through the central tower of the 1933 addition with the Rotunda on the ground floor, and on the top floor, what is now called the RBC Foundation Glass Room (with a glass floor designed to admit daylight to aquariums in the gallery below), Chapman and Oxley, 1930. *Page 91:* A section through the main entrance, Chapman and Oxley, 1930. Neither drawing indicates the four totem poles that were installed in the stairwells as construction was completed around them. *Page 92:* Construction begins on the 1933 addition. Much work was done by hand, including a significant portion of the excavation, so that as many people as possible would be employed during the Great Depression. *Page 93:* The Centre Block of the 1933 addition (right) connects the initial 1914 building with the new building along Queen's Park (left). *Page 94:* Detail, stonework, 1933 façade on Queen's Park.

Queen's Park Entrance, now the Weston Entrance

The tympanum is the semi-circular area above the 1933 building doors enclosed by an arch above the lintel of the entranceway. Its focal point is a seated female figure representing the liberal arts and sciences whose arms rest on shields carved with the coats of arms of the Province of Ontario and the University of Toronto, of which the ROM was a part until 1968. To her left is a scene representing the New World symbolized, most notably, by a totem pole, a tipi, and a buffalo. The Old World is represented on her right with the Winged Bull of Babylon, and images of ancient architecture: an obelisk, an arch, and a pyramid. The base is a series of gnome-like figures representing the building trades. The surrounding arch-band is carved with the signs of the Zodiac, and around this are the foliate rings of the main arch. Owls of knowledge rest on flanking promontories.

At the base of the three windows above the main doors are four allegorical figures corresponding to ceramic making, writing (panel and script), music (lyre, see right), and metalwork (the knight's helmet). They represent the decorative arts, and they also indicate how the ROM originally categorized subjects—as did the Victoria and Albert Museum at the time—by materials or technique rather than culture or geography.

Above the main doors, heraldic beasts, the royal lion and unicorn, borrowed from the Royal Arms of Britain, flank the Museum's name. As a "royal" institution, the Museum was allowed special distinctions such as this. There are incidental carvings of creatures from nature and mythology. To the left a procession of figures represents the ancient cultures of the Old World, and to the right, a similar procession depicts figures related to the New World including conquistadors and native peoples. This symbolism echoes that of the tympanum.

Sculptor Charles McKechnie (1865–1935) worked with Chapman and Oxley on several of their projects, most notably the angel and other figures on the Princes' Gates at the Canadian National Exhibition in 1927. For the Museum, he first created all the figures, full size, in clay. Plaster casts were then made of the forms and they were given to the stone carvers, who copied them, at times *in situ* high above Queen's Park on scaffolding.

Canadian architects of the time, especially John Lyle (1872–1945), who designed Union Station, were recommending contextually derived decoration as a way to create a Canadian style of architecture. Totems and other local motifs were considered as worthy of inclusion as traditional figures, for instance, figures from Greek mythology.

Above left: The 1914 building as completed. *Right:* An illustration of how the office building of 1914 was to be finished. *Below:* The office building was completed in 1937.

Page 98: The Chinese tomb complex, often referred to as the Ming Tomb, includes monuments from several dynasties. It was installed in the Garden Court wing from 1933 to 1959. This wing was demolished in 1978 to make way for the new curatorial centre (recently renamed the Louise Hawley Stone Curatorial Centre in honour of Mrs. Stone, whose bequest in 1998 remains the largest ever to the Museum). *Page 99:* When the Garden Court became a temporary exhibition space in 1959, the Chinese tomb complex was moved to the garden courtyard facing Bloor Street between the northeast and northwest wings of the Museum.

1933

Samuel Hall ❧ Currelly Gallery

The Armour Court (left) was renamed Currelly Gallery in 1946 in honour of C. T. Currelly, on his retirement. Sylvia Hahn, the artist of the murals in this space, which date to about 1940, depicted ROM staff members as jousting knights and spectators at a mediaeval tournament. Covered over in 1982 when the space became part of the Mankind Discovering theme gallery, the murals were once again revealed when the space was renovated for its current use. The space was renamed Samuel Hall ❧ Currelly Gallery in 1997 to recognize the major contributions to the ROM of Ernest and Elizabeth Samuel.

2007

Above: Looking into the 1933 Centre Block galleries. *Right:* 1933 stained-glass windows, Rotunda, restored in 2006. *Page 102:* The magnificent gold and multi-coloured mosaic Rotunda ceiling took eight months to assemble from small tiles cut from 12″ x 18″ sheets of glass from Venice, Italy. *Page 103:* Rotunda dome detail, the Elephant of India.

Rotunda Symbolism

The 1933 entrance is marked with a grand rotunda lobby with a balcony and mezzanine. It's an octagon with four two-storey arched openings supporting a decorative dome. The dome is red, blue, and turquoise Venetian glass mosaic set in a background of bronze, rust, and gold. The geometric patterns and figures give it a Byzantine quality.

The theme of the dome could be one of unity in diversity; the glory of creation is manifest in many divergent ways. The inscription in the centrepiece, from the *Book of Job,* suggests this theme succinctly: "That All Men May Know His Work."

The bands of the mosaic Rotunda ceiling represent the four major branches of historical development of art: Early man is indicated by a prehistoric cave dweller's conception of a buffalo, the Inca God of Thunder, and a totem pole evocative of North America before the Europeans arrived. The next band represents early Western civilization with an Egyptian falcon, a Greek seahorse, and a Roman she-wolf suckling Romulus and Remus. The third group illustrates the Asian cultural tradition with an Assyrian winged bull, the White Elephant of India, and a Chinese dragon. The fourth grouping suggests more recent history with the Christian symbol of the Lion from St. Mark's in Venice, the Moorish Fountain of the Lions from the Alhambra in Spain, and a heraldic griffin that contributes a Gothic European note.

In the hexagonal panels of the groins are images of the fundamentals of architecture: a ziggurat, an Egyptian temple, a Greek temple, and a Mayan temple.

STEL
BUDDHIST VO
DAT
GREY SANDST
PR

Page 104: The ROM's three Chinese temple paintings were acquired in 1928 and installed on the ground floor of the 1914 building in 1933. The largest of them, *The Paradise of Maitreya,* appears here. *Page 105: Venus the Mother* at the entrance to the 1933 second-floor hall of ancient Greek sculpture, pottery, and armour. *Page 106:* The Gallery of Ancient Greek Sculpture, second floor, Centre Block, with a Sylvia Hahn mural of an Aegean harbour. Opening (right) leads to stairs to the Rotunda. *Page 107*: The Gallery of Greek Pottery and Armour, second floor, Centre Block, with a Sylvia Hahn mural of a Greek domestic scene. Opening (left) leads to stairs to the Rotunda.

AN AEGEAN HARBOUR IN THE LATE GREEK PERIOD. MERCHANT SHIP TO THE LEFT. WARSHIP AND SHIPSHEDS TO THE RIGHT.

Page 108: The Egyptian Gallery (shown in the 1950s) on the second floor of the 1914 building was renovated as part of the 1933 expansion project. The original window was covered over with only the arched top remaining visible, the central portion opening for ventilation. Art Deco cornice details and light fixtures were added as well. *Page 109:* The Invertebrate Paleontology gallery, second floor of the 1933 addition. This space became the library in 1961. Murals were by Canadian artist George A. Reid (1860–1947). *Pages 110–11:* The Vertebrate Paleontology gallery, shown in 1960, on the second floor of the 1933 wing.

Page 112: The H. H. Mu Far Eastern Library was on the third floor of the office building at the southern end of the 1914 building. The library and offices for the new department of Chinese Studies opened when the third and fourth storeys were added to the office building in 1937. The evolution of exhibit design: *Page 113:* Geology Gallery, 1933 addition, north wing, first floor. *Pages 114–15:* The "new" Gallery of Geology in 1957, north wing of the 1933 addition (now the Daphne Cockwell Gallery of Canada: First Peoples). A highlight was the Bickell Globe illustrating the earth's mantle and core.

Pages 116–17: The "new" Gallery of Mineralogy in 1967, shown under construction and finished, used curving forms and completely obscured the architecture, including the windows in the 1933 building.

...ll globe of grey matter through which sp... ...r-changing conceptions of the universe.

1968

Page 118: The "new" Toronto City Hall, designed by Viljo Revell, opened in 1965 and symbolized the civic confidence that prompted the building of the planetarium. Page 119: The McLaughlin Planetarium seen from Queen's Park after it opened in 1968. The two buildings are architecturally similar in terms of their curvilinear form and concrete construction.

1968: The McLaughlin Planetarium

The idea of a planetarium for the ROM was first suggested in 1944 by Dr. C. A. Chant of the University of Toronto, but it was not until 15 years later that a planetarium was included in an informal ROM wish list. Its champion was Dr. V. B. Meen of the Department of Mineralogy at the University of Toronto. Public fascination with space exploration in the 1960s no doubt helped to rekindle interest in the project.

A key step was taken on October 1, 1964, when a proposal for *A Planetarium for the University of Toronto* was submitted to the president of the university. Colonel Sam McLaughlin, a pioneer of the Canadian automobile manufacturing industry, heard about it and wrote to the director of the ROM, Dr. W. E. Swinton, on November 27 with an offer to fund the project. He subsequently provided $2.5 million for the planetarium's construction and a further $1 million as an endowment fund.

A show that opened at the ROM in the summer of 1964, the *International Aerospace Exhibition,* jointly sponsored by the ROM and the Institute of Aerospace Studies of the University of Toronto, may have spurred the donation. Apparently Colonel McLaughlin attended the exhibition and was excited by it, but his interest in a planetarium for Toronto began prior to this when he saw the Hayden Planetarium in New York and, later, the Adler Planetarium in Chicago. Like the founders of the ROM after they had visited the great museums of Europe and the United States, Colonel McLaughlin had a dream: he was determined that one day Canada should have a planetarium to rival the ones he had seen in New York and Chicago. A planetarium was an architectural symbol of civic sophistication and progress, comparable to an opera house, albeit with a scientific rather than a cultural intent. For cities aspiring to be taken seriously, such as Toronto, they were *de rigueur.*

An initial plan had placed the planetarium in the south courtyard where the Curatorial Centre is now and had included a large parking garage, a 550-seat movie theatre, a tunnel to the subway, and provision for future development that might have included removal of the University of Toronto's Falconer Hall to the south. Needless to say, the garage, theatre, and subway tunnel were deleted from the project, and the building site was relocated. A house just south of the ROM, used by the university as the Blood and Vascular Disease Research Unit, was demolished; planetarium construction began in 1966.

Another site considered for the planetarium was the north courtyard on Bloor Street, where it would be more prominent, but Dr. Swinton felt that the planetarium dome would clash with the northern ends of the east and west wings. He preferred the Queen's Park location where he believed the juxtaposition of the historic ROM building and a contemporary planetarium would be less noticeable.

Colonel McLaughlin's ambition was for the planetarium to be "of the highest order and first class in every way." Dr. Thomas Clarke, who became the second head of the McLaughlin Planetarium in 1976, wrote in the summer 1982 issue of *Rotunda* that the proposal for the planetarium architectural style was to be "appropriate to the subject as a science and in relation to man's modern activities in space." We can assume that the planetarium was not to look like a CNE attraction—it was a serious business to study the stars.

The stolid modernism of the exterior did not convey the adventure of space exploration. The exhibits,

Space capsule from the ROM's *International Aerospace Exhibition,* 1964.

John P. Robarts Research Library, University of Toronto, a Brutalist concrete building designed by Warner Burns Toan & Leslie (New York) with Mathers and Haldenby, 1973.

CIBC Commerce Court, Toronto, a sleek tower designed by I. M. Pei & Partners and Page + Steele, Inc., 1973.

however, most particularly the Hall of Spheres, did convey with floating planet imagery, floor-mounted globe displays, and dramatic "space-age" lighting in darkened rooms, the romance associated with space travel in those days.

The concern that the planetarium be appropriately scientific and serious may explain why the design of the building is attributed, in most instances, primarily to Stone and Webster Canada Limited, an engineering firm. Allward & Gouinlock get secondary billing as the consulting architects for the 1965 plans.

Perhaps with a planetarium an engineer's efficiency or practicality overrides an architect's design concerns. The result was a fairly bland exterior enlivened only by the dome, a building not as successful in exploiting the drama of this novel architectural feature as the Hayden and Adler planetariums. The interior concrete work has a Brutalist style, although it is not as elegant as that Brutalist icon, Boston City Hall by Kallman, McKinnell and Knowles, Architects, completed in 1968. The John P. Robarts Research Library, completed in 1973, is a nearby example of the Brutalist style.

The dome rises 83 feet from the ground and has an outer diameter of 91 feet. Its structure is layered, with an outer waterproofed casing of reinforced concrete 2.5 inches thick, and an inner concrete dome insulated by a layer of urethane foam. Inside this is an interior dome, onto which the images were projected, approximately 75 feet in diameter, made from aluminum sheets, painted white, and perforated with 0.1-inch holes to let sound through, reduce echo, and allow ventilation.

After it was opened on October 26, 1968, the McLaughlin Planetarium attracted significant crowds and was a popular component of the ROM. Over the next decade, the McLaughlin Endowment was used to improve the theatre, including its sound and projection equipment. Not quite ten years after it opened, its north wing, or annex, was demolished to make way for the curatorial centre. This part of the planetarium had housed the workshop and studio, the sound studio, the theatre entrance, the passenger elevator, and about one-third of the display area. What remained of the gallery was retrofitted as a temporary replacement for the workshop and studio. A new circular stair was added to give access to the theatre.

The beginning of the end for the planetarium was the closure of the ROM during the construction of the new curatorial centre and Terrace Galleries additions. Planetarium attendance dropped dramatically and was never to recover. Compounding this, fascination with space peaked in 1969 with the first man on the moon; by the 1980s, planetariums seemed rather quaint, and most struggled to find audiences by broadening their programming to include music and non-astronomical shows.

The McLaughlin Planetarium closed on November 5, 1995. The building reopened on a three-year lease as the Children's Own Museum on December 6, 1998, but when the lease expired the building was converted to offices and storage. In 2006, the ROM proposed, with a development partner, to build condominiums and offices on this site. While the proposal did not proceed because of lack of support, the Renaissance ROM fundraising campaign anticipates the eventual redevelopment of this site.

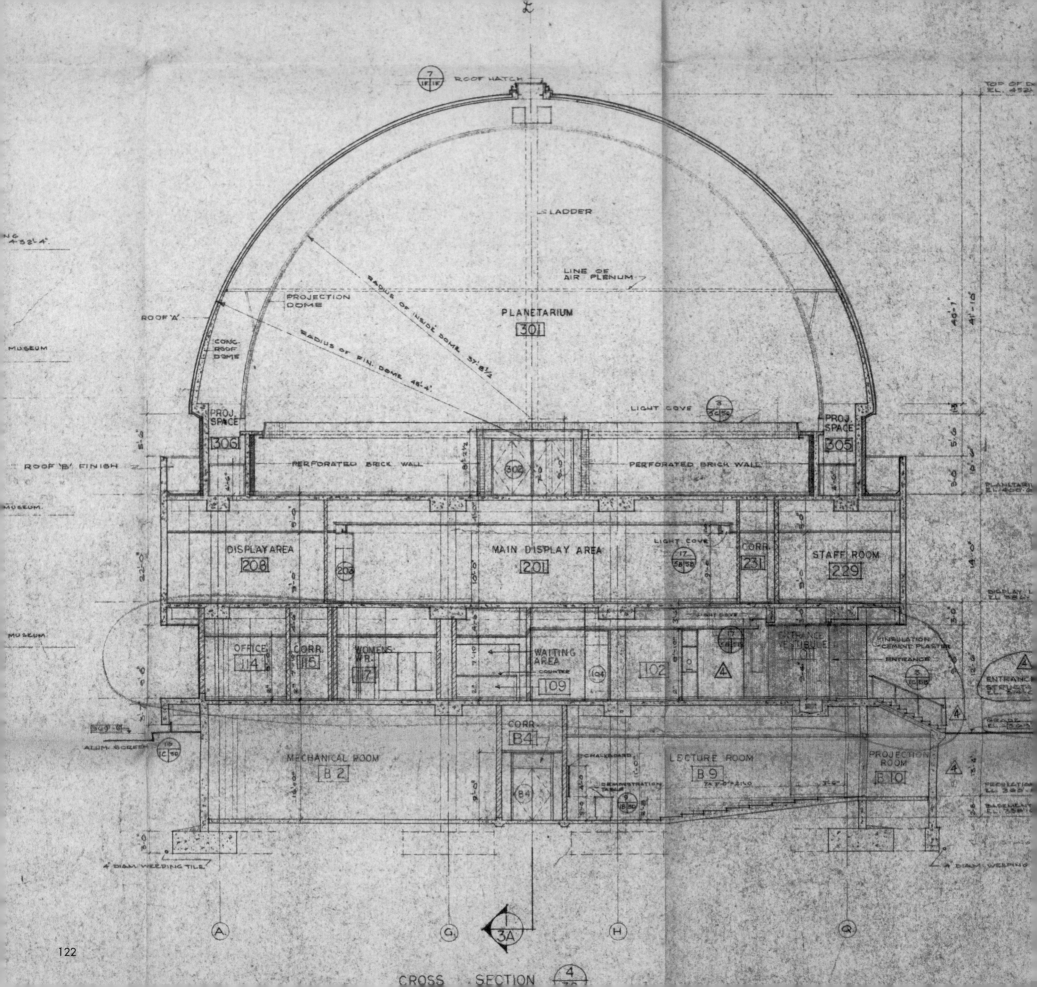

CROSS SECTION

Page 122: Section drawing of the planetarium. The engineers for the McLaughlin Planetarium, Stone and Webster Canada Limited, are given most of the design credit with Allward and Gouinlock credited as the consulting architects. Page 123: Construction of the McLaughlin Planetarium in 1967.

1984

Page 124: Eaton Centre, Toronto, designed by the Zeidler Partnership Architects and Bregman and Hamann, 1977 (phase one), 1979 (phase two). *Page 125:* The Terrace Galleries opened in 1982 and were "officially" opened in 1984 by the Queen when they became the Queen Elizabeth II Terrace Galleries.

1984: Curatorial Centre and Queen Elizabeth II Terrace Galleries

The *Royal Ontario Museum Act, 1968,* gave the Museum independence from the University of Toronto. The ROM became a self-governing institution, with its buildings and collections held in trust for the people of Ontario. In addition to a change in the way the Museum would be managed, this legislation signalled a shift from the University's research and teaching orientation for the Museum to one that recognized the Museum's increasing number of visitors and their importance, particularly as a revenue stream.

Accommodating its ever-growing public, including significant increases in organized school visits, meant creating more exhibit space and enhancing public amenities, while the continued growth of collections further fuelled the need for expansion. Adding more gallery space permitted more of the accumulating number of artifacts in storage to be displayed. It also required that the curatorial areas housed in the gallery wings be consolidated in a new building to allow these spaces to be used exclusively for display. Hence, the need for more exhibit space, along with the ambitions of the curators for consolidation of dispersed facilities, and better labs, offices, research areas, and storage, prompted the demand for a separate curatorial centre.

With the Museum's new-found administrational freedom, the first tangible steps were made towards expansion in 1969 when the ROM board commissioned the architects and planners Moffat Moffat & Kinoshita to do a feasibility study. Completed the following year, it demonstrated that the project was of a larger scope than already committed provincial funding could cope with, and so the initiative languished until 1974. In the meantime, a new Members' Lounge and a restaurant were added in 1970 overlooking the Chinese tomb complex in the Chinese Garden and accessed from the 1933 north wing. Then, with the prospect of additional funds from the Province, the ROM board appointed a project director, David Scott. Soon after, in 1975, the firms of Mathers & Haldenby and Moffat Moffat & Kinoshita were appointed architects for the expansion with Gene Kinoshita as design architect.

One of David Scott's first assignments was to prepare a planning report that would give a snapshot of the current Museum and describe what it might become, a mandate encompassing all aspects of its operations. *Guidelines for Planning* appeared in 1975. The most revolutionary ideas in it, the ones that were to have the most profound influence on the ROM's architecture, insisted that the Museum focus not solely on the past, but engage with present issues. The Museum was encouraged to adopt a cohesive and integrating content theme such as "Meaningful Survival."

This new attitude was summarized in a subsequent *Statement of Intent* and it was the seed for the later gallery reorganization in which objects were part of an overarching narrative whose purpose was to reveal social and cultural patterns. Galleries provided an overtly educational experience. They were no longer places solely to muse. This was an ambition many at the time decried as intellectual authoritarianism and turning history into sound bytes. To implement the new "cluster concept" approach, gallery planners wanted windowless galleries in which space could be manipulated to serve the storyline presented. Essentially, the less visible the architecture in galleries, the better.

Gallery planners wanted windowless galleries in which space could be manipulated to serve the storyline presented. Essentially, the less visible the architecture in galleries, the better

The grand Beaux Arts axis from the front door through the Currelly Gallery to Philosophers' Walk was gone. What blocked this vista now was the theme gallery, Mankind Discovering

This didactic focus, in retrospect, seems at odds with Gene Kinoshita's interest in providing a pleasant museum visit by reducing what he referred in general terms to as "museum fatigue," the endless march through windowless spaces to view objects. He spoke of natural light and its "mystical, ever-changing quality." He described his plans for atriums that would give "the space and environment for orientation and rest, and also a very important transition space for reorientation and a change in perspective."

In late 1975, the board asked Scott to prepare a report in which work to date could be consolidated. The *Interim Planning Report* was ready in 1976 and it outlined an ambitious project that would double the existing size of the Museum to 645,835 square feet and make it the second-largest museum building in North America, the Metropolitan Museum of Art in New York being the largest at 1,001,004 square feet.

Importantly, the report outlined the basic approach an expansion would eventually take: filling in areas to the north and south of the Centre Block that were originally conceived of as courtyards. A new curatorial centre would occupy the south courtyard (the Garden Court temporary exhibit hall would be removed), and in the north courtyard new galleries would be built facing Bloor Street. Both additions would be separated from the existing structures by skylight atriums.

Several months after the publication of the *Interim Planning Report*, the Ontario government reaffirmed its financial commitment to the project and increased its initial level of support. This, coupled with the promise of monies from Metro Toronto Council and private-sector support, meant that the project moved ahead. In 1978 the temporary exhibition hall was demolished and excavations for the new curatorial centre began. As renovations of the existing building started, the west wing closed to the public in 1980 and the east wing in 1981. The new curatorial centre opened in 1981.

When the Terrace Galleries and renovated galleries opened in 1982, the response was mixed. While the Terrace Galleries were impressive, they were mostly empty—there was no money remaining to install exhibits. By 1984, exhibits had been installed. The Queen was invited to open the addition officially, which at that point was rechristened The Queen Elizabeth II Terrace Galleries.

The major new public space, the north atrium, was not the greenery filled space Gene Kinoshita had imagined. Soon after the greenery was installed, it was realized that plants should not be permitted; they attracted insects that could find their way into collections and potentially damage them. As previously noted, lush spaces imagined as respites between forays into darkened galleries were instead harshly lighted and sterile areas, not ones that added positively to the visitor's experience.

The perception that little had been added was exacerbated by the sense of considerable loss: the grand Beaux Arts axis from the front door through the Currelly Gallery to Philosophers' Walk was gone. What blocked this vista now was the theme gallery, Mankind Discovering.

Much of what was accomplished was unseen. As Gene Kinoshita explained, "the whole complex of existing buildings has a new climate control, security and fire safety systems for the protection of both artifacts and visitors. Because the existing buildings had no cooling, humidity control or proper insulation, great care had to be taken to protect the exterior skin of the building from deterioration due to higher interior levels of

A rendering of an earlier scheme by Gene Kinoshita, April 1976, proposed a light-filled, almost totally glass addition that would be built between the two existing north wings of the Museum on Bloor Street. The concept of "terraced" galleries had not yet emerged. This proposal was considered inappropriate for the display techniques planned. *Page 129:* An earlier version, spring 1977, of the Terrace Galleries in which the terraces are conceptualized as hanging gardens. The lowest level (left) is a sunken garden for the Chinese tomb complex.

For some, the concrete aggregate finish appeared more appropriate to a shopping mall than a museum

humidity and air tightness." The beautifully vaulted plaster ceiling of the Currelly Gallery had to be demolished and then recreated at a lower level to accommodate the ducts and pipes above it. As well, the exteriors of the existing buildings were cleaned, and windows were repaired or, if infilled, made consistent with others that were similarly closed. The gift shop and other "encroachments," as Kinoshita referred to them, were removed from the Rotunda and it was taken back closer to its 1933 appearance. The Glass Room on the fourth floor was reclaimed from the Mammalogy Department.

Gene Kinoshita, in retrospect, had the best intentions. He wanted the Terrace Galleries to be part of a park fronting Bloor Street, and earlier versions of his plans show a hanging-gardens approach that would have produced a popular public space. He also wanted to harmonize the addition with the existing buildings and accomplished this by separating old and new with the atrium spaces and by cladding the addition, on the interior, in a very neutral manner. Unfortunately, neutral, perhaps because of budget constraints, became bland, and for some, the concrete aggregate finish appeared more appropriate to a shopping mall than a museum. While the curatorial centre remains, the Terrace Galleries were demolished 20 years after they were opened to make way for the Michael Lee-Chin Crystal.

Gene Kinoshita's comments in a 1982 article in *Rotunda* poignantly suggest that good intentions do not always equate with successful architecture: "My hope is that the ROM complex will again come to life, and that people from all over Canada and the world will visit and revisit, receiving lasting and loving images and experiences through its displays, its collections, its spatial experiences and its architecture."

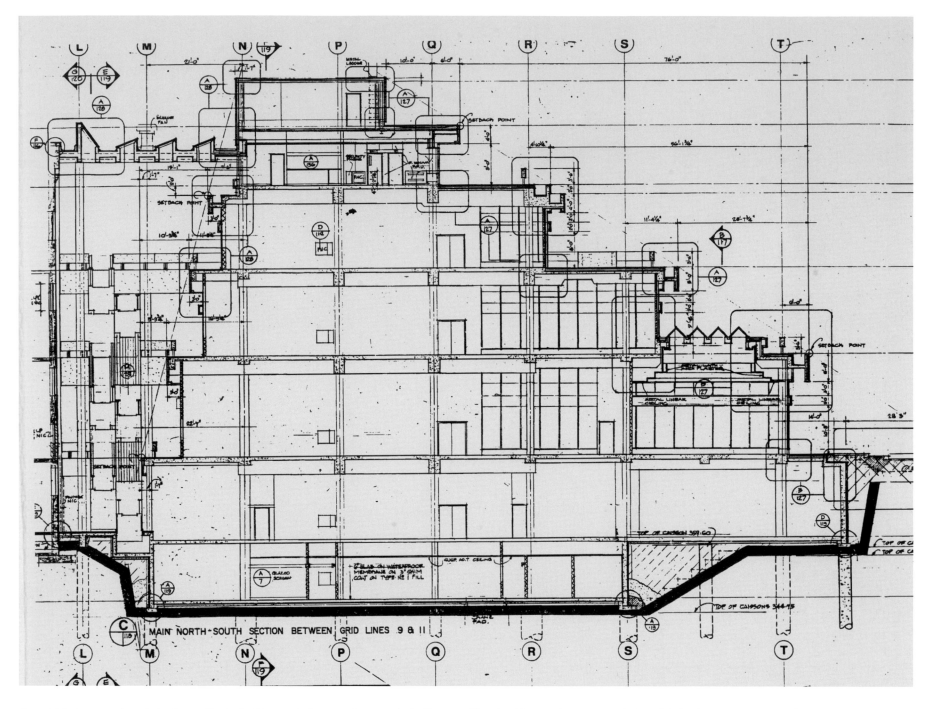

MAIN NORTH-SOUTH SECTION BETWEEN GRID LINES 9 & 11

Page 130: A section through the Queen Elizabeth II Terrace Galleries as they were built. The ground-floor level facing Bloor Street (right) has skylights for an area to house the Chinese tomb complex. *Page 131*: The skylight area of the Terrace Galleries facing Bloor Street designed for the Chinese tomb complex, 1984. *Page 132*: Architect's presentation drawing of the atrium joining the Terrace Galleries to the existing building, drawing by Michael McCann, 1977; the planting, critical to the concept, was removed because of conservators' concerns that insects might infiltrate the collections. *Page 133*: The Terrace Galleries, 1984, before the plants were removed.

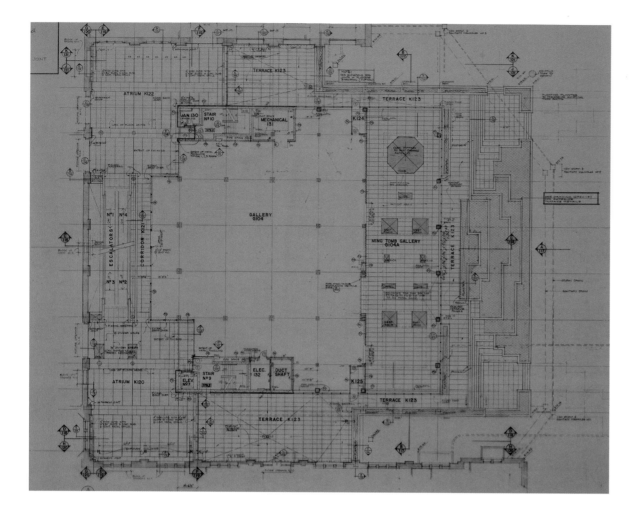

Page 134, top: The ground-floor plan for the Queen Elizabeth II Terrace Galleries. Bloor Street is to the right. *Bottom:* Dynamic Earth: INCO Limited Gallery of Earth Sciences created an experience for visitors that did not relate to the ROM's architecture, least of all to the 1914 building, where it was installed. *Page 135:* The Volcano Theatre in the Dynamic Earth gallery.

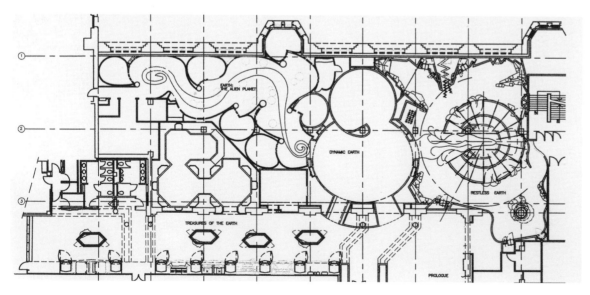

2007

Page 136: The Toronto Waterfront, 2006. *Page 137:* The Michael Lee-Chin Crystal from the corner of Bloor Street and Avenue Road, 2007.

2007: Renaissance ROM: Heritage Building Retrieval and the Michael Lee-Chin Crystal

The origins of RenROM (renaissance of the Royal Ontario Museum) predate the architectural selection process that first brought it to the public's attention in 2001. Before there was a "crystal," there were serious concerns about the future of the institution. In the mid 1990s, the ROM's board realized the public was losing interest. The Museum's traditional audience was dwindling, and potential supporters perceived it as irrelevant and/or a rather dreary place to spend an afternoon. Its ability to attract visitors, including tourists, was questioned—its long-term viability uncertain. Revenue generation was becoming increasingly important as government funding was a smaller percentage of its budget every year.

British-born Lindsay Sharp, the former director of Sydney, Australia's, Powerhouse Museum, was hired as the ROM's director in February 1997 with the anticipation that he would make radical changes to the ROM so that it could be a sustainable enterprise. As part of his mandate, the ROM board asked him to develop an institutional strategy that would renew the Museum. After several internally generated planning documents, which made it apparent that changes to the ROM's building were central to its revitalization, the ROM hired the Zeidler Roberts Partnership in January 2000 as the lead master-planning consultant. The Zeidler Roberts Partnership was also to translate the results of planning to date into building concepts that would be the basis for renovations or additions.

The Zeidler Roberts Partnership's master plan was approved by the ROM board in June 2000. It articulated principles that influenced the renovation and what was to become the Michael Lee-Chin Crystal, and it illustrated the principles with schematic building concepts that bear little correspondence to what was eventually built.

Among its recommendations, some were key: create an iconic presence that would invite people to the Museum and position it as an important civic attraction; move the main entrance to Bloor Street; ensure a central interior space that would "open up" the Museum (as the Hyacinth Gloria Chen Crystal Court does now); make the visitor experience a priority—it should be enjoyable rather than merely instructive and should be supported with enhanced retail and restaurant services; and retain the 1914 and 1933 heritage wings of the building. Building a condominium or a specialty hotel on the planetarium site as a source of revenue for the ROM's redevelopment was also suggested.

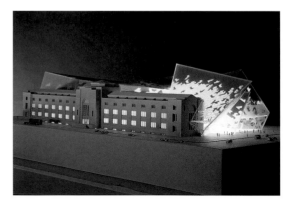

The finalists' submissions: Bing Thom Architects (top), Architetto Andrea Bruno (middle), and Studio Daniel Libeskind.

When William Thorsell became the Museum's director and CEO in August 2000, the master plan began to take concrete shape. Thorsell immediately found compelling language to express his new direction for the ROM, including coining the moniker "RenROM." He characterized the ROM at that time as having a "cliff on Queen's Park and a moat on Bloor"—a powerful image of its alienation from the public. And he said the ROM must transform itself into an institution integrated into the city fabric. It should become a spectacular example of civic confidence.

Thorsell and his colleagues translated the 2000 master plan into a concrete program. The new ROM would have 388,000 square feet of public space, including renovations to 75 per cent of the heritage galleries. RenROM would almost double the number of objects to be on view, including finding homes for collections never before shown. There was also to be a 20,000-square-foot increase in restaurant, retail, and event spaces

Much like the majestic cases filled with artifacts in the 1914 ROM galleries, Thorsell's vision was a return to a belief in the power of objects to captivate, to amuse, to create wonder, and to spark further learning about them

and a new 30,000-square-foot Learning Centre. The project was to retain and renovate the heritage galleries, the 1914 and 1933 wings, and it was left up to the imagination of the architects to determine what would happen with rest of the building, although it was broadly assumed that the Terrace Galleries would be demolished.

Thorsell had definite ideas about how the Museum should present itself: "The Museum should have very high standards. They should know who their audience is, and not lose faith in that audience, not dumb down, not turn themselves into a science centre or some post-modern version of what a museum should be." He concurred with Lindsay Sharp's priority of a renewed ROM that would focus on the visitor's experience as much as the housing of artifacts.

While the Museum was not to be "dumbed down," it was to be comfortable. This was a new idea that significantly influenced the ROM's architecture: it was not exclusively about the housing of objects, or the educational use of them, but about creating an institution that people want to visit perhaps for no other reason than that it's a pleasant spot to have lunch.

Most important, Thorsell did not believe that artifacts were props to be used in didactic displays, ones typically housed in dark, windowless, anonymous gallery spaces. Much like the majestic cases filled with artifacts in the 1914 ROM galleries, Thorsell's vision was a return to a belief in the power of objects to captivate, to amuse, to create wonder, and to spark further learning about them—a fascinating concept in a world where the *virtual* is the overwhelming reality, and the *real* a rare commodity.

This approach was a subtle rebuke to those who thought that the Museum's primary audience was children, or that the purpose of displays was overtly educational. RenROM was articulating a more inclusive experience, of prime interest to adults as it simultaneously accommodated children, especially through child-centric programming. This renewed sense of the ROM as a repository of culture and nature rather than an adjunct to schools was a significant influence on the architecture and the re-installation of exhibits.

The importance of "iconic architecture," as the master plan stated it, came to be called the *Bilbao Effect*. This phrase encapsulates the notion that if you build a captivating structure—such as Frank Gehry's Guggenheim Museum in Bilbao, Spain—people will flock to see it, even if it is, like Bilbao, remote and without a permanent collection. A good building design was not enough; what was required was a spectacular crowd magnet for both tourists and locals. William Thorsell recognized the need for iconic architecture but interpreted it differently. He believed that great architecture was necessary because he believes that the ROM is one of the world's most important museums (again, much like the optimism of the ROM's 1914 founders) and must be bold in whatever it does. Not only did the ROM need a bold building, but Thorsell influenced public opinion by his insistence that Toronto needed dynamic buildings such as the ROM if it was to be a contemporary city with a world presence.

To achieve this spectacular end product, with no funding in place for RenROM, Thorsell understood that the ROM also needed a fundraising campaign; a semi-public architect-selection process would be an opportune way to generate wide interest and launch the campaign. This dramatic beginning was inspired by a visit of senior ROM staff to MoMA in New York. Lessons were learned from MoMA's director, Glenn

Lowry, who had taken a "sketchbook approach" to MoMA's architect-selection process—architects' ideas were made accessible to the public for discussion via brief visual presentations, or sketchbooks.

Aside from the architectural significance of the Michael Lee-Chin Crystal, RenROM is also a fundraising landmark. At a time when most Toronto institutions (the Canadian Opera Company, the Art Gallery of Ontario, the Ontario College of Art and Design, the Royal Conservatory of Music, and the Gardiner Museum) were engaged in major fundraising campaigns, the ROM expected to fund 75 per cent of its capital costs from non-government sources.

The design-selection process generated 52 "expressions of interest" from its June 26, 2001, call, including some of the world's most prominent practitioners: Cesar Pelli, Kohn Pedersen Fox, Skidmore, Owings & Merrill, Foster + Partners, Jean Nouvel, and the eventual winner, Daniel Libeskind of Studio Daniel Libeskind.

The nine-member selection committee with its larger working group reduced this long list to a dozen and announced the names on September 7; five subsequently declined to continue. The seven semi-finalists, Architetto Andrea Bruno, Bing Thom Architects, Studio Daniel Libeskind, Kohn Pedersen Fox and Associates, Michael Hopkins and Partners, Rafael Viñoly Architects (with Architects Alliance) and Skidmore, Owings & Merrill, then presented their approaches in architectural sketchbooks, displayed at the ROM beginning November 23. (Daniel Libeskind's sketchbook was used only as a cover for a series of 12 conceptual sketches rendered on napkins from the ROM's restaurant.) The three finalists selected on December 14—Italian architect Andrea Bruno, Vancouver's Bing Thom, and then Berlin-based Daniel Libeskind—showed their designs at the ROM, in *Views of Our Future: Architectural Finalists,* starting on February 8, 2002. The public flocked to see the sketchbooks and many took the opportunity provided to give written comments. The architects presented their cases individually and answered questions from the public on three consecutive nights at the ROM, February 11, 12, and 13.

To ensure that the budget and construction assumptions of proposals were realistic, a construction-management firm was hired prior to the selection of an architect. Vanbots Construction Corporation became an important resource as finalists' proposals were reviewed. As well, it was decided that managing the project through a construction-management system, rather than a more standard contractor-client relationship, would offer more flexibility and cost control for a complex project with unique engineering and building issues.

And the winner is? William Thorsell explained the choice of Daniel Libeskind on February 26, 2002: "After technical reports on costs, disruption, maintenance, and programmatic fit, Libeskind was the cheapest, the fastest to build, the least disruptive, and met the program requirements for galleries most creatively and intelligently. Though his had the most dramatic appearance, it was the only one that didn't tear down the ROM's centre block." Most telling, it addressed the ROM's most basic architectural need at the time. "It created a landscape of desire inviting people to come in."

The winning scheme also permitted the ROM to remain open during construction, and it did. The lesson of the ROM's nearly two-year closure for the previous renovation and expansion had been profound—when you close it takes years to rebuild attendance.

Sharpe Centre for Design, Ontario College of Art & Design, Toronto, designed by Will Alsop of Alsop Architects, with Robbie Young + Wright Architects Inc., 2005.

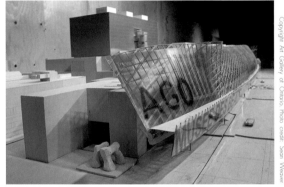

Art Gallery of Ontario, architectural model of the exterior by Frank Gehry.

Four Seasons Centre for the Performing Arts, Toronto, designed by A. J. (Jack) Diamond of Diamond and Schmitt Architects Inc., 2006.

Gardiner Museum, Toronto, alterations and additions by Kuwabara Payne McKenna Blumberg Architects, 2006. (Originally designed by Keith Wagland in 1984.)

On June 20, 2002, the ROM board of trustees approved phase one of RenROM's transformation project. Studio Daniel Libeskind would joint venture with Toronto-based Bregman + Hamann Architects to realize the project. The heritage architecture consultant would be Toronto-based ERA Architects Inc. Haley Sharpe Design, based in Leicester, England, were to be the exhibit designers. Glasbau Hahn GMBH & Co. of Frankfurt, Germany, was chosen for the enormous task of manufacturing the new display cases.

The Michael Lee-Chin Crystal was to add more than 56,000 square feet of new permanent gallery space, more than 93,000 square feet of additional public space, plus 24,000 square feet of support space for a total of almost 174,000 square feet.

The winning scheme continued to evolve as any initial proposal does when tuned to meet budget, program, and construction realities. One of the crystals, crystal six—it would have extended over the existing curatorial block and was primarily cosmetic, but it would also have housed new administration offices and meeting rooms—was eliminated. The main staircase and atrium, once entwined, were separated to become the J. F. Driscoll Family Stair of Wonders and the Spirit House. The total floor area was reduced by eight per cent to correspond with program requirements, although the remaining five crystal shapes were basically unchanged. On February 8, 2003, *Views of Our Future* exhibited an update of Libeskind's plans for the ROM.

Providing physical access for people with disabilities was a priority as the design for the Crystal addition evolved. Christine Karcza, a ROM trustee, spearheaded the initiative that included ROM staff and volunteers as well as designers from Studio Daniel Libeskind and Haley Sharpe. This project involved community consultations as well as research of international best practices. The goal was to create a world-class visitor experience through the application of universal design, that is, to make the building universally accessible. The Crystal began with an intrinsic accessibility advantage. Because the new plaza, beginning at the Bloor Street curb, would continue through the lobby to the existing Samuel Hall❖Currelly Gallery as a gentle upward slope, there were to be no steps on the ground floor. Karcza and her team built on this, reviewing every aspect of the building, and the exhibits, to ensure that best practices were implemented, ones that typically went beyond what current building codes required.

As the plans for the project were finalized there was a controversial change to the building's cladding. The jigsaw pattern of opaque, translucent, and transparent roofing material—it was never specified in the concept stage of the design—was reconsidered. This cladding was revised to become strips of silver-anodized aluminum extrusions approximately one foot in width and separated by 1.5-inch spaces (which function as conduits to the drainage system running underneath), with transparent, boldly framed windows. The translucent areas were eliminated and the transparent glass concentrated on the Bloor Street frontage. The original cladding approach allowed too much damaging light into galleries, particularly through translucent areas. As well, the initial surface could not effectively cope with drainage, an imperative concern, given the snow and ice of an Ontario winter.

In addition to the built-in drainage system under the new cladding, each band of anodized aluminum was slightly raised on edge, facing *uphill*, so that ice and snow could not easily slide down, creating an avalanche that sooner or later would impact pedestrians.

Libeskind maintains that the "crystal" moniker always corresponded to the crystal shapes rather than to the image of sparkling, transparent crystal. But the public's image was of a Crystal Palace–like structure, and it is understandable that many did not like what seemed to be an about-face when the design became more solid and metallic with the new cladding. The transparent image of the winning project was abetted by an internally illuminated model. Particularly in photographs that showed what the building might look like at night, it did suggest a mostly glass structure. Even though the change of cladding was just that, it robbed many of the building they believed had won the competition. For this constituency, the beginning of construction exacerbated their discomfort. As massive steel girders were lifted into place, the steel jungle emerging appeared to be just the opposite of the light, airy envelope the initial images had suggested.

With a project ready to build, a Jamaican-born entrepreneur, Michael Lee-Chin, jump-started the fundraising campaign by donating $30 million on April 2, 2003. The addition became the Michael Lee-Chin Crystal, and the interior atrium, the Hyacinth Gloria Chen Crystal Court, is named for his mother. The Honourable Hilary M. Weston, a former lieutenant governor of Ontario, was chosen to lead the fundraising campaign, with Hilary and Galen Weston and The W. Garfield Weston Foundation contributing a total of $20 million. On May 28, 2003, the project began with the demolition of the Terrace Galleries, which continued until November.

While every large, institutional project has its construction challenges, the Michael Lee-Chin Crystal's were unique, beginning with the complexity of the steel structure and the extraordinary joinery, where often five or six beams collide. Daniel Libeskind created form, and then the form was realized—technology determined little but was expected to facilitate a lot. This did not make for simple solutions. While the technology was conventional, its application was not because the level of precision required to implement it was unprecedented. ARUP, a London-based global company of designers, engineers, planners, and business consultants, provided the conceptual basis for structural, electrical, and mechanical engineering. They then worked with Canadian companies: structural engineers Halsall Associates, electrical engineers Mulvey and Banani International, and mechanical engineers The Mitchell Partnership.

Walters Inc., a steel company located in Hamilton, Ontario, was the steel fabricator, a key role as their job involved not only manufacturing the steel joists but being able to translate engineering plans via computers on the shop floor into precision-crafted materials that, when they were taken to the site, were allowed practically no tolerance for error. Lasers were used to sight position coordinates in order to move beams into correct alignment.

Beams jutting at all angles, sloped walls and windows, and the use of materials and construction techniques most workers had never before encountered—this was not a recipe for a stress-free building project. From the outset it was challenging; the building's design apparently allowed for the use of only one large crane. The operator often worked blind, relying on radio and hand signals from the crew below for guidance. Passersby on the site marvelled during construction at workers in safety harnesses and climbing equipment rappelled down the steel structure and then, later, on the waterproofed exterior, wearing soft-soled shoes to prevent damage to surfaces. The building's steel skeleton was officially marked by a "topping off" ceremony on July 12, 2005.

On December 26, 2005, ten galleries were opened in the ROM's renovated historic galleries, including the Daphne Cockwell Gallery of Canada: First Peoples and the Asian Suite of Galleries.

Beams jutting at all angles, sloped walls and windows, and the use of materials and construction techniques most workers had never before encountered—this was not a recipe for a stress-free building project

■ The tip of the Michael Lee-Chin Crystal is 120 feet or ten storeys high and overhangs the Bloor Street West sidewalk at a height equivalent of nine storeys above the ground. The base of the Crystal is 32 feet below grade.

■ Unlike most buildings, the Crystal has few walls that meet the floor or ceiling at right angles.

■ Approximately 3500 tons of steel and 38 tons of bolts were used to create the skeleton of the Crystal. Roughly 317,800 cubic feet of concrete were poured. There are 1800 square feet of glass on the exterior for its 52 windows. The cladding consists of approximately 90,000 square feet of extruded aluminum, one foot wide.

■ During peak construction periods, approximately 180 workers were on site, with up to 30 working on the steel structure alone. The confined size of the construction site did not permit all the materials to arrive at once. The steel beams, each unique and ranging in length from 3 feet to 82 feet, were typically on site for only a day prior to their installation.

In a conventional structural-steel building, part of the steel frame is erected and then the pouring of the concrete floors can begin. With the Crystal, all the steel had to be completely in place, and supported (shored), before the concrete could be poured and the cladding added. Until all the concrete was in place, the steel structure had to be temporarily braced because the concrete is intrinsic to the stability of the steel. This apparently added six months to the construction time compared to a standard steel and concrete structure.

Finishing the project's interior was no easier: there were many tight corners and even tighter ceiling-to-floor spaces where machinery was difficult to position or where it was awkward to work. Even tasks that do-it-yourself types manage at home were anything but standard. Dry-walling walls that overhang and slope away ten or more feet meant elaborate scaffolding had to be used. As any contractor will lament, it's not easy to create perfect seams when you have no right angles, and there are few in the Crystal.

While the new is never easy, the fact that the cladding or building skin was supplied via a design/build contract with Josef Gartner USA, L.P., and manufactured in Germany, did not help meet a schedule that was already as tight as possible to limit the time the Museum was not operating at full capacity. In 2006, the construction slowed; very little could proceed until the building was watertight, and frustration grew as the project fell behind schedule. The cladding was complicated; it has three layers and is more than three feet thick, the bottom layer being the moisture-proof seal. When the cladding did arrive, the extruded brushed aluminum had an unexpected variation of tone. While milled at the same plant, the aluminum came from different sources and included recycled material; hence, there are variations in its composition. The unintended tonal variation gives texture to the building's skin and inadvertently mimics the subtle variation in colour in the stone cladding of the historic wings.

Just as the building was nearing completion, two additional Libeskind elements were added. A new, limited-edition custom chair was created by the architect for the Spirit House and called, naturally enough, the Spirit House Chair. Constructed of 14-gauge stainless steel, it weighs 180 pounds and is manufactured by Klaus Neinkamper Ltd. of Toronto. Libeskind also designed a chandelier encrusted with Swarovski crystals to be installed over the grand staircase on the Michael Lee-Chin Crystal's fourth floor leading from the Roloff Beny Gallery to the Crystal 5 Restaurant Lounge.

The building had its "Architectural Opening & Building Dedication" at sunset on June 2, 2007. Governor General Michaëlle Jean officially opened the building in front of a crowd estimated at 40,000. The event also launched the first Luminato Festival in Toronto. While the Crystal's shell and main public areas were complete, most of the galleries were still to be installed. From the Saturday evening of the Crystal's opening, the Museum stayed open all night and through Sunday. Admission was free and more than 25,000 people streamed through to see the Crystal inside.

At the outset of the project, the expectation was that it would open for Christmas 2005. After reconsideration of the engineering approach, the opening was planned for December 2006 and the project, largely because of delays with the installation of the cladding, was ultimately six months late in terms of the revised schedule. This delay, coupled with significant increases in material costs, especially steel, pushed the final project cost from a budget of $216 million to $256 million, of which the Michael Lee-Chin Crystal represented $135 million.

While the public was fascinated by the Crystal, and many admitted that they liked it more after being inside, there was a divergence of opinion about the building. The range of opinion was reflected by the critic's reviews.

Lisa Rochon, architecture critic for the *Globe and Mail,* called the Crystal "hard, aggressive and in your face. It cantilevers dangerously over the street, shifting the ground from under our feet." Rochon also echoed the feelings about the building's not being the Crystal Palace–like structure some assumed it would be: "Had it been clad in glass with the cacophony of steel beams exposed to the public, the museum would clearly represent an astonishing triumph." As for the interior ambiance, she said, "There is more angst on the inside where windows cut like jagged scars across gallery walls, where steel grating makes for an uneasy, noisy floor on the many catwalks."

Christopher Hume, architecture critic for the *Toronto Star,* had a much more positive impression:

This is 21st century architecture at its most brilliant . . . Though he [Libeskind] can be rightly criticized for approaching architecture as an exercise in applied design, the Crystal shows Libeskind's remarkable ability to create beautiful spaces, if not exquisite objects . . . Libeskind has also managed to bring a sense of urbanity to the interior of the Crystal, which reads like a series of spaces joined by walkways, bridges, vantage points and windows. Clearly, the building was designed to provide maximum pleasure to visitors, to be an artifact in its own right, not simply a receptacle, the "black box" that obsessed curators for far too long.

Libeskind's architecture, according to Hume, is "an architecture of the unexpected, even provocative." Hume's summary of the Crystal likely represented the public consensus when it opened: "Though it won't thrill everyone, the advent of the Crystal will be good for Toronto. If nothing else, it reminds us that growth involves risk. It isn't just the institution that has taken a change here, it's the whole city."

Clearly, the building was designed to provide maximum pleasure to visitors, to be an artifact in its own right, not simply a receptacle, the "black box" that obsessed curators for far too long

Construction of the façade along Philosophers' Walk, 1911.

Looking from the south, the 1933 addition is to the right, along Queen's Park, and forms a "T" as it connects to the original 1914 building along Philosophers' Walk.

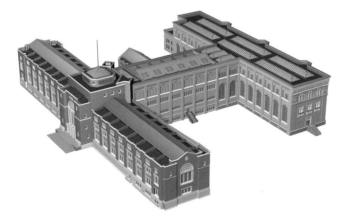

1933 | The 1933 addition (now called the Hilary and Galen Weston Wing and the Weston Family Wing) was designed by the Toronto firm of Chapman and Oxley. Their plan more than doubled the size of the Museum and moved the main entrance to Queen's Park, the front doors now opening to a remarkable mosaic-tiled rotunda. This second phase of the Museum was constructed during the Great Depression and it became a make-work project; much was done by hand that would not otherwise have been. The Province of Ontario also stipulated that building materials be local. The façade, for instance, was faced with Credit Valley and Queenston limestone.

View of the 1914 ROM from Bloor Street and Avenue Road, with main entrance, from Bloor Street, at right.

1914 | The Royal Ontario Museum's first building was designed by Toronto architects Darling and Pearson and was officially opened to the public by the Duke of Connaught, Governor General of Canada, in 1914. The Museum was a joint venture between the University of Toronto and the Province of Ontario. Its site, on the university campus, was north of the developed part of the city but was not considered too distant for Museum visitors. The entrance was on Bloor Street. The original windows along Philosophers' Walk, covered over in the 1970s, were reopened during the RenROM project.

Looking east towards Queen's Park, 1931, with the new Garden Court wing for the Chinese tomb complex in the foreground. This space became a hall for temporary exhibitions in 1959 and the Chinese tomb complex was moved outdoors.

The Queen Elizabeth II Terrace Galleries under construction, c. 1981.

The "conversation" between the Michael Lee-Chin Crystal and the Hilary and Galen Weston Wing is clearly heard from the corner of Bloor Street and Queen's Park.

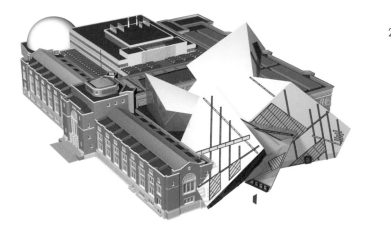

2007 | Planning for the Michael Lee-Chin Crystal addition and the renovation of the ROM's heritage buildings began with the finalization of a new master plan for the Museum in 2000 and a competition to select an architect for the project in 2001. Studio Daniel Libeskind with Bregman + Hamman Architects, a joint venture, were selected in 2002. The first phase of construction was the demolition of the Queen Elizabeth II Terrace Galleries, which began later that year. While the metal-clad Libeskind-designed addition is a contrast to the brick and stone 1914 and 1933 structures, the interior plan echoes the original Beaux Arts master plan prepared by Darling and Pearson and gives the 2007 ROM a renewed circulation logic. The 2007 addition moves the main entrance back to Bloor Street and provides significant new public amenities, as well as additional gallery space.

The Queen Elizabeth II Terrace Galleries from the north, between the northeast wing (1933, left), and the northwest wing (1914).

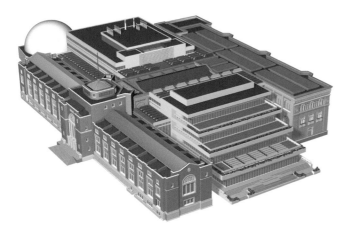

1968 | Colonel Sam McLaughlin, a pioneer of the Canadian automobile manufacturing industry, donated the funds in 1964 to build a planetarium. Stone and Webster Canada Limited, an engineering firm, designed the structure with Allward & Gouinlock as consulting architects. The McLaughlin Planetarium opened in 1968 and closed in 1995. The site will eventually be redeveloped as part of RenROM.

The next addition to the ROM began construction in 1978 and had two components. In the south courtyard, 1984 | a curatorial centre (now called the Louise Hawley Stone Curatorial Centre) was built with offices, laboratories, work areas, and collections storage. In the north courtyard, a new block of galleries was built facing Bloor Street, with a garden adjacent to the street. The Terrace Galleries opened to the public in 1982, and then were officially opened by the Queen in 1984, when they were renamed the Queen Elizabeth II Terrace Galleries.

First floor, 1914 building, 2005. The renovation stripped the heritage building back to its basic shell.

BOLD VISION: INTERVIEW WITH DANIEL LIBESKIND

If architecture fails, if it is pedestrian and lacks imagination and power, it tells only one story, that of its own making: how it was built, detailed, financed. But a great building, like great literature or poetry or music, can tell the story of the human soul. It can make us see the world in a wholly new way, change it forever. It can awaken our desires, propose imaginary trajectories, and say to a child who has seen little or been nowhere, hey, the world can be very different from what you ever imagined.

—Daniel Libeskind

Daniel Libeskind, Architect

Born in postwar Poland in 1946, Daniel Libeskind, B.Arch., M.A., BDA, AIA, became an American citizen in 1965. He studied music in Israel (on the America-Israel Cultural Foundation Scholarship) and in New York, becoming a virtuoso performer. He left music to study architecture, receiving his professional architectural degree in 1970 from the Cooper Union for the Advancement of Science and Art in New York City. He received a postgraduate degree in History and Theory of Architecture at the School of Comparative Studies at Essex University (England) in 1972.

In 1989, Libeskind won the competition for the Jewish Museum Berlin, which opened to the public in September 2001 to wide public acclaim and launched his international career. The city museum of Osnabrück, Germany, The Felix Nussbaum Haus, opened in July 1998. In July 2002, the Imperial War Museum North in Manchester, England, opened. Atelier Weil, a private atelier/gallery, opened in Mallorca, Spain, in September 2003. The Graduate Student Centre at the London Metropolitan University opened in March 2004, and the Danish Jewish Museum opened in Copenhagen in June 2004. Tangent, an office tower for the Hyundai Development Corporation, opened in Seoul, Korea, in February 2005. Memoria e Luce, a 9/11 memorial in Padua, Italy, opened on September 11, 2005. The Wohl Centre, Bar Ilan University, Tel Aviv, Israel, opened in October, 2005. And the Extension to the Denver Art Museum, Denver, Colorado, opened to the public in October of 2006.

Daniel Libeskind projects currently under construction include the Contemporary Jewish Museum in San Francisco; several of the components of the World Trade Center master plan; the Creative Media Centre for the City University of Hong Kong; a retail complex in Las Vegas, Nevada; and the Sukkah, an extension to the Jewish Museum Berlin.

Libeskind has taught and lectured at many universities. He has held such positions as the Frank O. Gehry Chair at the University of Toronto, Professor at the Hochschule für Gestaltung, Karlsruhe, Germany, the Cret Chair at the University of Pennsylvania, and the Louis Kahn Chair at Yale University. In 2004, Daniel Libeskind was appointed the first Cultural Ambassador for Architecture by the U.S. Department of State, as part of the CultureConnect Program.

Bold Vision: Interview with Daniel Libeskind, 2006, 2007

Kelvin Browne: What were your first impressions of the Renaissance ROM project? What interested you in the architectural competition?

Daniel Libeskind: I knew the ROM from when I first lived in Toronto, from 1971 to 1973, and then during the years 1977 and 1985 when I continued to teach at the University of Toronto. I took my children there many times. I certainly understood what the Museum wanted to do when I read the competition brief. I knew it was a brilliant place but a neglected site, a neglected museum in a wonderful city that required something powerful at such an important location. The brief addressed what needed to be done in a direct manner and I had complete and immediate empathy with the ROM's goals.

KB: What aspects of the brief most excited you?

DL: Great cities have great museums. The brief made this connection between Toronto and the Museum. The Louvre, The British Museum, the Metropolitan—the major museums are always centres of energy and places of pride for their cities. This translates into a responsibility for a museum to have a democratic responsiveness to people and to physically manifest a civic role. Today, a museum is more than the treasures inside; it's a generator of creativity. Fostering creativity is a central role of the contemporary city. A museum must spur the imagination and be accessible, emotionally and physically, to everyone.

The brief didn't mince its words describing what needed to be done. It said *we need something remarkable,* not just more gallery space. It was compelling and certainly made me want to get involved.

I responded positively to my client as well as the brief. I always say I'm only as good as my client. A great client is essential if an architect is to do great work. Inspired clients—ones who say more than *I like this* or *I don't like that,* ones who are deeply involved, who are culturally engaged with architecture and understand that architecture can be inspired by them—appreciate their role as collaborators.

KB: Where in the process did the crystal imagery emerge? Did you consider other approaches as you studied the programmatic requirements?

DL: When I walked through the Museum after reading the brief, my eye accidentally lighted on a crystal. Quite literally, that's when I got the idea. That's when I wanted to do some napkin sketches—very passionate sketches. I wanted these images to capture what I thought would be the right burst of energy on this site. It wasn't until I came back to the site that I thought, *how do we address all the issues, all the programmatic requirements, how do we make a building out of these sketches?* Interestingly, this initial wave of inspiration is very close in many, many ways to the final form of the building after all of the program and technical aspects had been resolved.

Today, a museum is more than the treasures inside; it's a generator of creativity

Jewish Museum Berlin, designed by Daniel Libeskind, completed in 1999, opened in 2001.

KB: You've said that something "spectacular" is required to attract all kinds of people to a museum, especially those who wouldn't typically go. Does this mean turning a museum into entertainment?

DL: The spectacular initiates you to the possibilities of the museum before you contemplate its depths. It draws you in. But there is at the ROM, and there should be, a blurring of the lines so there is a new perception of how all the aspects of the museum, including the commercial ones, the ones that let children play, and so on, come together. They're all part of the museum experience.

The museum remains a place of contemplation, of course, but the public wants to be entertained, wants to have a solitary experience, wants to interact, wants to go to restaurants, wants many things of a museum and, in these ways, the museum is a microcosm of the world. It can offer all these things and be spectacular too.

KB: What about architectural precedents for the ROM project?

DL: I don't think I had specific architectural precedents in mind. I was thinking of crystals—crystals are the most perfect forms and their shapes appear frequently in my buildings. They're luminous; they absorb light as they reflect and refract it.

There are many elements of public buildings that I love that are in the design, too, not literally, but they're there. Certain spaces are like the spaces of a cathedral. Or the Taj Mahal. I visited the Taj Mahal in 2004. The perfection of its form, the quality of light it radiates—I was totally overwhelmed. It reminded me of the Crystal. I joke that the Taj Mahal is retrospective proof that we did the right thing with the ROM.

Of course, I have many favourite museums. I like Sir John Soane's Museum in London, the Kimbell Art Museum in Fort Worth, the Castelvecchio Museum by Carlo Scarpa in Verona, the Museo Archeologico Nazionale in Naples—and of course, the Jewish Museum in Berlin. They're there, in the ROM's design. I can't get away from myself. I am who I am and I bring it all with me to a project.

KB: The ROM project has evolved from the proposal that won the competition. For some, it's become less of a crystal.

DL: Architecture is an evolutionary art. Bad architects build exactly what they proposed. The architects I admire work through the complexity of the project and navigate, sometimes through turbulent water. This kind of process makes architecture truly civic rather than just a folly on a grand scale. We've all worked very hard—the Museum staff, the technical experts—to evolve the project to meet all of its constituencies' needs.

For instance, the design of the ROM galleries evolved in consultation with curators. They've evolved to accommodate the collections and highlight special displays, such as the dinosaurs. But the galleries were not created by the objects so much as they have been refined to be a container adaptable to different and varied artifacts. The galleries accommodate but are not specific to the objects they display. They're not limited by the objects.

KB: The cladding changed and the amount of glazing is reduced from the original proposal. The crystal palace connection that many made with the original proposal isn't there.

DL: People often look at models as a miniature reality. You can't increase the size of even the most perfect model and expect that it is the building as it will be in space. This is the fundamental problem with a model relative to a real building, regardless of any changes that are made to the design. A model is only a simulation and for those who don't know architecture, they believe it's a confection that will be made real. But there's another reality to a built building.

Of course, the ROM has a different cladding then we initially thought, but the point of the model, the crystalline form, has not changed. There have been very few compromises. The intent of the model is the intent of the realized building.

KB: What impact have the ROM's collections had on your design?

The ROM's collections present an incredible challenge; it's like the Museum of Natural History and the Metropolitan Museum all in one building. I spent a lot of time thinking about this. The building certainly has to reconcile these two very different collections and be a meditation on the relationship of nature and civilization.

Circulation has been influenced by the collections. How will you use the galleries and in what sequence will you experience the objects? How do you make the galleries penetrate each other so that relationships between the spaces flow? You want the spaces to have generosity but also legibility, to accommodate and be directional.

It's a complicated building to understand, particularly in plan, yet it is easy to understand when you're in it.

KB: As you note, the plans for the ROM look complicated. Were computers an important design tool for you?

DL: Architects need plans. Le Corbusier said the plan is the generator of architecture, but I've never really agreed with this comment fully. The plan is merely a two-dimensional representation of architecture—you can't really design a sculptural form with a plan because sculpture is a moving space.

I recognize that many buildings today won't get built without computers. I work with computers, but I design in a very traditional way, by drawing. By hand. This is a gesture that comes from within and from without, that connects your mind with your eye, and the image of a building with the technical possibilities for it. Nothing will ever replace the hand as a design tool. The hand is still the most formidable extension of the mind.

I know many people create architecture by manipulating possibilities generated by a computer. Would they say I can't design a building because I have only a pencil? Of course, a computer has made it easier to build buildings: to rationalize the design process, to make it more economic, and to make it possible to coordinate various geometries so that a structure is producible.

Computers plague architecture. They're fast. They're fun. Architecture, however, is a cultural discipline. It's rooted in tradition and if you don't get in touch with that tradition, architecture becomes an odd experiment.

The spectacular initiates you to the possibilities of the museum before you contemplate its depths. It draws you in

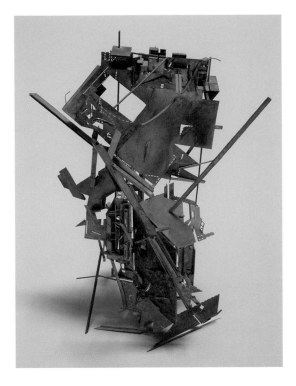

Micromégas, 1979, Model 2, #3 leakage (metal model, fragment), Daniel Libeskind.

Line of Fire, Geneva, 1988, Model 3, Daniel Libeskind.

Computers don't help you get in touch with that tradition necessarily. I said in *Breaking Ground* that "you can provide the chords and specify the vibrations, the music is elsewhere. Between the technique and the art is a mystery." What I mean is that if you hear the piano when you're listening to a performance, it's not a very good performance. When you hear the music, the technique disappears. I think the technique of making a building should disappear in its making and its construction. It's true in all the arts. Unfortunately, the computer is all too evident in many building designs today.

More than computers, models are important to me. There have been hundreds of them of all shapes and sizes for the ROM project. We worked with them to help us find ways to create spaces that glow with the crystal light. These models were both technical as well as architectural experiments. It's not only physical modes we're testing but emotional ones.

KB: Describe the ROM design or the most important components of it as you conceive them.

DL: The Museum is a kind of promenade through various elements—the entry, the Spirit House, the Stair of Wonders—it's an extension of the street, an extension of the city vibrating all around us. You will feel the building before you enter it, a vibration, from quite far. When you live in another city, see an image of it, and then come to visit, it will have a dramatic vector that will move it beyond what you expect it to be. The response will be visceral and not depend on precedence. Walter Benjamin mentioned the *aura* of a work of art. This isn't something we can understand easily in a deterministic, materialistic society where everything can be quantified and objectified. But it's this quality, this aura, that a great building like the ROM must have.

The ROM is a series of experiences. An architect is a choreographer of these experiences. How do the visitors come in the door, buy a ticket, check their coats, buy coffee, and so on. It's a continuum of finely nuanced and completely interconnected moments.

When you enter, the lobby and the Hyacinth Gloria Chen Crystal Court present the vertical organization. It's a web of mystery. It's not like some big museum buildings where you enter and see everything, but rather you enter, sense it, and understand it even though it's not all obvious or exposed. The heritage buildings will appear luminous and crystal-like, very chiselled, from the lobby, and you'll understand how it all fits together.

The temporary display area [Garfield Weston Exhibition Hall], one floor below the lobby, could have been a typical anonymous space. Instead, it has qualities similar to the galleries above. This isn't space that adds nothing to a show. Rather, it has a character and will enhance each show installed there. Every blockbuster here will be definitely at the ROM and not feel like it could be in any big, empty place.

KB: What were the challenges of designing the Crystal?

DL: A building like this has never been built before. There is no precedent for structure at these angles. There is no precedent for dealing with snow loads on these kinds of roofs or on surfaces that jut out the way these do or galleries that cantilever, literally, over one of the main streets of a city. There's little precedent for the relationship between scales, between the grandiose and the very intimate, a corner that's made for one or two people.

The cladding is not merely cladding but three-dimensional architecture people will see; this is new. The new is always a challenge.

KB: The Crystal addition to the ROM elicits a strong reaction from people, positive and negative. Did you anticipate this?

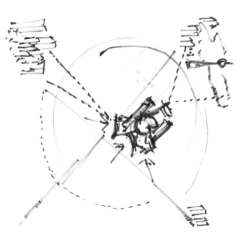

DL: Any artistic thought, if worthy of creation, is not going to fit right in because it isn't going to be like something else; it's not more of the same thing. It's got to be a bit difficult, at least at first. It's going to jump at you. Friction is inevitable if it's good because it's something that wakes you up. Public discourse and even controversy are good things. I don't intend to shock but I believe an encounter with the unfamiliar is liberating. It opens you to fresh experiences and allows a new relationship with the past and all the remarkable things the ROM houses.

KB: Renaissance ROM is both a new building and a renovation to a heritage structure. Did relating to an existing building change your approach compared to how you might consider a tabula rasa project?

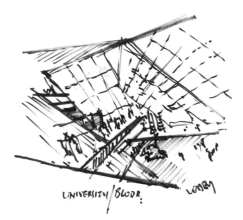

DL: I never saw the Crystal addition as a stand-alone building. I've seen many additions where the new building is just something else, not part of a whole. As an architect, I've worked with many heritage buildings, including the Jewish Museum. I think it's a true advantage to have an existing building, certainly much better than having an empty site. Building on a vacant site is like building on an island, in a sense, or building what might otherwise be a free-standing sculpture.

KB: When you were preparing your competition entry, were there aspects of the design you thought central to addressing the brief or essential to the building's success?

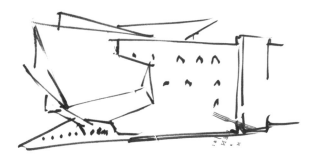

DL: I was aware in the existing ROM of the difficulty visitors had orienting themselves. Because of this, I was not initially focused on creating an incredible space for the Chinese collection, for instance, but rather on making a promenade—both topographical and mental—that allows visitors to sense the totality of the collection and orient themselves without having to resort to masses of signage. This promenade would give an experiential understanding of the place, and people would feel comfortable as they began their visit. There is the pleasure of discovery when there's an underlying order; this was my goal for a visitor's experience.

Another focus is more difficult to describe. A museum is not merely a collection of functions. It has to have a certain atmosphere—you can put different names to it—spiritual, exciting, awe-inspiring. However you describe it, the crucial thing is that it must be there. It's this vibration that makes us respond to more than just the objects and, instead, to the totality of the experience and what the collections symbolize. I think this is evident in all the great museums. It's this atmosphere that shapes the way people perceive themselves in relation to the artifacts on display. It helps visitors open themselves up to a new experience.

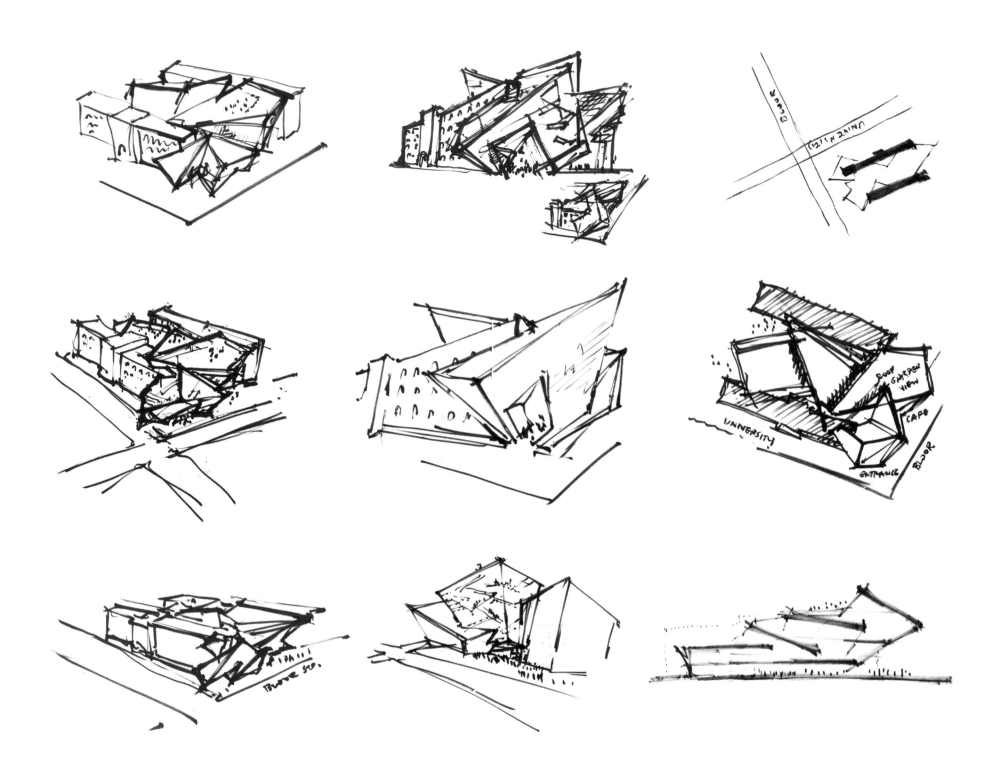

Pages 152–53: Daniel Libeskind's napkin drawings—his "sketchbook" submission—went on display at the ROM with the submissions of six other semi-finalists on November 23, 2001.

KB: How does your approach to the ROM correspond to other projects? The Denver Art Museum seems to have many similarities, at least on the surface. Or the proposed addition to the Victoria and Albert Museum. There seems to be a similar relationship proposed between the new and the existing building.

DL: Every musical composition is made with notes but each composition can still be very different, even though they are made of these similar components. I certainly have a signature, harmonies that I respond to and that I use in my work. So yes, there are similarities; if there weren't, it would be anonymous architecture or architecture that a committee could create.

That said, while there are similarities, the minute you see the Denver Art Museum or especially when you step inside the Frederic C. Hamilton Building, you know it is a very different building from the ROM. In fact, the proposed additions to the V & A, the Denver Art Museum, and the ROM have quite different conceptual starting points. There's a progression. The Jewish Museum was a plan that became 3-D. The V & A was a ribbon, a path that unfolded to create a spatial discourse that we then enclosed. Denver was two paths, two lines that went for a walk, which we then combined with volumes. It's a hybrid of the V & A and ROM approach. The ROM is formed with volumes, crystals, and the spaces between them.

KB: What about your approach to the ROM's historical galleries? You've mentioned the conversation of the new with the existing, but what about the interior specifically? I've heard this described as a retrieval rather than restoration or renovation?

DL: I like the term retrieval for the interiors of the historic wings. There's no sense of creating a historic stage set, a place suitable for a museum a hundred years ago. However, there is a spirit in those spaces that I believe the renovation has liberated and that recovers the initial vision of the Museum. We recreated a comparable feeling to that of 1914, although, of course, to create this similar feeling requires a different space as our sensibilities are different now from what they were then.

The conservation requirements are handled on an individual-case basis, so this allows the space significant flexibility. And the sunlight through the windows is wonderful, and controllable, and objects are placed in relation to sun depending on their tolerance for it. I think the sun streaming in brings the historical wings alive.

KB: What were your impressions of the building when it was completed versus your idea/images of it while you were designing it?

DL: Architecture isn't an approximation. What is built is what was designed although there are some unexpected pleasures when you see the building from angles you didn't imagine. That said, a new building has a certain mood; it's like a newborn. It's a new being that will grow and mature and take on meaning over time. The building has tremendous energy and this will help shape its evolution.

Frederic C. Hamilton Building, Denver Art Museum, Denver, Colorado, Studio Daniel Libeskind, 2006.

People forget that harmony isn't about playing the same note over and over again—that's monotony—it's about different notes, and this is true for architecture, too

KB: The building prompted a wide range of comments when it opened, especially from architectural critics who were either very positive or very negative. What's your reaction to the reactions?

DL: Many comments seem to be about the person making the comment rather than about the building—the Crystal can be like a Rorschach test. A crystal has many facets—everyone can see something different when they look at the same thing. But isn't it wonderful that people have an emotional reaction to a building and aren't passive when they engage with it? Think of all the reactions to the most enduring works of art—most didn't begin with easy acceptance.

KB: Some said the building was a copy of the Denver Art Museum completed the year before.

DL: The people who think the ROM is like Denver have never looked at either building. They're different. Mozart isn't Haydn. Le Corbusier isn't Mies van der Rohe. My work has a signature. It's the way I think. Mies made it clear he did one kind of building. We don't think of that as a deficiency but as the core of his integrity as an architect.

KB: What are your favourite elements of the Crystal?

DL: The Crystal has so many moments. It's a collection of great moments, a collage of experiences. I recognize pieces—the Stair of Wonders, the Spirit House, the unique gallery spaces—but rather than as isolated elements I think of them as part of a total experience.

KB: A lasting impression of this project?

DL: This project had great karma. It was a true collaboration. A genius client like William Thorsell was part of this, but the whole team fostered a creative atmosphere. The city was fascinated by what we were doing— maybe my most wonderful memory is of Toronto and what a fantastic place it was to build this building.

2001–2007: THE MICHAEL LEE-CHIN CRYSTAL EMERGES

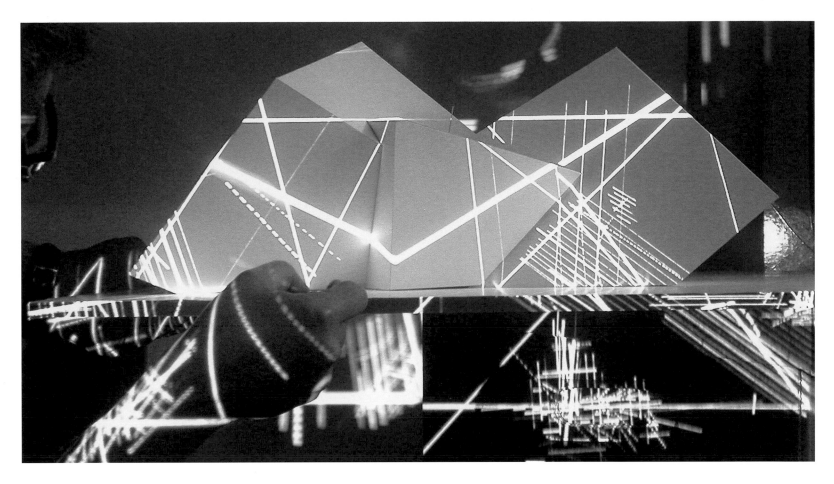

In the August/September 2002 issue of *Building*, the project architect for RenROM, Stephane Raymond of Studio Daniel Libeskind, described the process of designing the Crystal façade: "It began with the design team's crude explorations and observations of how light might land and pass through the geometry of the building by studying a piece of Russian crystal we found in a shop in Berlin. As a very rough starting point we took one of Daniel Libeskind's drawings. We made a slide of it and began to project it on the crystal."

The design team then moved to projecting the same slide on a model of the building in many iterations. From these explorations, Raymond said, a language for the skin of the Crystal began to emerge, "one where the windows or cuts sometimes wrapped planes or sometimes reflected off one plane and showed up unexpectedly on another. The language carries equally over all planes . . . on what might be considered a wall, a roof, or both, or neither, creating windows or skylights."

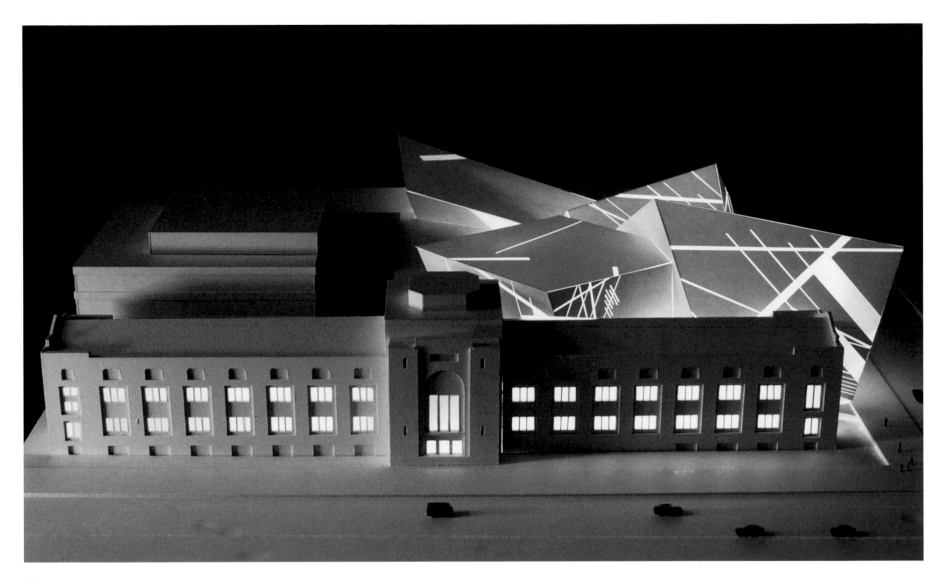

Page 158: A larger-scale model of the Michael Lee-Chin Crystal to help finalize design details, 2003. *Page 159:* A preliminary design model, 2002.

Pages 160–61: Computer-based renderings by finest-images were very accurate in describing the completed structures as can be seen when this 2007 photograph (above) of the finished building is compared to a computer-generated image created from a similar viewpoint (opposite).

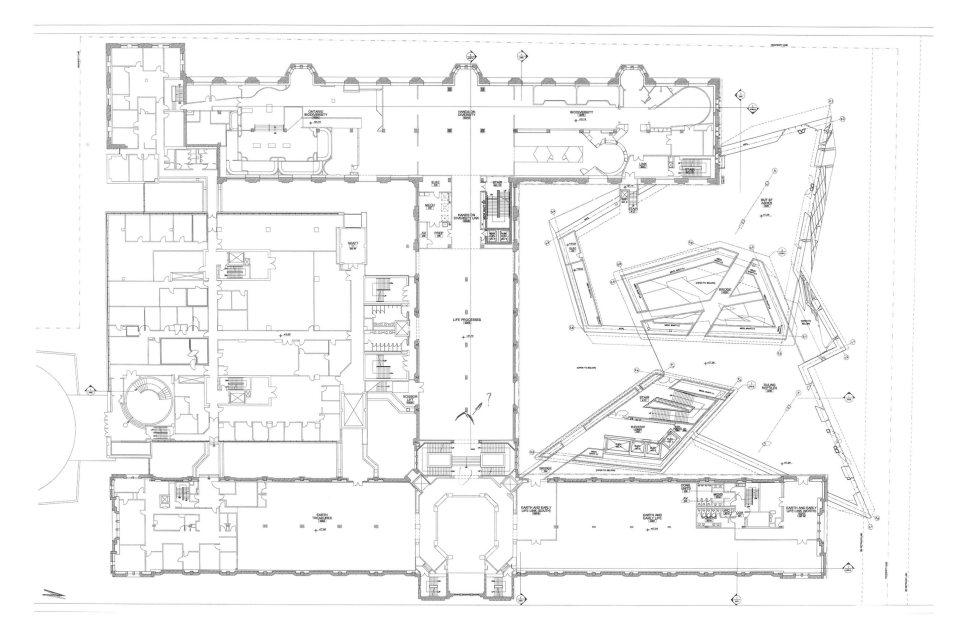

A working drawing of the Michael Lee-Chin Crystal in the context of the existing second floor. In general, two-dimensional drawings were inadequate as the sole means for designing a building as complex as the Crystal. A combination of digital-design technologies and traditional model-building skills were used instead. Physical models were constructed from digital models, and digital "3-D" models were unfolded into two dimensions.

While some companies such as Hamilton-based steel fabricator Walters Inc. had software to work from detailed digital models, most contractors required two-dimensional drawings to estimate costs and for construction purposes. Ultimately, each floor had three floor plans: A principal or general reference drawing (shown above) indicated the finished top of slab for each floor. A second plan, called a "finished floor setting-out point drawing," gave key points specified as coordinates in a three-dimensional form with each corner of the slab marked as a coordinate. A third plan, the "lower slab setting-out point drawing," used three-dimensional coordinates relating to the perimeter concrete curb. None of these plans had conventional dimensions because the crystal shapes could not be represented in a traditional manner.

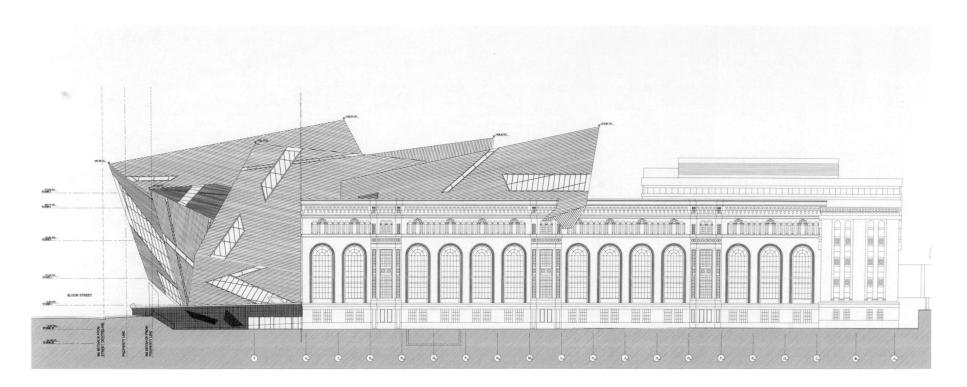

Top: An elevation from the west or Philosophers' Walk perspective that was part of the mammoth final working drawings package. *Bottom:* One of the working drawings was described as an "unfolded" model and would be cut and "folded" to create a three-dimensional rendering of the crystal structure as in this illustration.

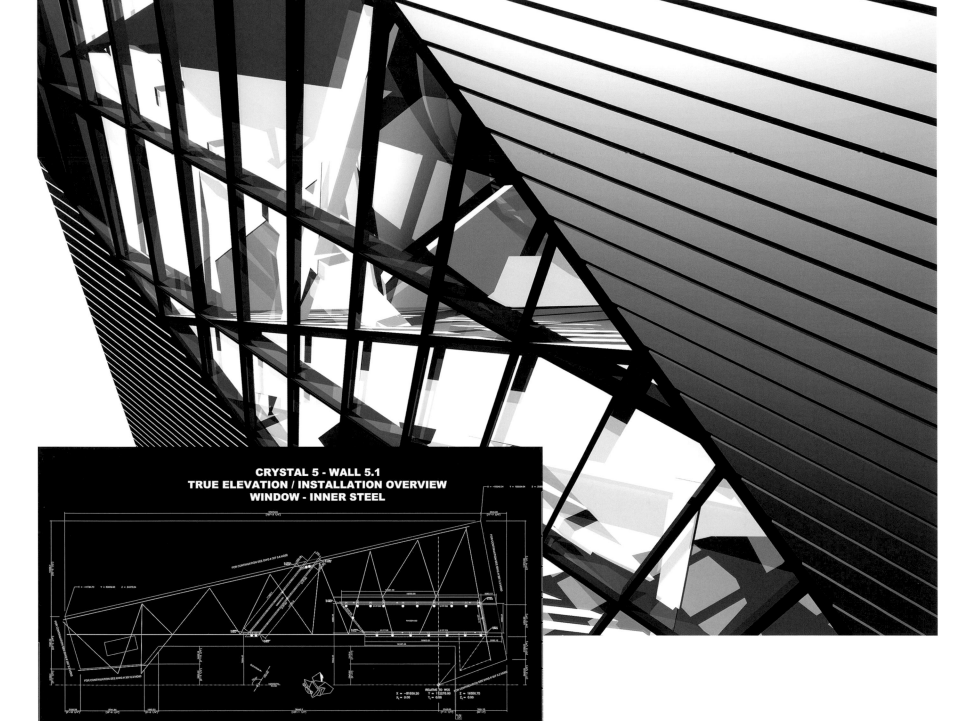

CRYSTAL 5 - WALL 5.1
TRUE ELEVATION / INSTALLATION OVERVIEW
WINDOW - INNER STEEL

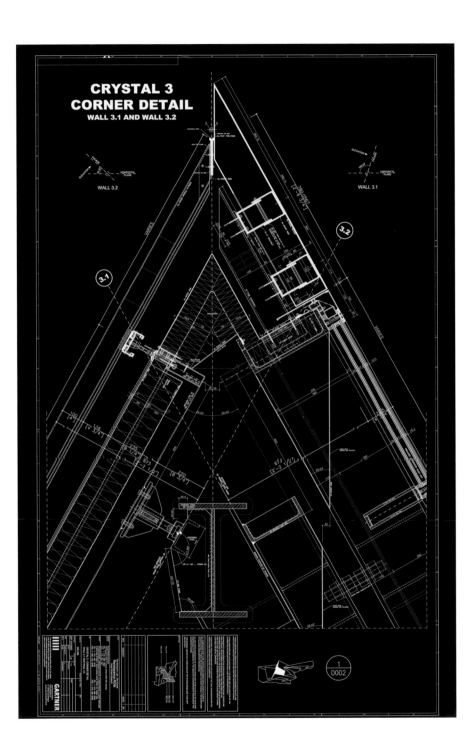

Page 164, left: A shop drawing or detailed fabrication drawing by the cladding design/building contractor Josef Gartner USA, L. P., 2006. Page 164, right: Computer-generated window study by Studio Daniel Libeskind, 2005; studies such as this helped finalize the design. Page 165, left: A shop drawing by Josef Gartner USA, L. P. details the complicated gutter system under the first layer of roofing. Page 165, right: To ensure it could cope with rain, snow, and ice, the cladding and drainage system was tested during a Canadian winter (2003) by RWDI Air Inc., an engineering consulting firm in Guelph, Ontario. Pages 166–67: The fabrication of the steel structure by Walters Inc. required detailed shop drawings that were then transposed to three dimensions with the results carefully documented by on-site photography.

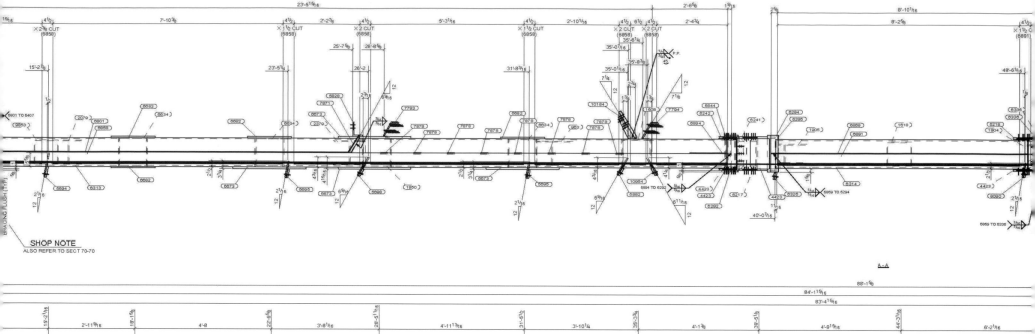

A-A

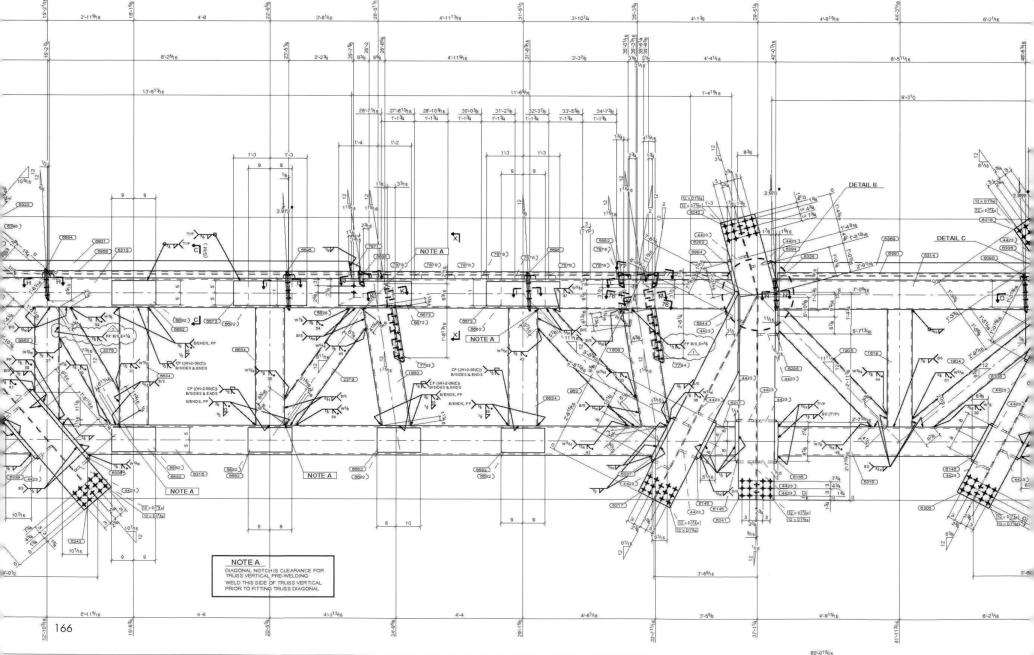

SHOP NOTE
ALSO REFER TO SECT 70-70

NOTE A
DIAGONAL NOTCH IS CLEARANCE FOR
TRUSS VERTICAL PRE-WELDING
WELD THIS SIDE OF TRUSS VERTICAL
PRIOR TO FITTING TRUSS DIAGONAL

DETAIL B

DETAIL C

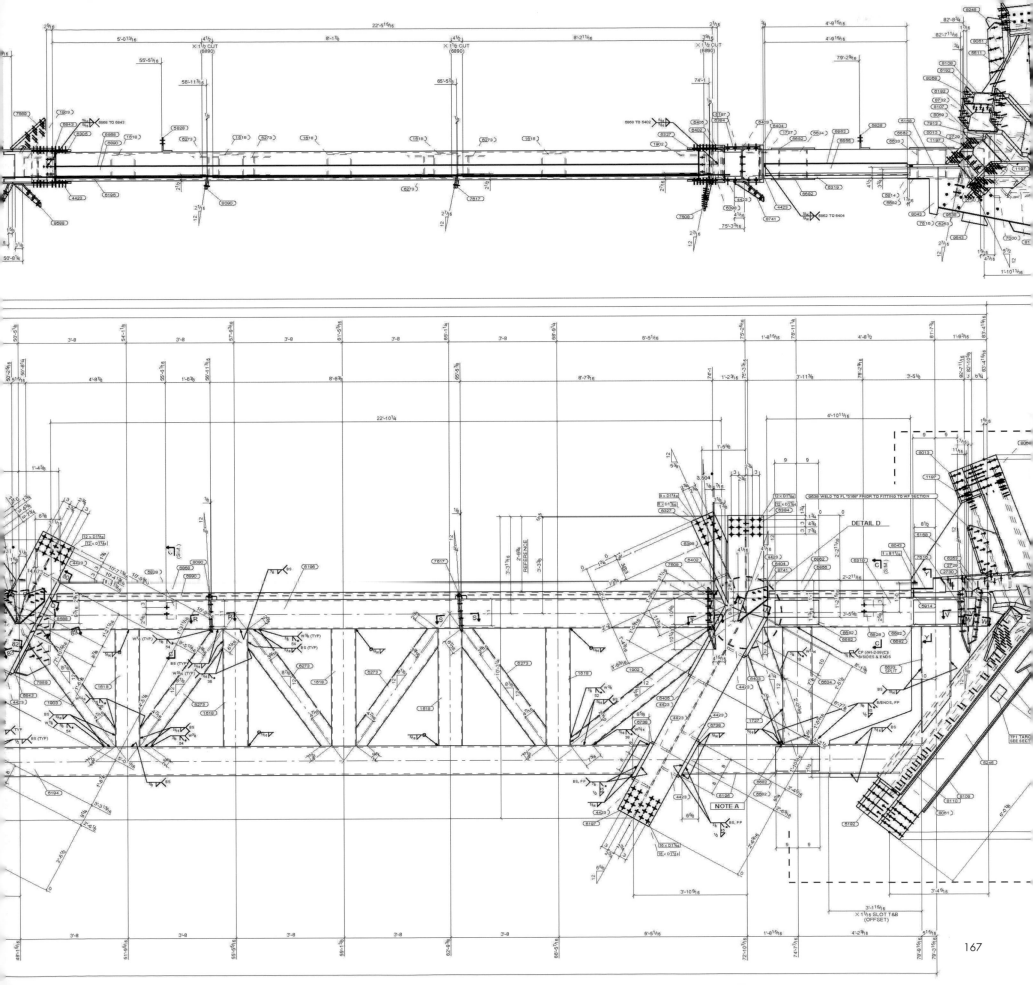

167

Page 168: Coloured three-dimensional shop drawing of the steel structure; each colour represents a different stage of construction. *Page 169:* On-site photography corresponded exactly to the computer-generated shop drawings. *Pages 170–71:* The lows and highs of the steel structure. *Page 170:* Structural steel in Level 2B, the foundation of the Michael Lee-Chin Crystal's Spirit House, 32 feet below grade. *Page 171:* The Crystal peak emerges.

2003

July 2003

October 2003

February 2004

March 2004

August 2004

March 2005

May 2005

August 2005

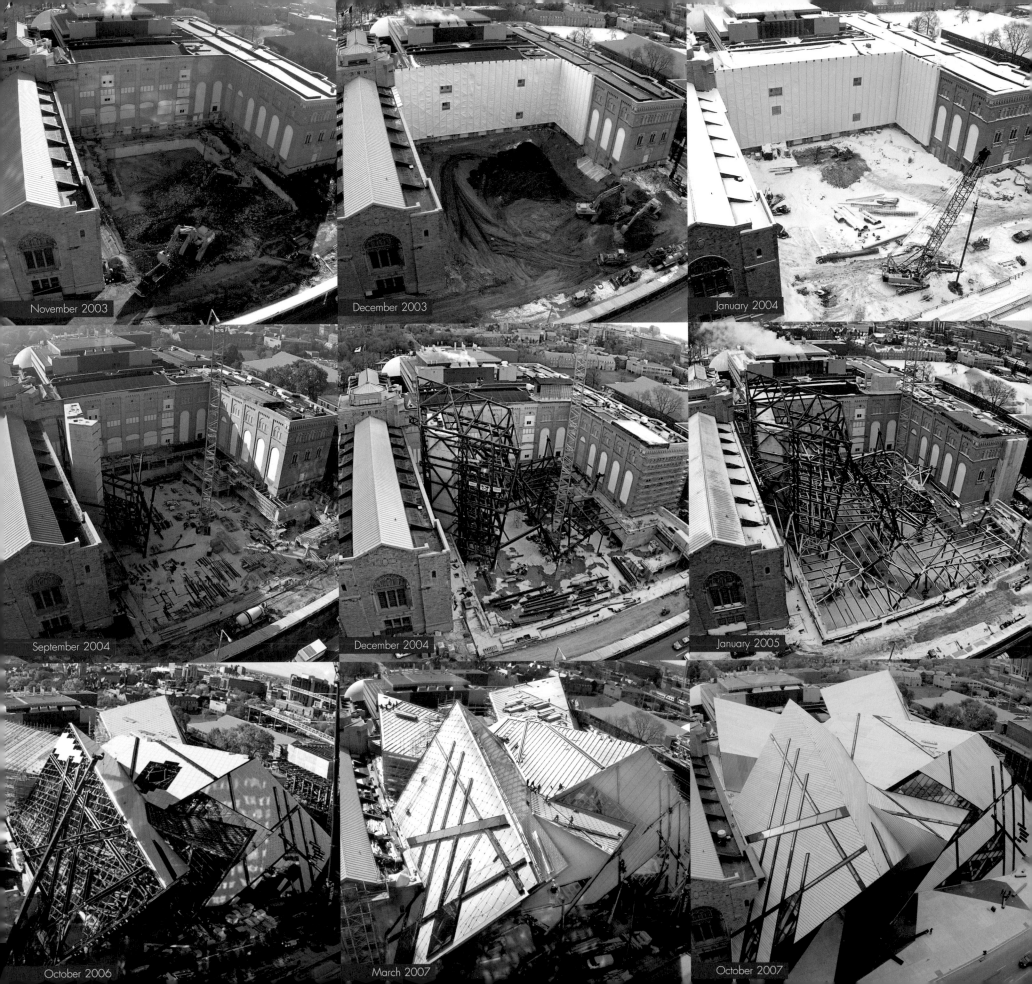

November 2003

December 2003

January 2004

September 2004

December 2004

January 2005

October 2006

March 2007

October 2007

Pages 175—76: The Michael Lee-Chin Crystal in "conversation" with the north façade of the 1914 building, 2007. *Page 177:* The soaring points of the Crystal on Bloor Street, 2007. The peak to the extreme top right contains the Patricia Harris Gallery of Textiles and Costume. *Page 178:* Just inside the ROM's new main entrance from Bloor Street, 2007. The Spirit House is to the left and the coat-check to the right. *Page 179:* The Hyacinth Gloria Chen Crystal Court connects the ROM's heritage buildings with the Crystal; two "shard" skylights are the dramatic focal point of the space.

Pages 180–81: In the new blockbuster exhibition space, Garfield Weston Exhibition Hall, the massive steel structure supporting the Michael Lee-Chin Crystal is boldly visible. Few visitors will perceive it as structure, seeing instead a forest of dramatic columns. Page 182: The Matthews Family Court of Chinese Sculpture on the first floor of the 1914 Philosophers' Walk Building, 2007. Page 183: RenROM has gloriously restored the Rotunda and the magnificent view from the Weston Entrance, through Samuel Hall❧Currelly Gallery, to the central bay window in the 1914 Philosophers' Walk Building.

183

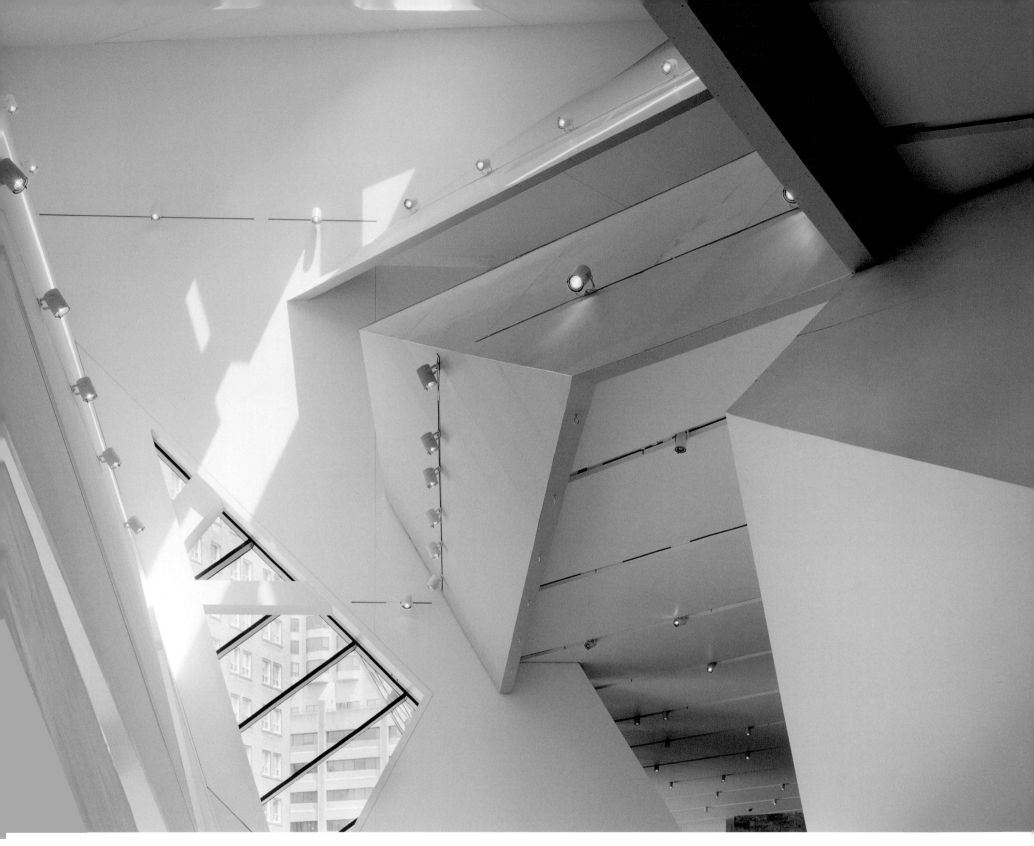

Pages 184–85: The J. F. Driscoll Family Stair of Wonders, 2007, with a glimpse of one of the showcases, a "cabinet of curiosities" embedded in the wall. *Page 186:* View from the west crystal upwards into the atrium known colloquially as "the beak" because it protrudes outwards between the east and west crystals. *Page 187:* Looking across one of the bridges in the Spirit House into the second floor of the west crystal, now the James and Louise Temerty Galleries of the Age of Dinosaurs.

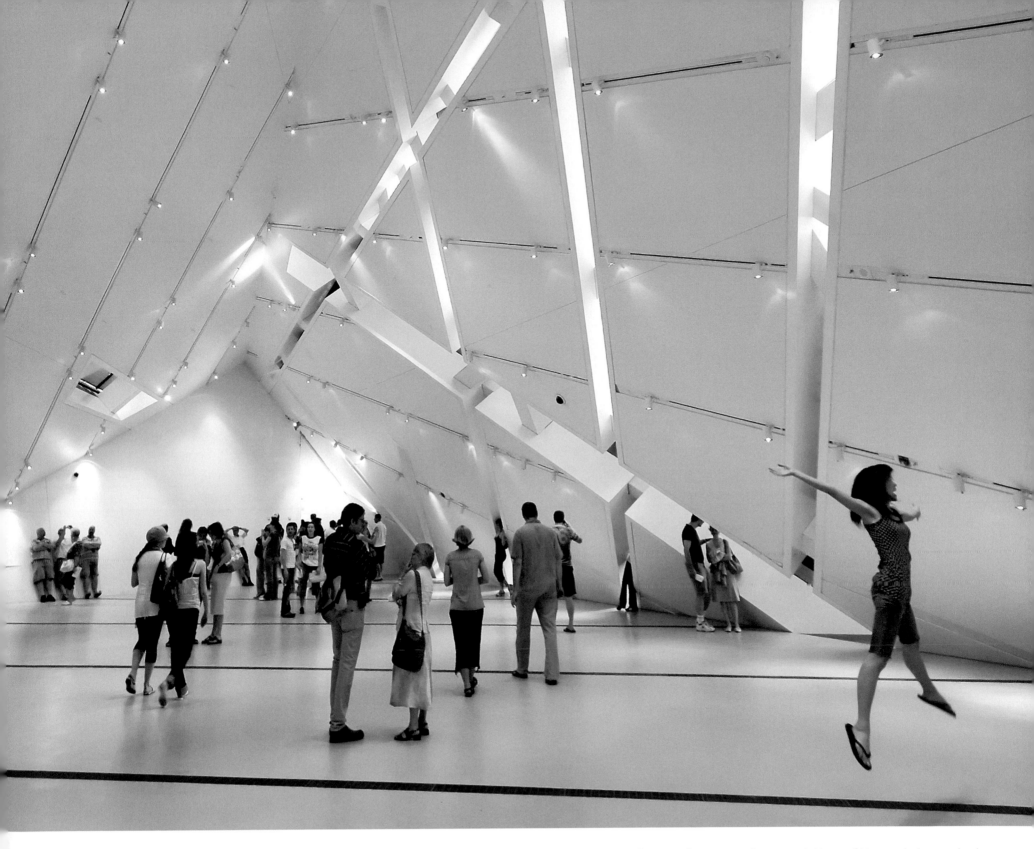

Page 188: The first installation by the Institute for Contemporary Culture at the ROM in the Michael Lee-Chin Crystal's Roloff Beny Gallery was Hiroshi Sugimoto's *History of History,* which opened with the Michael Lee-Chin Crystal in June 2007. The massive curved wall was temporary and was designed by the artist for this exhibition. *Page 189:* The galleries were "naked" during the joyous opening weekend when more than 25,000 people visited the ROM for free. The Patricia Harris Gallery of Textiles and Costume occupies the space shown here. *Page 190:* As viewed from Philosophers' Walk, the peak of the Crystal 5 Restaurant Lounge (C5), the ROM's new fine-dining restaurant, is in bold juxtaposition to the 1914 building. *Page 191:* Michael Lee-Chin Crystal, eve of the June 2, 2007 Architectural Opening & Building Dedication. The Crystal's Bloor Street façade can be a dramatic screen for projection.

Royal Ontario Museum
The ROM
100 Queen's Park
Toronto, Ontario
M5S 2C6

www.rom.on.ca

Library and Archives Canada Cataloguing in Publication

Browne, Kelvin
    Bold visions : the architecture of the Royal Ontario Museum / Kelvin Browne.
A condensed edition of this title was also published.
ISBN 978-0-88854-457-5 (bound).–ISBN 978-0-88854-458-2 (pbk.)

    1. Royal Ontario Museum. 2. Museum architecture—Ontario—Toronto.
3. Museum buildings—Ontario—Toronto.
4. Architecture—Ontario—Toronto.
5. Toronto (Ont.)—Buildings, structures, etc.
I. Royal Ontario Museum. II. Title.

AM101.T67B76 2007a   727'.60009713541   C2007-907175-9

Kelvin Browne (M. Arch., University of Toronto) is the Executive Director, Marketing & Commercial Development, Royal Ontario Museum.

Project Manager: Glen Ellis
Editor: Andrea Gallagher
Architectural Consultant: Dave Hollands
Art Director: Kelvin Browne
Designer: Tara Winterhalt
Principal Photographers: Brian Boyle, Steven Evans
Production Coordinator: Virginia Morin

Special thanks to Michael Allen, George Baird, Meg Beckel, Nicole Eaton, Thore Garbers, Paul Gogan, Lee Jacobson, Peter Kaellgren, Daniel Libeskind, Nancy Lockhart, Gail Lord, Julia Matthews, Michael McClelland, Dan Rahimi, Stephane Raymond, Larry Richards, and William Thorsell.

Printed on acid-free paper by Friesens Printers

Printed and bound in Canada

The Royal Ontario Museum is an agency of the Ontario Ministry of Culture.